Imagining the Age of Goethe in German Literature, 1970–2010

Studies in German Literature, Linguistics, and Culture

Imagining the Age of Goethe in German Literature, 1970–2010

John D. Pizer

CAMDEN HOUSE
Rochester, New York

First published 2011
by Camden House

Camden House is an imprint of Boydell & Brewer Inc.
668 Mt. Hope Avenue, Rochester, NY 14620, USA
www.camden-house.com
and of Boydell & Brewer Limited
PO Box 9, Woodbridge, Suffolk IP12 3DF, UK
www.boydellandbrewer.com

ISBN-13: 978-1-57113-517-9
ISBN-10: 1-57113-517-0

Library of Congress Cataloging-in-Publication Data

Pizer, John David.
   Imagining the age of Goethe in German literature, 1970–2010 / John D. Pizer.
     p. cm. — (Studies in German literature, linguistics, and culture)
   Includes bibliographical references and index.
   ISBN-13: 978-1-57113-517-9 (acid-free paper)
   ISBN-10: 1-57113-517-0 (acid-free paper)
   1. Historical fiction, German—History and criticism. 2. Biographical
fiction, German—History and criticism. 3. Historical drama, German—History
and criticism. 4. Goethe, Johann Wolfgang von, 1749-1832—In literature.
5. Authors in literature. 6. Künstlerromane—History and criticism. 7. German
literature—18th century—Appreciation—Germany. 8. German literature—20th
century—History and criticism. 9. German literature—21st century—History
and criticism. I. Title.
   PT747.H5P59 2011
   833'.08109092—dc22
                                                                    2011007403

This publication is printed on acid-free paper.
Printed in the United States of America.

Contents

Acknowledgments   vii

Introduction   1

1: Staging Violence and Transcendence, Embracing Feminism:
    The Instantiation of Kleist and German Romanticism   28

2: Hölderlins East and West   56

3: Between Feminism and National Identity:
    The Historical Novels of Renate Feyl   87

4: Goethe Contra and Pro   111

5: Savaging and Salvaging the German Enlightenment   156

Conclusion   187

Bibliography   193

Index   205

Acknowledgments

THIS BOOK IS THE PRODUCT OF a number of years of research and writing. I would like to acknowledge the College of Arts & Sciences (recently renamed the College of Humanities and Social Sciences) of Louisiana State University for providing me a sabbatical research leave in the spring 2009 semester, during which time I was able to compose two chapters. A number of people have been very helpful with advice, suggestions, and encouragement, including colleagues at LSU, Katharina Gerstenberger (from whom I first heard the name Renate Feyl), Paul Michael Lützeler, Azade Seyhan, Stephen Brockmann, and David Kirshner (who, when I expressed difficulties in coming up with a title for this book, made a joke that helped me make a final decision in this matter!). Special thanks are due as well to Ina Pfitzner, who arranged an evening literary salon in Berlin in August 2008 devoted to the topic that is the focus of the current book, and arranged for my interview with author Renate Feyl, an interview incorporated into chapter 3. Thanks as well to Renate Feyl herself, who graciously granted me the interview during the course of a delightful evening at her house. I appreciate the efforts of the editorial staff of Camden House for facilitating this book, especially those of editor Jim Walker, who was very encouraging throughout the whole process. I appreciate as well the helpful suggestions of the anonymous manuscript readers.

Portions of three of the chapters in this book have been published in an earlier form in journals. Chapter 1 represents an expanded version of an article that was printed in *German Studies Review* 33.1 (February 2010): 1–22, "Staging Violence and Transcendence: Reading Christa Wolf through German Romanticism." Much of chapter 5 was first published in a special issue, "Alexander von Humboldt's Transatlantic Personae," of *Atlantic Studies* 7.2 (June 2010): 127–42, under the title "Skewering the Enlightenment: Alexander von Humboldt and Immanuel Kant as Fictional Characters." Special thanks here go to the guest editor Vera M. Kutzinski, who made a number of suggestions for the article that were incorporated into the book chapter version. My colleague in the Department of Geography and Anthropology at LSU, Kent Mathewson, was helpful in steering me toward some useful works of Humboldt scholarship. The section on Rafik Schami in chapter 4 constitutes a small portion of an essay, "Moving the *Divan* Beyond Orientalism: Rafik Schami's Instrumentalization of Goethe," that originally appeared in the journal *Seminar*, special issue, 41.3 "Reassessing

Orientalism in German Studies," edited by Friederike Eigler (September 2005): 261–74. My thanks to the editors of these journals, Diethelm Prowe, William Boelhower, and Raleigh Whitinger respectively, for their permission to reprint.

This book is dedicated to my family: wife Patricia, daughter Jasmin, mother Roselle, sister and brother-in-law Liz and Bill Quicksilver, their children Matthew and Laura, and my wife's extensive family. They have always been supportive, not to mention gracious in conceding to me the role of Germanics scholar with respect to the division of labor in the family!

John Pizer
May 2011

Introduction

THE EIGHTEENTH AND EARLY NINETEENTH centuries have long been considered the "Golden Age" of German literature. This was never more the case than in the years immediately following the Second World War, when Germany's reputation was at its lowest ebb as National Socialist atrocities were being revealed in their horrific dimensions. By contrast, the Germany of the so-called *Goethezeit*, or Age of Goethe, seemed truly golden. Even before the war, Goethe and his fellow writers of the period named after him were upheld as model cosmopolitans who eschewed the rigid nationalism marking the Third Reich and focused on the ideals of acculturation (*Bildung*) rather than national conquest.[1] It was a period when Germany gained the reputation of being the land of poets and thinkers, as Germaine de Staël famously surmised in her *De l'Allemagne* (1813), a brief period of intense intellectual ferment with dreams that seemed to idealize Enlightenment utopias of universal peace and widespread individual intellectual development before a reactionary phase set in after Napoleon was definitively vanquished in 1815. Repressive measures enacted at the Congress of Vienna and in Restoration Germany caused this later era's most famous poet, Heinrich Heine, to claim his nation had been transformed from the land of poets and thinkers (*Dichter und Denker*) into the land of judges and executioners (*Richter und Henker*). With the exception of the brief progressive literary and political blossoming preceding the revolutionary year 1848, one could justifiably claim that Germany has never experienced such a hopeful, progressive, artistic, and idealistic period as the Age of Goethe either before or since. It is therefore no wonder that the late 1940s saw intellectuals such as Fritz Strich, in his *Goethe und die Weltliteratur*[2] (Goethe and world literature, 1946), call upon his fellow German speakers to inaugurate a new age of global cosmopolitanism following the model of Goethe's world literary ideals, and Robert Lohan, in 1945, to title the anthology of representative works from the period he edited the *Golden Age of German Literature*.[3]

The veneration for Goethe exhibited by leading German intellectuals in the wake of the Third Reich suggests a revival of the ideal of this country as a *Kulturnation*, a nation forged through culture, now that it was subject to foreign occupation. In his study *Weltbürgertum und Nationalstaat* (Cosmopolitanism and the national state, 1907), Friedrich Meinecke had famously defined the common cultural treasures (*Kulturgüter*) of a nation, its shared language, religion, and literature, as those elements constituting the cultural nation and holding it together.[4] However, his book as a whole praises the development of the political/national state as the mark of its maturity. The "cosmopolitanism" in the title marks Germany's historically less advanced stage, signifying a period when *only* the elements of the *Kulturnation* held it together and, politically divided, cosmopolitanism appealed to its men of letters. In other words, the "national state" was, in Meinecke's early perspective, superior from a political point of view to a merely cultural state. However, after the war, in his 1946 study *Die deutsche Katastrophe* (The German catastrophe), Meinecke nostalgically recollects radio broadcasts during the Third Reich as an almost sacral escape from the horrors of Nazi Germany, and recommends reinstituting such "Feierstunden" (solemn hours) devoted to the poetry of Goethe and Schiller. He believes that, in the midst of the fatherland's misery and destruction, its citizens may feel thereby something indestructible in the German character in their hour of need.[5] Meinecke's tacit change of heart about Germany as a *Kulturnation* immediately after the war suggests that this is the paradigm some intellectuals wished to deploy for the spiritual regeneration of the country, a regeneration to be achieved through an immersion into the works composed during its literary apex in the Age of Goethe.

Goethe and the other authors who wrote during the period named after him have not always been treated with such reverence; the literary school classified under the rubric *Junges Deutschland* (Young Germany) in the 1830s, particularly its adherent Ludwig Börne, heaped scorn on the so-called "poet-prince," seeing in him and other writers of the period reactionaries who supported the post-Napoleonic restoration of the *ancien régime*. However, given the prominence of *Goethezeit* intellectuals in the cultural and scientific history of the country, it is not surprising that leading figures of the age also became the heroic protagonists of historical fiction. Much of this work in its early phases was marked by a hagiographic and/or sentimental approach to these iconic personages. While some imaginative historical literature that was focused on Age of Goethe figures was richly nuanced and achieved canonic status, it was not until the 1970s that a significant body of works began to emerge that made this period and its intellectuals the object of serious historical fiction. Although these works have attracted critical attention individually, some in substantial volume, this corpus has never been analyzed as a cohesive, coherent subgenre. The articulation and analysis of German Age-of-Goethe fiction written from the 1970s to the present day — the examination of the style and substance of such works, their commonalities, divergences, and the motivations inspiring their composition — is the focus of the current book. As Katharina Gerstenberger has noted: "Since the eighteenth century literature has played a significant role in Germans' understanding of their culture and national identity."[6] *Imagining the Age of Goethe* is inspired by the supposition that the understanding of German culture and national identity since the 1970s by some of its leading authors is largely accessible through the literature of this period that imaginatively constellates the nation's eighteenth- and early nineteenth-century intellectuals, particularly its creative writers. By examining the unique but broadly developed subgenre of historical fiction focused on Age-of-Goethe intellectuals, the following book will enable new insights into the understanding alluded to by Gerstenberger. Although drawing on the vast previous scholarship on German Age-of-Goethe fiction written since the 1970s, my book shows for the first time in a sustained manner the powerful hold the *Goethezeit* continues to exercise on the imaginary of many of Germany's leading writers. This inner-German dialogue across the ages provides an important corrective to the dominant critical view that contemporary German-language literature, literature written since the 1970s but especially in the last two decades, is composed primarily under the sign of globalization and the influence of mass American culture.

The Question of Genre

The question of genre is central to our concerns. The uniqueness of the body of works this book will explore is the result of their situatedness between two frequently discussed literary types: historical fiction and artist fiction. Sometimes artist fiction can be subsumed under historical fiction when the protagonists are historical artists, writers, and musicians known to posterity. However, most historical fiction does not revolve around real-life intellectuals and artists from the past; most well-known artist fiction — referred to in its novel-length variant by the German term *Künstlerroman* even in much English-language scholarship[7] — is centered around entirely fictional protagonists, even if, as is frequently the case, these protagonists lead lives closely patterned after those of their authors, so that works like James Joyce's *Portrait of the Artist as a Young Man* (1916), and, to a lesser extent, Thomas Mann's *Tonio Kröger* (1903) are imaginatively veiled autobiographies. Because the body of works explored in this book is constituted between the poles of historical fiction and artist fiction, the character of this corpus as an admixture of discrete though sometimes interrelated genres must be examined.

Georg Lukács's comprehensive analysis of historical fiction, *Der historische Roman* (The historical novel, 1938; first German publication 1955) is still considered the most significant work on the subject, but his perspective clearly reveals the impossibility of subsuming the literature examined in *Imagining the Age of Goethe* under the category he analyzes, quite apart from the fact that a number of the works I examine are dramas rather than epic prose. Singling out Walter Scott as the exemplary practitioner of the genre, Lukács argues that the historical novel — he sees the sweeping eighteenth-century society novel, the *Gesellschaftsro-man*, as a precursor here — dynamically represents social crises in the past that foreshadow the present. A Marxist, Lukács finds that the crises in the social strata of a nation articulated in the historical novel should create the ambience of historical necessity inherent in the Hegelian dialectic. He eschews static description in favor of sweeping narrative panoramas informed by objective realism, a mirroring of past social life in its great conflicts. Based on these criteria, most fiction treated in my book would be dismissed by Lukács on all counts, for these works are frequently marked by static detail. They focus on significant personages rather than on the sweep of dialectically developing German society (though the context of these lives as rooted in social crises in the Age of Goethe is almost never entirely neglected), and the delineation of inner lives is frequently highlighted at the expense of narrating external sociopolitical events of the period. At the outset of *Der historische Roman*, Lukács asserts that the historical novel emerged early in the nineteenth century contemporaneously with the fall of Napoleon, citing Scott's *Waverly* (1814) as an initial exemplar of the genre. He claims the "so-called" historical novels of the seventeenth century are only historical through their external thematic, their "costume," and generally reflect the mores and psychology of the age in which they were written: "Es kommt hier allein auf die Kuriosität und Exzentrizität des geschilderten Milieus an, nicht auf die künstlerisch getreue Abbildung eines konkreten historischen Zeitalters"[8] (Here it only depends on the curious character and the eccentricity of the portrayed milieu, not on the artistically faithful illustration of a concrete historical period). What Lukács describes here as characteristics of seventeenth-century historical fiction not infrequently applies to the works examined in the following chapters of this book: Detailed portraits of milieus are often included to strike the reader with their curious and — from a twentieth- or twenty-first-century perspective — eccentric features. Also not infrequently, these works tend to reflect contemporary psychological perspectives rather than the psycho-social mores of the Age of Goethe. Particularly in the case of such politically engaged authors as Peter Weiss, fiction anchored around the *Goethezeit* reflects the writer's own political, social, and even (in the case of Daniel Kehlmann) environmental stances on present-day issues, a practice Lukács strongly frowned upon. This is the reason he preferred conservative realist authors such as Honoré de Balzac over writers more ideologically in harmony with his own leftist politics, like Emile Zola.

While Lukács's book on the historical novel was groundbreaking, other scholars who have analyzed this genre have created other standards of judgment that are radically at variance with those of the prolific Hungarian intellectual. Hans Vilmar Geppert's *Der 'andere' historische Roman: Theorie und Strukturen einer diskontinuierlichen Gattung* (The 'other' historical novel: Theory and structures of a discontinuous genre, 1976), the most widely referenced work on the genre composed in the late twentieth century, valorizes precisely the kind of historical novel scorned by Lukács. Geppert defends playful, self-referential fiction where the narrating consciousness underscores the imaginative nature of the historical representations, which may include radical distortions of the temporal period focused upon in the work. He articulates this variation on the structure and narratological approach in the historical novel in conscious opposition to Lukács's orthodoxy.[9] Writing two decades after the appearance of *Der historische Roman* and having been exposed to contemporary postmodernism, Geppert allows for the kind of experimentation and narratological subjectivity engaged in by some of the authors examined in *Imagining the Age of Goethe*. He privileges approaches to the genre antithetical to Lukács's poetics. However, even Geppert's more capacious attitude does not broadly encompass the kind of literature analyzed here. While Geppert makes a "categorical" distinction between fiction and history, the authors I examine — while sometimes indulging in the absolute freedom with historical realities allowed by Geppert — tend to adhere to a greater extent to the facts and figures of the period they imaginatively constellate. This remains the case regardless of whatever narratological experimentations or (in the case of Peter Härtling) subjective self-insertions they deploy, and is due to their realization that the Age of Goethe is still the most valorized — indeed, to some Germans, sacrosanct — cultural period in the nation's history. They may invent episodes in their protagonists' lives, but their awareness of contemporary reverence for the *Goethezeit* still causes most of them to respect the broadly established contours of these figures' biographies and intellectual histories. They realize that only by keeping an at least rough adherence to the lives of figures like Goethe, Kleist, and Kant can they challenge the critical orthodoxies that still surround these figures in the popular imagination, especially when — as was the case in the German Democratic Republic but also in the early years of the Federal Republic of Germany — those orthodoxies are underwritten by the state.

One of the more recent books to examine the genre of the historical novel in a comprehensive fashion is Hugo Aust's *Der historische Roman* (The historical novel, 1994). This work offers a categorization scheme outside the dichotomies presented by Lukács and Geppert that is of some value to understanding the literary subgenre my book addresses. Aust distinguishes between the parabolic and the reconstructive historical novel. He defines the reconstructive historical novel as a work focused on the precise or "authentic" bringing back to literary life (*Wiederherstellung*) of a temporal epoch, world or personage. He finds this particular kind of subgenre exemplified by the "professor novel," by which he means not fiction with academics as protagonists but rather works betraying a scholarly attention to historic detail, evident in Scott's antiquary inclinations, the archaeological ambitions of a Georg Ebers, and the semiotic scholarliness of an Umberto Eco; all these men were profoundly learned and, in the case of Ebers and Eco, professional academics. One example of such an author from this study, who has sought to resurrect major intellectual figures from the Age of Goethe through imaginative literature, is Renate Feyl, the focus of chapter 3, who is very precise in her recreation of period ambience and detail while setting forth a specific feminist and German national (but not nationalist) agenda. Aust's definition of the parabolic form as an attempt to use history to mirror the present[10] is certainly the case with Peter Weiss and Peter Härtling, who are examined in chapter 2. Weiss's play about Friedrich Hölderlin betrays a powerful sociopolitical agenda only slightly more veiled than in the dramas he sets in the late twentieth century, while Härtling, as noted, actually inserts himself as narrator into his Hölderlin novel in order to underscore filiations between Swabia past and present, and between his life and that of his literary precursor.

What Aust terms the parabolic historical novel is associated by David Roberts specifically with its twentieth-century variant. He refers in this regard to the "modern German historical novel," the title of his introduction to a volume of essays published in 1991 and bearing the same name, when he notes that "the consciousness of temporal difference, of the interaction, the 'vertical simultaneity' of past and present is integral to the hermeneutics of the historical novel."[11] We will see that the instantiation of such "vertical simultaneity" extends into the twenty-first-century German historical novel as well, even if, in one novel by Feyl, without intention. On the other hand, looking back to the body of historical fiction produced in West Germany from the 1970s up to reunification, we will be able to refute Osman Durrani's assertion that this nation was marked by "Geschichtsmüdigkeit" (weariness of history) to such an extent that only East German authors "alighted on exemplary figures from the Age of Goethe onwards as vehicles for their discussions of social and political developments closer to home."[12] While we will see that GDR authors were indeed prompted to create a rich corpus of fiction situated in the *Goethezeit* in response to a wave of political repression and censorship in that nation in the mid-1970s, we will also find that FRG authors were extremely productive within this subgenre as well.

If our brief survey of engagements with the genre of the historical novel indicates that the works examined here cannot unproblematically be classified as historical fiction, a glance at analyses of artist fiction shows that this literary type also fails to fit our subgenre exactly. We have already noted that much artist fiction — including the most celebrated works, such as those of Joyce and Thomas Mann — bring into literary being writers like Joyce's Stephen Hero, who are the product of pure invention even if they have a thinly veiled autobiographical character. In other words, they have no relationship to historically antecedent creative figures. Also, my book does not restrict itself to authors of imaginative literature. Daniel Kehlmann's novel *Die Vermessung der Welt* (Measuring the world, 2005), a fictional double biography of the lives of the *Goethezeit* explorer/geographer Alexander von Humboldt and the mathematician/astronomer Carl Friedrich Gauß, as well as Klaas Huizing's novel on Kant and the philosopher/visionary Johann Georg Hamann, *Das Ding an sich* (The thing-in-itself, 1998) do not belong to the *Künstlerroman* category. They are included because the writing of their protagonists contributed greatly to the intellectual ferment that made this age such an era of veneration for subsequent generations of educated Germans. On the other hand, fictional accounts of painters, sculptors, and composers are excluded from consideration because they only indirectly impacted the writing of the age. I focus on works written on the writers themselves, regardless of genre and whether they produced fiction, nonfiction, or both. Even with these restrictions, my book cannot be completely comprehensive; there have been simply too many works published within the subgenre it addresses since the 1970s for all of them to be included. I generally address works that have garnered at least a modicum of critical attention.

As with the historical novel, critical engagements with the *Künstlerroman*, and artist fiction in general, are voluminous, and can receive only brief consideration here. Roberta Seret's study *Voyage into Creativity: The Modern* Künstlerroman (1992) excludes virtually all novels from the genre that are not informed by a strongly autobiographical dimension: The "voyage" here is the author's personal development into a creative writer as revealed through the acculturative formation (*Bildung*) of his or her primary protagonist. Novels such as Thomas Mann's *Dr. Faustus* (1948), which contains a strong historical and philosophical dimension not always linked to Mann's personal development as an artist as filtered through the figure of his primary creative protagonist, Adrian Leverkühn, are excluded from her typology.[13] The works I examine in this book *cannot* be autobiographical (unless, as in the case of Härtling, the author inserts himself or herself directly into the narrative) because they focus on historical personages, even if the authors sometimes betray a sympathetic identification with their protagonists. Seret would presumably therefore exclude all of them from her *Künstlerroman* typology. While Evy Varsamopoulou justifiably criticizes Seret for the narrowness of her definition in her own book on the female artist novel,[14] she still assumes "that the *Künstlerroman* with a writer or poet protagonist discloses a critical awareness of the *métier* of literary art, blurring the boundaries between fiction and criticism, as the novelist becomes critic of his/her own creative process or product."[15] While, as the full title of her book — the *Poetics of the* Künstlerinroman *and the Aesthetics of the Sublime* (2002) — indicates, she goes beyond Seret's definition by examining the engagement with the sublime by female authors at a metafictional level, the historical

distance between the authors I examine and their eighteenth- and early
nineteenth-century protagonists sometimes precludes a metatheoretical
engagement with writing in the contemporary age, quite apart from the
fact that the creative process often constitutes a secondary, and even neg-
ligible, area of exploration in these works.

Like Varsamopoulou, Hans Ester and Guillaume van Gemert, in
their introduction to a volume of essays focused on imaginative engagements with the creative personality, assume that artist fiction contains a
metatheoretical dimension that makes art and artistry the objects of artistic endeavor. The thematization of an artist's life presupposes an empathetic engagement with the life of a creative individual, an artist, though
even such subjective identification must be informed by objectivity and
verifiability (*Überprüfbarkeit*) to be historically credible. Nevertheless,
legitimate artist fiction can still employ the narrated lives of past artists to
reflect contemporary aesthetic and social issues, according to these editors, who also find that the thematizing of genuine art and artistic figures
constitutes an essential component of contemporary literature.[16] These
are all valid generalizations concerning artist fiction, but, again, metatheoretical aesthetic discourse is not always a significant feature in the works
analyzed in my book, and empathetic identification is far from evident in
much of them, particularly in some of the ironic treatments of Goethe
discussed in chapter 4.

In his recent magisterial overview of the European artist novel, *Der
europäische Künstlerroman* (The European artist novel, 2008) from
Romanticism to the present day (virtually all scholars of this genre trace
its beginnings to the Romantic age), Peter Zima seems to sustain a perspective antithetical to that of Ester and van Gemert. This is evident in
the subtitle of his book: *Von der romantischen Utopie zur postmodernen
Parodie* (From romantic utopia to postmodern parody). A parodist
approach to historical artist figures — and there are a number of works
analyzed in *Imagining the Age of Goethe* that contain a strong mixture of
parody — would appear to at least mitigate the element of empathetic
identification on the part of the contemporary author. Zima asserts that
while even in Romanticism's artist novels the position of the artist and his
creative output within society came to be articulated increasingly as prob-
lematic, leading to the portrayal of art as marginalized in the late-modern
era, this domain has been so devalued in the contemporary postmodern age, reduced to an "epiphenomenon of the economy," that parody
becomes the only viable approach to writing artist novels in the twenty-
first century. The utopian and idealist dimension of the genre evident
even in the late-modern novels of a Thomas Mann, Marcel Proust and
Jean-Paul Sartre, where art can still be articulated as a weapon against the
bourgeois utilitarianism of the father's generation, loses its credibility in
a contemporary age marked by radical pluralism and indifference toward

(totalizing) aesthetic ideologies. The only criterion for judging art in this age is "value-indifferent exchange value." Radical doubt toward the ideal of art as a calling, an ideal exemplified and articulated by Joyce's *A Portrait of the Artist as a Young Man* but considered illegitimate and irrelevant in the current age marked by an all-encompassing commercialism, comes to expression in the contemporary artist novel. Nevertheless, Zima finds the critical spirit of late modernism is still evident in the contemporary novelist's enactment of all possible writerly means to resist the "postmodern 'brave new world.'" However, by parody, Zima does not refer to the ironic imitation or persiflage of previous authors but the broad critique of aesthetic idealism evinced by earlier ages and of literature's possible elevating efficacy, its enriching of public discourse.[17] In the works I examine, writers from the Age of Goethe tend either to be positively constellated as martyrs to such idealism (particularly in the case of Hölderlin fiction) or as cynical manipulators of elevated art, who act as the vanguard of bourgeois commercialism (evident, for example, in Peter Weiss's portrayal of Goethe in his play on Hölderlin). Thus, Zima's examination of the postmodern parodistic *Künstlerroman*, which highlights works in the German-speaking world by Thomas Bernhard and Christoph Ransmayr, does not provide a theoretical model for an engagement with the unique subgenre undertaken in the following chapters of my book.

It is clear from the foregoing that the body of work examined in *Imagining the Age of Goethe* cannot easily be subsumed under the various typologies associated with the historical novel and the artist novel, quite apart from the fact that some of the works I analyze are dramas. A more conducive approach is provided by Ralf Sudau's *Werkbearbeitung, Dichterfiguren: Traditionsaneignung am Beispiel der deutschen Gegenwartsliteratur* (Work treatment, poet figures: The appropriation of tradition as exemplified by contemporary German literature, 1985). The term "Aneignung" possesses a range of nuances not translatable by one English term. Appropriation, occupancy, incorporation, and adoption are all denoted by this German word, and, in combination, they suggest some of the variety of tactics pursued by German authors in their fictionally enacted encounters with writers from the Age of Goethe. Sudau's book examines both literary adaptations of earlier German texts, thus encompassing the kind of *Twentieth-Century Reworkings of German Literature* discussed by Gundula Sharman in her more recent (2002) monograph with this title, and the sort of biographical fiction treated in my book. Sudau's typology is based on the sort of intertextual/intergenerational varieties he encounters in the works he examines, whether they trend toward parody, idealizing, pastiche, or disavowal as approaches (among others) toward previous figures and models. Two of the chapters included in the biographical fiction portion of Sudau's book address works of Hölderlin literature also examined in *Imagining the Age of Goethe*: Peter

Härtling's novel *Hölderlin* (1976), which Sudau casts, appropriately, as an example of "Vergegenwärtigung," a term traditionally translated as "realization" but etymologically suggesting a "making present," a tactic pursued by Härtling through his constant present-day narrative interventions, and Peter Weiss's drama of the same title (1971). Sudau cites this latter work as exemplary of a literary "Vereinnahmung," another term difficult to translate but indicating an instrumentalizing interpretation/appropriation of a text or figure, an engagement with a personage or work for specific, frequently political purposes.[18] Once again, Sudau's characterization is quite apt here, as we will see, and his book brings us beyond the genre poetics of artist and historical novels — poetics that are not as productive for our purposes.

Another fruitful approach with respect to the subgenre examined in the following chapters of this book is provided by the editors of a collection of essays entitled *The Author as Character: Representing Historical Writers in Western Literature* (1999). Broadly speaking, this title identifies the subgenre of my book: The main characters of all the works analyzed in *Imagining the Age of Goethe* are authors, even if their authorial activities and their position as writers are not always a focus in the biographical fiction in which they are brought back to life. In their introduction to the volume, Paul Franssen and Ton Hoenselaars note that any autobiographical element in author-as-character fiction is mitigated by the need to maintain at least some semblance of historical accuracy.[19] As we have seen, this is not the case with the broader *Künstlerroman*, which some critics see as primarily a veiled imaginative autobiography. Author-as-character fiction, by contrast, constitutes a kind of dialogue across time with past writers, even if, we might add, the present-day author's role in the dialogue is marked by hostility. With respect to the question of genre, Franssen and Hoenselaars's thesis that "the phenomenon of the author as character should be situated at the crossroads between the historical novel, biography, and the *Künstlerroman*"[20] is as accurate a representation as any concerning the generic body of work the following book attempts to elucidate.

Literary Precursors

The 1970s did not mark the beginning of a German literary engagement with intellectuals from the Age of Goethe, although this current epoch is the only one in which a consistent, voluminous stream of noteworthy works belonging to this subgenre was, and is being, composed. Already during the *Goethezeit* itself, well-known contemporary authors were being cast as characters in plays. Goethe's brief farce *Götter, Helden und Wieland* (Gods, heroes and Wieland, 1774) attacks the venerable neoclassical author Christoph Martin Wieland, whom Goethe had earlier held to be one of his few genuine mentors and who was to become one of his associates at Weimar's "Court of the Muses" not long after the play's publication. It satirizes Wieland for his supposed emasculation of classical Greek values and deities in both his adaptation of Euripides' play *Alcestis* (438 B.C.E.), entitled *Alceste* (1773), and in his "Briefe an einen Freund über das Singspiel" (Letters to a friend on the singspiel, 1773), in which he asserts that his singspiel is superior to Euripides' original play. Written during Goethe's Sturm und Drang period, the farce's Wieland is forced to endure the invective of such figures as Alcestis, Hercules, Mercury, and even Euripides for allegedly softening the latter's powerful tragicomedy into an altogether overly temperate *plaidoyer* for moderation and virtue. Goethe himself becomes a character in Jakob Michael Reinhold Lenz's *Pandämonium Germanicum* (1775). Like Goethe's farce, this satire is a Storm-and-Stress invective against what is perceived to be the mediocrity of most contemporary German writers, and Goethe, much adulated at that time by his younger friend, is presented as an almost divine figure who literally towers above his and Lenz's rivals as they both stand on a mountaintop and endure — Goethe amusedly and Lenz with some trepidation — the utterly ineffective stone-throwing and insults hurled at them by the mob of writers below. These brief dramatic sketches by Goethe and Lenz are justifiably considered quite minor works in the context of their respective oeuvres, but they already illustrate a trend evident in the contemporary literature explored in the following chapters: the use of *Goethezeit* authors as fictional characters for polemical purposes.

Most imaginative literature of this kind composed from the nineteenth century up to the 1970s has not stood the test of time. Some works were quite popular in their age but are forgotten today. Perhaps the most notable is Luise Mühlbach's *Fürsten und Dichter* (Princes and poets, 1867), which constitutes four volumes of the seventeen-volume *Deutschland in Sturm und Drang* (Germany in storm and stress, 1867–68). Mühlbach's novels tended to be very popular in the English-speaking world, and *Fürsten und Dichter* achieved great success in its translation as *Goethe and Schiller*, which appeared in 1898. It is full of pathos and emotional exclamations in its poetic recreation of the two poets, and clearly was written with a large, popular audience in mind. What Brent O. Peterson has said of her historical fiction concerning Friedrich the Great and those who devalued this work applies to *Fürsten und Dichter* as well: "Mühlbach seems unthreatened by questions of aesthetic quality, and she makes not the faintest attempt at distancing herself from the mass of readers to whom she appeals."[21] Worthy of noting in passing as well is the Goethe fiction published in Germany during the Third Reich and then in the immediate postwar years, particularly in the 1950s. In separate articles, Jens Kruse has shown that the former body of works instrumentalized the figure of Goethe to underwrite the policies and proclivities of the

Nazis,[22] while the latter corpus is marked by the tendency of its authors to draw upon Goethe's veneration of Napoleon, as well as his duplicitous erotic dalliances, in order tacitly to excuse their own Hitler worship and other culpable behavior during the Third Reich.[23]

An exception to the 1950s tendency to treat Goethe as an object of veneration consistent with the Goethe cult at that time (discussed in chapter 4), or as a literary predecessor whose behavior and political views tacitly exculpate German authors who towed the party line during the Third Reich, is constituted by Arno Schmidt's novella *Goethe und Einer seiner Bewunderer* (Goethe and one of his admirers, 1957). In this story, Goethe is a revenant brought back to life in contemporary Germany for fifteen hours as part of a program that allows prominent present-day individuals this brief time span to learn the truth about the lives and work of the revived historical personages through direct personal contact. Prior to the temporary resurrection of Goethe, noted authors from his age who interact with the 1950s Germans include E. T. A. Hoffmann, who behaves in a boorish manner, and Christoph Martin Wieland, who tells a previously unknown tale about Goethe's eccentric attempt to make the Duchess of Weimar laugh. This already clues the reader that Schmidt intends to subvert the cult of Goethe and his age. Both Goethe and his narrator companion Schmidt employ the latter's unique idiolect, infused with dialect, puns, and ribald salacious humor, to poke fun at this cult and to attack contemporary artistic and political trends. Allusions are made to Buchenwald as both the site of a Nazi death camp and a place to which those who revere the Age of Goethe make pilgrimages, and to the looming threat of a nuclear war. Goethe expresses his contempt for the bourgeoisie and the peasants, showing the inappropriateness of his iconic status in the socialist GDR, and there are irreverent conversations concerning authors and their works from the past and present, including Goethe and Schmidt. At one point Goethe claims "Wir sind Alle Heinis"[24] (We are all twerps). In the press conference summarized by the fictional Schmidt at the novella's conclusion, which consists of his answers to questions posed by various noteworthy individuals about the views Goethe expressed during his brief resurrection, Goethe is said to hold West Germany's contemporary foreign policy in contempt, and to believe a new war is imminent. The newspaper reports on the event conclude that Schmidt was a poor choice to question Goethe, and then add negative comments concerning the actual Schmidt's own fiction. Schmidt's sacrilegious treatment of Goethe and his age was unusual in the 1950s, but has become commonplace today.[25]

Only two works of *Goethezeit* fiction written prior to the 1970s have attained, and sustained, canonic status, although they are separated by a wide chronological gap and by vastly disparate styles, purports, and lengths. The first is Georg Büchner's fragmentary novella *Lenz* (composed in late 1835, first published in 1839), and the second is Thomas Mann's novel *Lotte in Weimar* (Lotte in Weimar, 1939; translated as *The Beloved Returns*). Mann also published an early story on Schiller, "Schwere Stunde" (A difficult hour, 1905). These three works merit some attention, as they anticipate certain trends explored later in this book. Büchner's novella is based largely on the diary observations of the Alsatian pastor Johann Friedrich Oberlin, at whose home the already schizophrenic playwright Lenz resided early in 1778. Like some of the Hölderlin literature we will examine in chapter 2, Büchner's tale chronicles the descent of a sensitive poetic soul into incurable madness. Sigrid Damm's book on Goethe's sister Cornelia discussed in chapter 4, which also highlights a frustrated, lonely individual's lapse into a deep depression marked by bouts of delirium (particularly as she nears death), blurs the line between historical biography and fiction, as does Büchner's story. There is a major difference, however: Damm's Cornelia and the Hölderlin portrayed in a number of literary works are clearly victims of a cold, overly rational, deceitful, uncaring social, and, to some extent, familial milieu, while the philanthropist Oberlin treats Lenz in a friendly, sympathetic manner. Büchner's novella is marked by an unadorned, detached, objective, almost clinical style, which is why it is frequently cited as an early exemplar of both literary realism and naturalism. The concluding lines, typical of the narrative's paratactic expository syntax and a structure eschewing dramatic development and resolution, clearly illustrate Büchner's almost journalistic approach, a style quite unlike that found in most Age-of-Goethe fiction written since the 1970s:

> Am folgenden Morgen bei trübem regnerischem Wetter traf er in Straßburg ein. Er schien ganz vernünftig, sprach mit den Leuten; er tat Alles wie es die Anderen taten, es war aber eine entsetzliche Leere in ihm, er fühlte keine Angst mehr, kein Verlangen; sein Dasein war ihm eine notwendige Last. — So lebte er hin.[26]

> [On the following morning, marked by dreary rainy weather, he entered Strasbourg. He seemed completely rational, spoke with the people; he did everything like the others did, but there was a dreadful emptiness in him, he felt no more fear, no desire; his existence seemed to him a necessary burden. — in this way he lived on.]

Maurice Benn argues "that Büchner really had much in common with Lenz and that the extraordinary power and authority of his Novelle is largely due to this natural affinity,"[27] but the work's detached style, lack of parody, irony, or overt narrative engagement — sympathetic or hostile — with its eponymous protagonist distinguish it from most of the work examined in *Imagining the Age of Goethe*. Büchner's tale inspired a number of other imaginative narratives in which sensitive, alienated artistic figures are driven to madness or near madness, though I am aware of only one such work, Robert Walser's dramatic sketch *Lenz* (1912), which revolves around the historical figure of the dramatist himself.[28]

Thomas Mann's quite brief story "Schwere Stunde" employs his typically complex, frequently hypotactic syntax punctuated by fragmented exclamation, declamation, free indirect style, and interior monologue to compose a sympathetic portrait of a gravely ill Friedrich Schiller struggling late at night to write his drama *Don Carlos* (1787) as he ruminates on his physical pain, his creative struggles, and his jealousy of the "Other," his friend and rival Goethe, for whom creative output seemed so effortless. Mann's well-known identification with Schiller at this time as a writer who — like himself — had to engage in a titanic effort of will to produce a single page of acceptable verse, drama, or epic prose, and his thinly veiled resentment at geniuses like Goethe from whom great writing seemed simply and naturally to flow, come to expression in the story. The creative struggle of Mann and Mann's Schiller, and Mann's admiration, tinged with jealousy, of Goethe, are evident in the following passage: "Wunder der Sehnsucht waren seine Werke, der Sehnsucht nach Form, Gestalt, Begrenzung, Körperlichkeit, der Sehnsucht hinüber in die klare Welt des anderen, der unmittelbar und mit göttlichem Mund die besonnten Dinge bei Namen nannte"[29] (His works were wonders of yearning, the yearning for form, shape, boundary, physicality, the yearning to cross over into the lucid world of the other one, who with immediacy and divine mouth named the glowing things by name). With respect to syntax, lexical choices, narrative style, and clear empathetic identification with the historical writer who is the object of his story, Mann and Büchner could not be more opposite. As Hans Vaget has argued, Mann's tale, written in response to a request to contribute a piece for the journal *Simplicissimus* to mark the centenary of Schiller's death, can be regarded "as an act of literary self-fashioning by an author who took the occasion of the centenary to don the mask of Schiller in order to understand more clearly what kind of a writer he himself wanted to be."[30] Such direct use of a *Goethezeit* author as a model for "literary self-fashioning" is not much in evidence in the works examined in this book's subsequent chapters, though, as we will see, empathetic *spiritual* identification and sympathy for the plight of fellow writers from an earlier age are often discernable in this corpus. Mann was, after all, the last writer who saw himself as the second coming of Weimar-Classical genius.

Lotte in Weimar was written much later in Mann's career, when the model for his literary self-fashioning had become Goethe, though it is also reasonable to assert, as Gamin Bartle has, that "In this novel, Mann invokes Goethe in order to break free from him" after having spent years imitating this genius.[31] *Lotte in Weimar* is a long and complex novel, and the image of Goethe that emerges from its pages is highly ambiguous. It is a fictional account of the 1816 Weimar visit of the widowed Charlotte Buff Kestner, the woman with whom Goethe was infatuated as a young man and whom he used as the model for the beautiful but betrothed Lotte, whose unavailability drives the eponymous hero to suicide in his wildly successful first novel, *Die Leiden des jungen Werther* (The sorrows of young Werther, 1774). The historical Goethe took only brief laconic note of this visit, but Mann employs the perspectives of a variety of visitors intimately connected with the great man, including his son, as they visit Kestner in her hotel in Weimar. Later, the fictional Goethe's own interior monologue is interspersed with conversations with his assistant. These passages, as well as Kestner's subsequent encounter with her former admirer at a party he holds for her and in a coach ride back to her hotel, flesh out a more unmediated portrait of the artist as an old man. This Goethe is by turns courteous and haughty, outgoing and secretive, brilliant and eccentric to the point of ridiculousness. While Mann's Goethe with his foibles and peculiarities cuts a sometimes amusing figure — albeit far less sympathetic than the frail but courageous and determined Schiller of "Schwere Stunde" — Mann nevertheless instrumentalizes the ever-authoritative figure of the "poet-prince" for ideological and political purposes in the novel, just as writers who advocated National Socialism were also doing at that time in Germany.

In doing so, Mann is prone to distort the historical record, a tendency certainly understandable under the circumstances and one not uncommon in today's *Goethezeit* fiction. This is especially the case as the fictional Goethe expresses his views concerning the Jewish people at the soirée given for Kestner. He speaks of a pogrom in Eger during which many Jews were murdered after a sermon by a monk blaming the Jews for all ills. Goethe characterizes the Jews as having become wise, skeptical, and ironic, marked by a pathos sometimes impressing outsiders as grotesque, through the venerable age of their race.[32] The allusion to the pogrom is an example of what Barbara Molinelli-Stein refers to as using Goethe as a mouthpiece to enunciate a critical-negative stance toward contemporary Germans throughout the novel, a circumstance, she notes, that led a British prosecutor at the Nuremberg Trials to cite an individual whom he thought was Goethe in railing against German atrocities but who turned out to be Mann's Goethe in *Lotte in Weimar*. As Molinelli-Stein argues, Goethe's comments on Judaism during the dinner table conversation allow Mann to make an admonitory reference to contemporary (late 1930s) circumstances in Germany in coded form.[33] The historical Goethe's attitude toward Jews, particularly with regard to the controversial issue of Jewish emancipation, was considerably more negative, as a recent essay has shown.[34] Mann's Goethe displays the same horror at the xenophobia and anti-French fervor — Napoleon's defeat had putatively liberated the German body politic from the enervating, debilitating, and overly refined influence of its western neighbor — that Mann was experiencing on the eve of the Second World War. He even prophesizes, alluding to the pogrom against the Jews of Eger, that worldwide hatred toward the Germans will be unleashed to a degree that will make the one evening of murder seem like a "Miniaturvor- und -abbild" (733; miniature model and likeness). In a different vein, Mann's Goethe reflects on parody as the highest form of art in one of his interior monologues, an ironic refraction of Mann's own proclivity toward parody considering that Goethe himself, through the amusingly ornate efflorescence of his stream of consciousness diction, is himself being parodied: "Das Geliebte, Heilige, Alte, das hohe Vorbild auf einer Stufe und mit Gehalten zu wiederholen, die ihm den Stempel des Parodischen verleihen und das Product sich späten, schon spottenden Auflösungsgebilden wie der nacheuripideischen Komödie annähern lassen . . ." (680–81; To repeat the beloved, sacred, old, the high exemplary at a level and with contents that lend it the stamp of the parodistic and allow it to approach the product of late, already mocking images of dissolution such as the post-Euripidean comedy . . .). Mann's conflicted distancing and approximation, ironic treatment as well as instrumentalization, and parody and appropriation of Germany's most venerated writer is unique in the corpus of *Goethezeit* fiction. The body of work examined in the subsequent chapters of this book is marked by a rather different set of proclivities, styles, and attitudes.

Another canonic work featuring Goethe as a fictional character, albeit in a minor role, was written by Mann's contemporary Hermann Hesse. Hesse's *Der Steppenwolf* was published in 1927, some twelve years prior to *Lotte in Weimar*, but achieved its greatest popularity among young people in the 1960s and 1970s. The disaffected youth in this period saw a role model in the book's central protagonist, Harry Haller — the "wolf of the steppes" of the title — for his rejection of bourgeois values, nationalism, and militarism in his quest for a harmonious existence, a search involving the ingestion of psychotropic drugs and a certain sexual abandon. These pursuits, of course, found favor among the 1968 generation in Western Europe and the United States, a generation that widely emulated these aspects of Harry Haller's lifestyle. However, unlike the 1968 generation of German writers, who largely associated Goethe with stultifying middle-class values or the kind of decadence they regarded as amoral, as chapter 4 will show, Haller the Steppenwolf encounters a playful, joking, immortally wise Goethe in a brief dream sequence in the first half of the novel. Like Mann in the late 1920s and 1930s, Hesse regarded Goethe at that time as a cosmopolitan humanist whose genuine values were contrary to those of the militarist and nationalist Germans whose shrill voices dominated the political and academic milieu in the first half of the twentieth century. Academic mandarins who supported such militarism tended to represent Goethe as a titanic, lonely but stolid exemplar of their own bourgeois worldview. Precisely this image of Goethe is utterly repugnant to Haller when he encounters it in the tacit perspective, and even the painting, of a professor and wife whose home he visits.[35]

When Haller falls into a dream shortly after fleeing the professor's house and plunging into the demimonde of a local tavern, he finds himself as a journal correspondent in the presence of Goethe, who at first seems to embody the professor's view of him, stiff and officious, with an order of merit on his "classical breast." Indeed, Haller begins his conversation with the dream Goethe by claiming that his generation of youth finds the poet too pompous, vain, and ceremonious. However, Haller then realizes the man before him is the author of the verse "Dämmrung senkte sich von oben" (Twilight descended from above, 1827), with its Romantic evocation of a nocturnally holistic world. While Haller goes on to accuse Goethe of an inauthenticity rooted in a shallow optimism that denies the profound despairing truth recognized by Beethoven and Kleist, even, indeed, by the poet himself, Goethe disarms him by citing Mozart's opera *Die Zauberflöte* (The magic flute, 1791), Haller's favorite work (as he angrily confesses) as an example of an authentically realized optimism and belief. Goethe confesses to having pursued, in life, the immortality of which Haller had accused him, but reveals his childlike, playful, curious nature.

Haller is irritated by Goethe's joking ripostes, even as the poet's visage becomes young and rosy, resembling that of Schubert and Mozart. Goethe tells Haller that he should not take him so seriously, that the immortals don't like such a reception, and that they love fun. Goethe dances about and proffers a tiny female leg that Haller suspects is the scorpion he had encountered at the outset of the dream, a suspicion that pleases Goethe and prompts him to further tease the Steppenwolf. His dream ends with an image of a thousand-year-old Goethe laughing to himself with a profound old man's humor (*Greisenhumor*).[36] As Henry Hatfield has noted, the dream Goethe, along with a dream Mozart, play a role in guiding Haller away from his destructive solipsism toward a guilt-free embrace of the erotic, toward an enjoyment of the present, and toward laughter.[37] Hesse is unique in creating a fictional Goethe who, through the Steppenwolf's accusations, not only reflects contemporary critiques of the poet and anticipates the late-twentieth-century fictional persiflage of this author, but allows his Goethe to deflect such criticism and emerge as an ideal archetype, the venerable, indeed immortal old man who teaches one to live joyfully in the present.

Looking Ahead

Of all the Age-of-Goethe fiction composed between Goethe's death in 1832 and the 1970s, only the Büchner and Mann works discussed above have stood the test of time by their continuous inclusion in an ever-shifting canon. Other works belonging to this genre, such as Mühlbach's novel on Goethe and Schiller, remain of interest mostly to scholars like Peterson, who are interested in issues raised by cultural studies, the relationship of literature to history, and reception theory. It is, of course, impossible to know the future critical and commercial fate of the *Goethezeit* fiction that is discussed in the subsequent chapters of this book. Far and away the most successful of these works, with respect to popular acclaim and sales figures, is Kehlmann's *Die Vermessung der Welt*. However, one of Germany's most eminent Humboldt scholars, Ottmar Ette, criticizes this work for its alleged grotesque distortion of the historical record and surmises that it may ultimately lapse into obscurity like another piece of Humboldt fiction he considers to be a literary hatchet job, Eugen Hermann von Dedenroth's novella "Ein Sohn Alexander's von Humboldt oder der Indianer von Maypures" (A son of Alexander von Humboldt or the Indian from Maypures, 1858). As the title indicates, Dedenroth's fictional Humboldt is the father of an illegitimate son, which Ette believes was based on the rumors, commonplaces, readings, facts, and half-truths then in currency concerning the explorer — a mixture Ette believes created the basis for Kehlmann's novel[38] — though, one must add, the Humboldt of *Die Vermessung der Welt* is a homosexual with absolutely no sexual interest in women. Whether or not Kehlmann's novel and other texts examined in the rest of my book will be forgotten or become part of the German literary canon (if canons continue to exist), their analysis provides a window onto the insights, proclivities, and styles of recent and contemporary German authors and, most uniquely, on their relationship to Germany's most celebrated literary and intellectual period through the guise of their fiction. Opening this window is the goal of my book.

My exploration begins with an analysis of what is currently the most canonic work of *Goethezeit* fiction written since the beginning of the 1970s: Christa Wolf's *Kein Ort. Nirgends* (No place on earth, 1979). In this short novel, Wolf creates a fictional encounter between the authors Heinrich von Kleist and Karoline von Günderrode. Unlike the numerous prior treatments of this work, chapter 1 accords significant attention to another key writer from the period, who makes only a brief appearance in this work but plays a major role in its historical allusions: Bettine Brentano. Because of the novel's radical decentering of voice, it is uniquely engaged in a covert dialogue with the oeuvre of these three authors. Therefore, unlike in subsequent chapters, I examine relevant works by these *Goethezeit* writers themselves in some detail in order to situate Wolf's ideological position, which is also grounded in the famous epistolary debate between Lukács and Anna Seghers in the 1930s. I compare Wolf's treatment of Kleist with that of other authors, particularly the West German Karin Reschke in her 1982 novel *Verfolgte des Glücks: Findebuch der Henriette Vogel* (A woman persecuted by happiness: The diary of Henriette Vogel). This novel narrates the life of the title figure, with whom the historical Kleist committed joint suicide, through fictional diary passages and letters. Chapter 1 concludes by contrasting Wolf's fictional treatment of Bettine Brentano with that of Günter Grass's *Der Butt* (The flounder, 1978), which is also informed, albeit to a lesser degree and from a quite disparate perspective, by a yearning for a gender-transcending social holism.

Chapter 2 continues the comparison between DDR and FRG voices by looking at Hölderlin fiction composed by two authors associated with each country: Stephan Hermlin and Gerhard Wolf (Christa's husband) from the East and Peter Weiss and Peter Härtling from the West. All four authors recuperate Hölderlin from his unfortunate deployment as a battlefield inspiration and fatherland poet by the Nazis during the Second World War. The chapter opens with a discussion of Lukács's essay on Hölderlin, which is somewhat ambivalent with respect to the poet's political stance and which impacted subsequent engagements with the poet. The chapter then focuses on Hermlin's radio play *Scardanelli* (1970), a relatively apolitical text that charts Hölderlin's gradual lapse into insanity through a series of fifteen rather incohesive scenes. This analysis is followed by an examination of Wolf's novel *Der arme Hölderlin* (Poor Hölderlin, 1972), a somewhat experimental work that deviates from GDR socialist realism in shuttling between first- and third-person narrative perspectives to evoke the intersection between the personal and the political; both domains, in tandem, are shown to bring about the poet's madness. Weiss's play *Hölderlin* (1971) paints the poet as a radical supporter of the French Revolution and as a tragic victim of the reactionary German forces who are supported by Goethe and Hegel — both of whom are portrayed as sycophants of the nobility and the emerging bourgeoisie. The West German Härtling's novel *Hölderlin* (1976) blends personal autobiography (the narrator follows the young Härtling's retracing of Hölderlin's paths through Swabia) with an imaginative account of the poet's life. Hermlin, Wolf, Weiss, and Härtling all provide sympathetic portraits of the poet, but create quite disparate works with respect to style, genre, faithfulness to the historical record, and personal (authorial) identification.

The third chapter looks at a series of historical novels by Renate Feyl, who began writing Goethezeit fiction in the GDR and continues to do so today as a resident of unified Berlin. Her work is shown to be informed by both the effort to shape German national identity in the current global age and to articulate a nascent feminist struggle among women who wrote in the eighteenth and early nineteenth centuries. Her primary protagonists are all women of letters who lived in the shadows, and often under the domineering tutelage, of men, their husbands and/or other male literary figures of the time. These include Luise Gottsched, the wife of the highly influential mid-eighteenth-century literary theorist Johann Christoph Gottsched, who treated her tyrannically and was jealous of her own literary success after the bloom of their initially happy marriage had worn off (in *Idylle mit Professor* [Idyll with professor, 1986]); Sophie La Roche, the first famous German-language woman writer (in *Die profanen Stunden des Glücks* [The profane hours of happiness, 1996]); and Caroline von Wolzogen, whose primary fame was based on her status as Schiller's sister-in-law but who has become more recently examined as an author of note (in *Das sanfte Joch der Vortrefflichkeit* [The gentle yoke of exemplarity, 1999]). Feyl's historical novel on the relationship between Prussia's first queen, Sophie Charlotte, and the early Enlightenment philosopher Gottfried Wilhelm Leibniz (*Aussicht auf bleibende Helle: Die Königin und der Philosoph* [Prospect for enduring luminosity: The queen and the philosopher, 2006]) is also shown to be relevant to the elucidation of Feyl's poetics situated between nationalism and feminism. I was able to interview Feyl at her Berlin home in August 2008, and I draw upon our conversation in my analysis of her historical novels. Chapter 3 concludes by briefly contrasting her approach to this genre with that of another significant GDR feminist, Brigitte Struzyk, who wrote a novel set in the Age of Goethe, *Caroline unterm Freiheitsbaum: Ansichtssachen* (Caroline under the freedom tree: Perspectival matters, 1988), on the irreverent Caroline Böhmer-Schlegel-Schelling, a central figure among the early German Romantics.

The figure of Goethe plays a central role in many of the works examined in chapters 2 and 3, and, to a lesser extent, in chapter 1, but chapter 4 looks at fiction centered primarily on this personage. Like Mann's *Lotte in Weimar*, these works tend to exhibit a conflicted attitude toward the poet, sometimes highlighting his foibles and tyranny (particularly toward his factotum Johann Peter Eckermann) through parody and persiflage, while at other times evoking his extraordinary, overarching, often spontaneously manifest genius. These works are sometimes marked by satiric humor, as in the highly irreverent depiction of Goethe as an absent lothario through the eyes of his erstwhile lover Charlotte von Stein in a monologue by East German playwright Peter Hacks, *Ein Gespräch im Hause Stein über den abwesenden Herrn von Goethe* (A conversation in the Stein house concerning the absent Goethe, 1974). He comes across as a rather tactless lover in a novel focused on Frau von Stein by the East German writer Johanna Hoffmann, *Charlotte von Stein: Goethe und ich werden niemals Freunde* (Charlotte von Stein: Goethe and I will never be friends, 1988), and as a manipulative, selfish brother in Sigrid Damm's semi-fictional biography of his sister Cornelia, *Cornelia Goethe* (1987). An even more caustic parody of Goethe as a senile but lascivious despot is evident in an Eckermann-focused radio play by Martin Walser, *In Goethes Hand: Szenen aus dem 19. Jahrhundert* (In Goethe's hand: Scenes from the nineteenth century, 1982). Walser goes on to treat Goethe more sympathetically — but still somewhat comically — as an aging lover in his novel *Ein liebender Mann* (A loving man), published in 2008. Like Walser, Jens Sparschuh explores Eckermann's relationship with Goethe in his novel *Der große Coup: Aus den geheimen Tage- und Nachtbüchern des Johann Peter Eckermann* (The great coup: From the secret day and night diaries of Johann Peter Eckermann, 1987). However, here Eckermann becomes the first-person narrator who, unlike Walser's Eckermann, possesses genuine agency and is able to use it to shape Goethe's posthumous reception as Germany's most immortal writer. In the humorous novel *Faustinas Küsse* (Faustina's kisses, 1998), Hans-Josef Ortheil recreates Goethe's long sojourn in Italy through the eyes of a fictional Italian laborer, who latches onto the poet as a hoped-for meal ticket after Goethe arrives in Rome. A novella by Henning Boëtius, *Tod in Weimar* (Death in Weimar, 1999), portrays Goethe as utterly debauched even on the verge of death. Common to all these texts seems to be the effort finally to put an end to the German cult of Goethe.

To be sure, there is a countertrend in recent German fiction on Goethe that tends to present the poet in a positive, though still not hagiographic, manner. Otto Böhmer's novel *Der junge Herr Goethe* (The young Mr. Goethe) — also published in 1999 on the 250th anniversary of Goethe's birth — imagines the young poet as dynamic and full of energy, albeit plagued somewhat by self-doubt. Rafik Schami's novel of the same year, *Der geheime Bericht über den Dichter Goethe, der eine Prüfung auf einer arabischen Insel bestand* (The secret report on the poet Goethe, who passed a test on an Arabian island), which was coauthored with Uwe-Michael Gutzschhahn, displays a highly positive treatment of Goethe. Though the poet himself is not a character, he is still a prized source of wisdom for the residents of the fictional island of Hulm in the late nineteenth century. Schami and Gutzschhahn uphold Goethe as a model of multicultural probity for a contemporary young German audience, though the novel's bleak, indeed dystopian, conclusion somewhat reduces the effectiveness of his presentation as a paragon. In Robert Löhr's novels *Das Erlkönig-Manöver* (The earl-king maneuver, 2007) and *Das Hamlet-Komplott* (The Hamlet conspiracy, 2010), Goethe is presented as a cautious but brave leader to bands of illustrious literary contemporaries in campaigns against the Napoleonic occupation of Germany.

In addition to undermining the hagiographic status still accorded Germany's most famous writer, a major goal of German postmodernism has been the deconstruction of the Age of Enlightenment. Works exhibiting this tendency include Kehlmann's novel on Humboldt and Gauß, as well as Huizing's lesser-known *Das Ding an sich*, which depicts the Enlightenment paragon Kant's relationship with the visionary language philosopher Hamann, centering on their attempt to disenchant a magically potent shard from the time of Adam. Another focus of chapter 5 is Gert Hofmann's novel on the brilliant scientist/aphorist Georg Christoph Lichtenberg's liaison with a preadolescent girl, *Die kleine Stechardin* (translated as Lichtenberg and the little flower girl, 1994), which adopts a fairy-tale tone to underscore Lichtenberg's childlike side and to disarm the suggestion of sexual abuse against a minor that would otherwise come into play. The chapter draws on the work of philosopher Hans Blumenberg in contextualizing the fictional treatments of Humboldt, Kant, and Lichtenberg. It opens with a brief examination of GDR playwright Heiner Müller's drama *Leben Gundlings Friedrich von Preußen Lessings Schlaf Traum Schrei: Ein Greuelmärchen* (Gundling's life Friedrich of Prussia Lessing's sleep dream scream: A horror story, 1976), the pioneering work of postmodern anti-Enlightenment fiction. This Enlightenment critique is also taken up by Sparschuh in his novel *Lavaters Maske* (Lavater's mask, 1999), set in contemporary Germany and Switzerland but with flashbacks to the life of the eighteenth-century Swiss physiognomist Johann Kaspar Lavater. The blending of past and present turns Lavater into a kind of forerunner and model for the all-encompassing surveillance techniques Michel Foucault famously traced to the late eighteenth-century Age of Enlightenment.

By way of contrast, fictional prose on Humboldt by Christoph Hein and a recent novel on Lichtenberg by Boëtius are works that underscore the positive aspects of the Age of Enlightenment. Hein's story "Die russischen Briefe des Jägers Johann Seifert" (The Russian letters of the hunter Johann Seifert), part of the collection *Einladung zum Lever Bourgeois* (Invitation to the Lever bourgeois, 1980), portrays Humboldt as a courageous Enlightenment visionary by creating an imaginative account of his Russian travels. Boëtius's *Der Gnom: Ein Lichtenberg-Roman* (The gnome: A Lichtenberg novel, 1989) highlights Lichtenberg's courage as a scientific researcher and exposer of charlatanism.

Age-of-Goethe Fiction and the Contemporary Nation(s)

Though this book engages in a few brief discussions of works by Austrian and Swiss writers, the vast majority of writers examined are products of the three post-war Germanies: the Federal Republic of Germany, the German Democratic Republic, and the contemporary unified state popularly known as the Berlin Republic. An obviously relevant question concerns the degree to which texts were shaped by the politics and cultural ambience of the three nations in which the various authors resided. In certain instances, the influence exerted by the sociopolitical landscapes of the three countries was not inconsiderable. The chapter on Hölderlin fiction is organized according to the citizenship of its authors. Contemporary political perspectives strongly shaped the Hölderlin play of Weiss, who resided in the West, and played a more subtle background role in the thematics and structure of Gerhard Wolf's *Der arme Hölderlin*. *Imagining the Age of Goethe* argues on several occasions that the Romantic "turn" in East German Age-of-Goethe fiction was largely triggered by that country's expulsion of singer/songwriter Wolf Biermann, as well as by a conscious decision to side with Seghers in her defense of the German Romantics rather than Lukács in his preference for Goethe (the debate between these two celebrated Marxists is discussed in chapter 1). The playfully ironic, humorous treatment of serious subjects — such as Goethe's sojourn in Italy in Ortheil's novel and the proleptic ambience of impending environmental catastrophe in Kehlmann's best-selling send-up of Humboldt and Gauß — are treated as hallmarks of contemporary Berlin Republic postmodernism.

Nevertheless, this book deliberately resists the temptation to assume a seminal link between the approach of the authors explored here and their affiliations with the three Germanies in which, by choice or birth, they resided or reside. Such a one-sided orientation would very likely lead to inaccurate generalizations. Let us consider, for example, the examples of feminist *Goethezeit* literature: It is safe to say that this subset of texts highlights the unequal treatment of women in eighteenth- and early nineteenth-century Germany by the patriarchy who dominated the cultural and political institutions of the small states constituting the pre-1871 fatherland. In her 1986 study of women's literature in the Federal Republic of Germany, Karin Richter-Schröder argues that a focus on contemporary life (the 1970s and early 1980s) in works with a strong autobiographical component is the hallmark of FRG "Frauenliteratur" during what we can now term its last decades.[39] Richter-Schröder may be accurate with respect to broad trends in that country's feminist literature, but her analysis does not necessarily apply to West German fiction featuring women authors of the Age of Goethe. While it may be argued that all fiction has an autobiographical component, Reschke's novel on Henriette Vogel and Kleist, and Struzyk's on Caroline Böhmer-Schlegel-Schelling, are by their very nature historical biographical fiction rather than autobiographical, even though Reschke's Vogel is possessed of a West German feminist consciousness drawn from her author's world view. In her book on GDR feminist writing, Lorna Martens claims that, contrary to the writing of Western feminists, East German fiction by female authors tended not to portray women as victims, due to the socialist context of the country, which created more equal working opportunities for women through well-developed institutional networks. Thus, in Martens's view, GDR feminist literature differed from that of the West in tending to represent women as competent and possessed of fortitude.[40] While this latter characterization certainly applies to the chief protagonists of Feyl's novels, they also are sometimes, like Wolf's Günderrode, portrayed as victims lacking the benefits Martens believes were available to their gender in the socialist GDR state. In sum, while national affiliation did, in certain instances, impact the form and content of Age-of-Goethe fiction from the 1970s to the present, it was not usually decisive, and I found it more productive to focus on the discrete proclivities of individual authors and works. When these works display similar tendencies — allowing them to be grouped into cohesive subsets — the unifying factors tend to be grounded in similar thematic, formal/structural, and psychological elements rather than in national/political factors. Although this brief overview indicates widely disparate attitudes and styles in the fictional engagements with the intellectuals of the Age of Goethe from the 1970s to the present, it also underscores that a continuing obsession with this period marks the work of contemporary German authors.

Notes

[1] A good example is Thomas Mann's embrace of Goethe as an exemplary citizen, educator, and man of tolerance during the years of the Third Reich. This politically motivated perspective is summarized by Manfred Dierks in his "Thomas Mann's Late Politics," in *A Companion to the Works of Thomas Mann*, ed. Herbert Lehnert and Eva Wessell (Rochester, NY: Camden House, 2004), 207–10.

[2] Fritz Strich, *Goethe und die Weltliteratur* (Bern: Francke, 1946).

[3] Robert Lohan, ed., *The Golden Age of German Literature* (New York: Frederick Ungar, 1945).

[4] Friedrich Meinecke, *Weltbürgertum und Nationalstaat*, 6th ed. (Munich: R. Oldenbourg, 1922), 3.

[5] See Karl Robert Mandelkow, *Goethe in Deutschland: Rezeptionsgeschichte eines Klassikers. Band II: 1919–1982* (Munich: C. H. Beck, 1989), 136.

[6] Katharina Gerstenberger, *Writing the New Berlin: The German Capital in Post-Wall Literature* (Rochester, NY: Camden House, 2008), 2.

[7] See, for example, Roberta Seret, *Voyage into Creativity: The Modern Künstlerroman* (New York: Peter Lang, 1992), and Evy Varsamopoulou, *The Poetics of the* Künstlerinroman *and the Aesthetics of the Sublime* (Burlington, VT: Ashgate, 2002).

[8] Georg Lukács, *Werke*, vol. 6, *Probleme des Realismus III: Der historische Roman* (Neuwied: Luchterhand, 1965), 23.

[9] Hans Vilmar Geppert, *Der 'andere' historische Roman: Theorie und Strukturen einer diskontinuierlichen Gattung* (Tübingen: Max Niemeyer, 1976), 1–15.

[10] Hugo Aust, *Der historische Roman* (Stuttgart: J. B. Metzler, 1994), 33.

[11] David Roberts, "The Modern German Historical Novel: An Introduction," in *The Modern German Historical Novel: Paradigms, Problems, Perspectives*, ed. David Roberts and Philip Thomson (Oxford: Berg, 1991), 16.

[12] Osman Durrani, "Introduction," in *Travellers in Time and Space: The German Historical Novel/Reisende durch Zeit und Raum: Der deutschsprachige historische Roman*, ed. Osman Durrani and Julian Preece (Amsterdam: Rodopi, 2001), iii.

[13] Seret, *Voyage into Creativity*, 1–12.

[14] Varsamopoulou, *Poetics of the* Künstlerinroman, xiv.

[15] Varsamopoulou, *Poetics of the* Künstlerinroman, xii–xiii.

[16] Hans Ester and Guillaume van Gemert, "Zum Geleit," in *Künstler-Bilder: Zur produktiven Auseinandersetzung mit der schöpferischen Persönlichkeit*, ed. Hans Ester and Guillaume van Gemert (Amsterdam: Rodopi, 2003), 7–8.

[17] Peter V. Zima, *Der europäische Künstlerroman: Von der romantischen Utopie zur postmodernen Parodie* (Tübingen: A Francke, 2008), xi–xv.

[18] Ralf Sudau, *Werkbearbeitung, Dichterfiguren: Traditionsaneignung am Beispiel der deutschen Gegenwartsliteratur* (Tübingen: Max Niemeyer, 1985), 118–63.

[19] Paul Franssen and Ton Hoenselaars, "Introduction. The Author as Character: Defining a Genre," in *The Author as Character: Representing Historical Writers in Western Literature*, ed. Paul Franssen and Ton Hoenselaars (Cranbury, NJ: Fairleigh Dickinson UP, 1999), 11–35, esp. 20 and 28.

[20] Franssen and Hoenselaars, "Introduction," 18.

[21] Brent O. Peterson, "Mühlbach, Ranke, and the Truth of Historical Fiction," in *A Companion to German Realism 1848–1900*, ed. Todd Kontje (Rochester, NY: Camden House, 2002), 69. For a broader discussion of Mühlbach as an author who (as she herself asserted in the preface to *Deutschland in Sturm und Drang*) was more an illustrator and popularizer of history for a broad public than a writer with serious aesthetic ambitions, see Hartmut Eggert, *Studien zur Wirkungsgeschichte des deutschen historischen Romans 1850–1875* (Frankfurt am Main: Vittorio Klostermann, 1971), 69–77.

[22] Jens Kruse, "The Political Uses of 'Goethe' during the Nazi Period: Goethe Fictions between 1933 and 1945," *New German Review* 19 (2003–4): 12–29.

[23] Kruse, "'Goethe' und Adenauer als Dioskuren: die Goethe-Fiktionen der fünfziger Jahre," *Germanic Review* 63 (1988): 189–96.

[24] Arno Schmidt, "Goethe und Einer seiner Bewunderer," in *Das erzählerische Werk in 8 Bänden* (Bargfeld: Arno Schmidt Stiftung, 1985), 6:48.

[25] Schmidt's fantastic projection of Goethe into a twentieth-century time frame was repeated by the Austrian author Thomas Bernhard in his short story "Goethe schtirbt" (Goethe dies, 1982), in which the poet's last wish is to have the man he admires most in the world, the twentieth-century philosopher Ludwig Wittgenstein, brought from Oxford or Cambridge to his deathbed. Bernhard also wrote a play, *Immanuel Kant* (1978), which portrays the philosopher on a late twentieth-century cruise ship journeying to New York, where he is to receive an honorary degree from Columbia University and have his glaucoma cured. As Bernhard's Kant claims to be a friend of the philosopher Gottfried Wilhelm Leibniz, who died eight years prior to the historical Kant's birth, Bernhard can be said to have bent the play's historical time frame backwards as well as forwards. However, because the play concludes with Kant being assisted from the ship on its arrival in

New York by doctors and assistants from an insane asylum, Bernhard suggests this Kant is a crazed impostor who parrots the historical philosopher's ideas and spouts grotesquely abridged citations from his work, much as the fictional Kant's parrot Friedrich repeats snippets of his master's dialogue on the ship. Thomas Bernhard, "Goethe schtirbt," *Die Zeit*, 19 March 1982: 41–42; "Immanuel Kant," in *Die Stücke 1969–1981* (Frankfurt am Main: Suhrkamp, 1983), 595–684.

[26] Georg Büchner, "Lenz," in *Werke und Briefe* (Munich: dtv, 1980), 89.

[27] Maurice B. Benn, *The Drama of Revolt: A Critical Study of Georg Büchner* (Cambridge: Cambridge UP, 1976), 193.

[28] For an analysis of Walser's dramatic sketch, see my essay, "'Man schaffe ihn auf eine sanfte Manier fort': Robert Walser's *Lenz* as a Cipher for the Dark Side of Modernity," in *Space to Act: The Theater of J. M. R. Lenz*, ed. Alan C. Leidner and Helga S. Madland (Columbia, SC: Camden House, 1993), 141–49. For a discussion of the "Lenz narratives" inspired by Büchner's novella, see Timm Reiner Menke, *Lenz-Erzählungen in der deutschen Literatur* (Hildesheim: Georg Olms, 1984). Consistent with his book's focus on short prose narratives, Menke's chapter on Robert Walser does not examine the Lenz drama but rather Walser's story "Kleist in Thun" (1907), which evokes this author's alienation and isolation. I will briefly discuss "Kleist in Thun" in chapter 1.

[29] Thomas Mann, "Schwere Stunde," in *Gesammelte Werke in zwölf Bänden* (Oldenbourg: S. Fischer, 1960), 8:377.

[30] Hans Rudolf Vaget, "Thomas Mann, Schiller, and the Politics of Literary Self-Fashioning," *Monatshefte* 97 (2005): 494.

[31] Gamin Bartle, "Displacing Goethe: Tribute and Exorcism in Thomas Mann's *The Beloved Returns*," in *The Author as Character*, 198.

[32] Mann, "Lotte in Weimar," in *Gesammelte Werke*, 2:727–30.

[33] Barbara Molinelli-Stein, *Thomas Mann: Das Werk als Selbstinszenierung eines problematischen Ichs. Versuch einer psycho-existenziellen Strukturanalyse zu den Romanen* Lotte in Weimar *und* Doktor Faustus (Tübingen: Stauffenburg, 1999), 17–18.

[34] See W. Daniel Wilson, "'Humanitätssalbader': Goethe's Distaste for Jewish Emancipation, and Jewish Responses," in *Goethe in German-Jewish Culture*, ed. Klaus L. Berghahn and Jost Hermand (Rochester, NY: Camden House: 2001), 146–64.

[35] See Hans-Joachim Hahn, "Hermann Hesse's Goethe," in *A Companion to the Works of Hermann Hesse*, ed. Ingo Cornils (Rochester, NY: Camden House, 2009), 399–400.

[36] Hermann Hesse, *Der Steppenwolf*, 40th ed. (Berlin: S. Fischer, 1931), 106–14.

[37] Henry Hatfield, *Crisis and Continuity in Modern German Fiction: Ten Essays* (Ithaca: Cornell UP, 1969), 69–70.

[38] Ottmar Ette, *Alexander von Humboldt und die Globalisierung: Das Mobile des Wissens* (Frankfurt am Main: Insel, 2009), 314.

[39] Karin Richter-Schröder, *Frauenliteratur und weibliche Identität: Theoretische Ansätze zu einer weiblichen Ästhetik und zur Entwicklung der neuen deutschen Frauenliteratur* (Frankfurt am Main: Hain, 1986), 1–8.

[40] Lorna Martens, *The Promised Land? Feminist Writing in the German Democratic Republic* (Albany: SUNY P, 2001), 18–22. Of course, not all scholars of West German feminist literature would agree that works belonging to this category treated women as victims. For contrary perspectives, see Leslie A. Adelson, *Making Bodies, Making History: Feminism and German Identity* (Lincoln: U of Nebraska P, 1993), 36, and Richard W. McCormick, *Politics of the Self: Feminism and the Postmodern in West German Literature and Film* (Princeton, NJ: Princeton UP, 1991), 76.

1: Staging Violence and Transcendence, Embracing Feminism: The Instantiation of Kleist and German Romanticism

THIS CHAPTER IS PRIMARILY DEVOTED to an examination of the most canonic work of the subgenre that is the focus of *Imagining the Age of Goethe*: Christa Wolf's novel *Kein Ort. Nirgends*[1] (No place on earth, 1979). In order to understand Wolf's fictional treatment of the Age-of-Goethe authors Heinrich von Kleist and Caroline von Günderrode, Wolf's essays on Kleist and Günderrode will be frequently cited. This will also be the case with Wolf's article on Bettine Brentano. This latter personage appears to be a minor figure in Wolf's novel, but plays a more significant, albeit tacit role, than previous critics have realized. While earlier engagements with the novel have examined Wolf and the Romantics primarily as a subject-object relationship, that is to say, with how the subject (author Christa Wolf) creates an object (the world of early nineteenth-century German Romanticism[2]), I will reverse the terms of this agency. In other words, instead of explaining once again how Christa Wolf projects a Romantic world view, I will show how German Romanticism itself stages — which is to say, brings about — the writing of Christa Wolf. This is not as radical a process as it might sound and involves neither a genuine dialectical reversal nor a shift to the passive voice, as though Wolf were merely an inert object performed by the Romantic past. Although I will indeed draw on the discourse of performativity, as the constructed character of genre (elucidated by Judith Butler[3]) is a key factor in the composition of Wolf's novel, my methodology is counterintuitive primarily through its inversion of the chronology governing other examinations of Wolf and German Romanticism. That is to say, rather than beginning with Wolf and immediately examining the Romantics through the filter of her reading, this chapter will commence with the examination of a key motif, violent conflict and war, in selected works by the authors who are the key protagonists in *Kein Ort. Nirgends*: Günderrode, Kleist, and (again, at a subtextual level), Brentano. For although violence receives, at the surface level, only marginal treatment in Wolf's novel — and although such works as *Kassandra* (1983) and *Störfall* (Accident, 1987) have justly established her reputation as a pacifist — belligerent confrontation and revolution receive a psychic staging in *Kein Ort. Nirgends*. This subtle enactment of violence is tied not only to the future suicides of its main protagonists and their general fate as social outcasts, but to the novel's employment of gender reversal and androgyny with respect to both Günderrode and Kleist, as well as its concomitant evocation of social transcendence. This dimension of Wolf's relationship to German Romanticism has been largely ignored, and can only be established by first looking at the treatment of violence by Kleist, Günderrode, and Brentano. (Brentano's voice also articulates the novel's utopian projection of transcendence.) Only then can we proceed to examine not only Wolf's novel and essays on these three figures, but also the somewhat misunderstood origins of her initial engagement with German Romanticism in the famous debate on realism between Georg Lukács and Anna Seghers. I will also consider the contrast between Wolf's treatment of Kleist and that of Karin Reschke in her novel *Verfolgte des Glücks: Findebuch der Henriette Vogel* (A woman persecuted by happiness: The diary of Henriette Vogel, 1982).[4] This section begins with a brief examination of two earlier fictional characterizations of Kleist by Robert Walser[5] and Günter Kunert[6] to demonstrate the consistency of twentieth-century German novelists in drawing upon the figure of Kleist as an exemplar, like Hölderlin, of the gifted but tragically marginalized author, the paradigmatic literary outsider. I will conclude the chapter by contrasting *Kein Ort. Nirgends* with Günter Grass's novel *Der Butt*[7] (The flounder, 1978), in which another coterie of German Romantics (also including Bettine and her brother Clemens Brentano) is imaginatively recreated, but with a rather disparate treatment of the utopian gender transcendence evident in Wolf's nearly contemporaneous, albeit considerably shorter, work.

Violence and Enthusiasm in Kleist, Günderrode, and Brentano

Wolf's uniquely intersubjective style, her attempt to understand her characters and engage with them rather than simply make them fictional objects, makes her novel a dialogue with her protagonists, one which cannot be understood without drawing upon the historical work of her dialogue partners. Additionally, the motif of violence in Wolf's novel can only be elucidated by showing where in the works of Kleist, Günderrode, and Bettine Brentano this motif is articulated, indeed valorized, because this valorization becomes tacitly integrated into *Kein Ort. Nirgends.* The intersection between violent contestation, including warfare, and the employment of the motif of androgyny in the service of transcending traditional constructed/constricting gender roles in the works of these three authors has recently been explored in scholarly monographs by Elisabeth Krimmer[8] and Patricia Simpson.[9] Krimmer has argued that Kleist attempts to inscribe the female body as a locus of truth and identity within a stable framework, thereby grounding gender in nature in an age when sign systems were beginning to be harnessed in the service of creating a socially normative, regulated relationship between the sexes. However, Krimmer finds that Kleist's doubts regarding an overarching truth invested in gender cause him to employ the motif of cross-dressing in order to deconstruct this very stability in his drama *Die Familie Schroffenstein* (1803). In Simpson's reading of Kleist's *Penthesilea* (1808), Achilles is the figure who insists on the stable division of the sexes, but both he and the eponymous heroine reject their social orders' regulative models of desire within the domain of war, with transcendent, transgressive, but concomitantly tragic results for both. Both Krimmer and Simpson argue that Günderrode, with her poetic world of feminized men and manly women, tacitly dismissed the normative gender dichotomies deconstructed by Kleist out of hand, but Simpson argues that some female characters in Günderrode not only adopt traditionally male sexual roles, but also the values of male hierarchies. As with Kleist, the transgression of sexual boundaries leads to a tragic fate in Günderrode's dramatic works, and the unrealizable desire to transcend highly constrictive class-based, as well as gender-based, limitations drove her to suicide. Indeed, these parallels in the artistic and personal lives of Kleist and Günderrode inspired Wolf to imagine their meeting in *Kein Ort. Nirgends.*

War, aggression, revenge, and bloodletting are, of course, constant motifs throughout the range of Kleist's oeuvre, and have been exhaustively treated.[10] However, the basis for the seeming valorization of violent conflict on the part of Günderrode and Brentano has been less widely explored, so that Krimmer and Simpson are most innovative in this regard. More cogently than previous scholars, Krimmer shows that the instantiation of physical battle in Günderrode and Brentano is grounded in the ability of warfare — or at least its poetic enactment — to destabilize conventional notions of gender roles, to expose their culturally driven, artificial constructedness, which is in fact the role assigned by Butler to transsexuals and transvestites in her engagement with boundary-crossing gender performativity. In Krimmer's view, belletristically driven cross-dressing in Brentano's poetry, thought, and even personal life plays a key role in her attempts to destabilize the rigid gender boundaries characteristic of her age. While the free-spirited Brentano valiantly struggled to overcome gender and class hierarchies personally and artistically throughout the course of her long and productive life, her more reticent, introverted friend Günderrode could not sustain this battle. In Krimmer's reading, Günderrode's frequent use of gender role reversal in her protagonists stems from her own sense of impotence as "a male spirit trapped in a female body,"[11] an emotion reflected in the tragic, violent demise of her heroines as well as her own suicide. For Simpson, Günderrode's poetic enactment of warfare and dueling constitutes the articulation of a desire to negotiate a role for the feminine in the fight for a fatherland, and is inscribed within the structure of a martial erotics that Simpson identifies with German Romanticism *tout court*. She sees Brentano's poetic engagement with warfare as her attempt to construct a "postenlightenment universal feminine."[12] Although Brentano, on the surface level, plays only a secondary role in Wolf's novel, this dimension of her political volition is evident in Wolf's essay on her, and can be read back into *Kein Ort. Nirgends* in such a way that Wolf's own purpose in articulating a socially and sexually transcendent imaginary can be brought to the fore.

Krimmer and Simpson highlight elements of the art and lives of Kleist, Günderrode, and Brentano that are evident in Wolf's essays on these figures and in *Kein Ort. Nirgends*, as I will show. However, I will also examine works of these Romantic authors relevant to understanding how and why these writers are treated in Wolf's imaginative and essayistic engagements with them from within a rather different order of signification, one that has only recently come to the fore in understanding the Enlightenment and what Simpson terms the "postenlightenment." This area of discussion, constituted by Kantian and post-Kantian debates concerning the dichotomy between enthusiasm and fanaticism, has not been previously applied to Wolf's engagement with German Romanticism. While Kant was ambivalent about enthusiasm, owing to its psychic relationship to a fanaticism that he linked to a solipsistic belief in an unmediated communion with divine authority,[13] he also believed that enthusiasm allows the subject to transcend his or her isolation and be part of a larger whole. Both Günderrode and Brentano constantly evoke their sense of isolation and the need to spiritually overcome it in Brentano's epistolary novel *Die Günderrode* (1840), a somewhat fictional recreation of Brentano's correspondence with her friend at the turn of the century. War and conflict, with their potential to transcend personal, social, and gender boundaries, allow the correspondents a self-overcoming on a poetic level through the enthusiastic spectatorship of martial violence, a spectatorship enabled by reading and writing. It is not an exaggeration to claim that the longing for such a transcendence of deeply felt psychic isolation is the core thematic element binding and motivating the epistolary exchange. Similarly, in Brentano's earlier novel *Goethes Briefwechsel mit einem Kinde* (Goethe's correspondence with a child, 1835), enthusiasm is the constant sentiment that allows her first-person narrator to overcome the physical and emotional distance separating her from Goethe, the idolized beloved who inspires the sentiment. A discourse on enthusiasm is also evident in Günderrode's enactment of violent contestation in her verse and dramatic sketches. Wolf's novel and her essays on both authors illustrate more poignantly than purely academic scholarship could — because these works directly reflect her own personal predicament — the socio-historical, largely gender-driven basis for the isolation faced by Günderrode and

Brentano. Thus, Wolf's claim, in the penultimate sentence of her long essay on Günderrode: "Die Literatur der Deutschen als ein Schlacht-feld — auch das wäre eine Weise, sie zu betrachten,"[14] (The literature of the Germans as a battlefield — that would also be a way to regard it), reflects a choice of trope — the battlefield — designed to evoke the pathos of tragedy with respect to Günderrode's ultimate fate, but also to hint at the subversive sublation Wolf articulates in the poet's work.

War in the form of the immediate threat posed to the German lands by the French Revolution lies at the heart of Kant's reflections on enthu-siasm and revolutionary fanaticism. Kant sought to make a distinction between violent revolution as the overthrow of an established juridical-political government, which he rejected as self-contradictory, and the enthusiastic reception, via spectatorship, of such an event. The revolu-tionary events themselves have no legal justification because a constitu-tion already establishes all rights and laws, making revolution, ipso facto, lawless. Enthusiasm, on the other hand, constitutes the sublimation of violent insurrectionary impulses that lead to revolution when unmedi-ated: Under the influence of enthusiasm, these impulses create an emo-tional but idealistic identification with the revolutionaries and their goals, one that can be successfully contained and channeled through academic and governmental oversight into an affective moral sphere. The emo-tions, in other words, may thereby be steered toward individual and social ethical improvements rather than allowed to veer toward revolution-ary violence.[15] While the enthusiasm for revolutionary goals transports the spectator into the domain of pure morality, Kant describes war, in *Der Streit der Fakultäten* (The conflict of the faculties, 1798), as "das größte Hinderniß des Moralischen" (the greatest hindrance to morality), which can only eventually be eliminated through wise intervention from above.[16] Although the debate on what differentiates appropriate belief and morally grounded enthusiasm from fanaticism (*Schwärmerei*) can be traced back to Luther and his time,[17] the French Revolution imposed an obvious political urgency to this strain of philosophical discourse, and profoundly influenced Romanticism.

Among those at least indirectly influenced by this revolution-inspired discourse was Kleist. Andreas Gailus, in reading Kleist's response to Honoré de Mirabeau's speech directed against Louis XVI's master of ceremonies, establishes the speech as the moment when the nation, rather than the king, becomes sovereign, giving orders rather than taking them. Thus, for Kleist, "Mirabeau's France is the productive site of historical novelty."[18] In Gailus's analysis of *Michael Kohlhaas* (1810), Mirabeau's regency-destroying speech is seen as the inspiration for the novella's "narrative insurrection against the stultifying machinery of political bureaucracy," as well as its rechanneling of Kantian Enlightenment cosmopolitanism into the service of an emerging nationalist discourse (*Passions*, 25–27). Furthermore, Gailus reads *Michael*

Kohlhaas as a melodramatic illustration of the impasses in Kant's attempt to regulate enthusiasm institutionally through an allied juridical and educational apparatus and funnel it into selfless service of the larger community. Kohlhaas is as committed to principle as the ideal Kantian agent. However, Kleist projects Kant's abstract postulation concerning regulated enthusiasm, and his grounding of freedom and reason within the sphere of universalized public service, into a domain Kant avoids — namely, the particular case of a specific individual crystallized into a personal instance rooted in a materiality Kant does not address: the grievous injury to Kohlhaas's horses and the principle that the state must redress this grievance. Thus, Kohlhaas's commitment to Kantian principle overwhelms the containment mechanisms for separating enthusiasm from a passionate, indeed fanatic, commitment to an ideal (*Passions*, 116–22).

Wolf's *Kein Ort. Nirgends* also foregrounds this impasse of philosophical abstractions in the face of concrete facticity. With its occluded narrative voice that tends to deliberately obscure the specific bearer of thoughts and purveyor of dialogue, one can only assume that the following line is addressed by Günderrode to Kleist: "Daß man die Philosophie nicht beim Wort nehmen, das Lesen am Ideal nicht messen soll — das ist Gesetz" (63; that one cannot take philosophy at its word, should not measure reading on the ideal — that is law). Like Kleist's Kohlhaas, Wolf's Kleist is presented as a man whose rigid adherence to ideals, as well as his attempt to apply them to particular instances in his own life, marginalize and destroy him. To be sure, during the narrative time of Wolf's novel, June 1804, Kleist had not yet published *Michael Kohlhaas*, or much else.[19] Nevertheless, his emerging nationalism and concomitant ambivalence toward the French Revolution are also evident in Wolf's novel, as we will see. This ambivalence came to inspire Kleist, via his figure Kohlhaas, to conceive of himself "as a German Mirabeau, who, with the energy of his eventful prose, will rouse the public from its moribund slumber and stimulate its enthusiasm for the national cause" (*Passions*, 26–27). However, it is Friedrich Wilhelm Schelling and Hölderlin who will allow us to elucidate how the pathos of enthusiasm helped shape Günderrode's gender-transcending poetic instantiation of violent conflict, an instantiation that is manifest in Wolf's imaginative and critical portrayal of this author. Before turning to the works of Günderrode and Brentano, though, I will briefly examine in this context Kleist's *Penthesilea*. For although, like *Michael Kohlhaas*, this work was written after the 1804 narrative time of Wolf's novel — he began to write it in Königsberg in 1805 — *Penthesilea* constitutes Kleist's own most overt performance of gender transcendence within the domain of war. It is also the filter through which Wolf read Kleist's own apparent sexual ambiguity in *Kein Ort. Nirgends*, as is evident in her own essay on *Penthesilea* that, published in 1982, belongs to the same period of Wolf's artistic life as the novel.

For Wolf, as for most readers, it is Penthesilea's killing and cannibal-
istic consumption of Achilles, who is both mortal enemy and object of
desire, that arouses the most intense, albeit horrified, fascination. In this
scene, violent combat permits the Amazon warrior to transgress all the
boundaries of gender and desire, allowing her to feel, though only briefly
before guilt sets in, "wonderfully content, sated, as it were, basking in
the afterglow of her conquest,"[20] as Simon Richter puts it. The Amazon queen's ecstasy is described at second hand by Princess Meroe, who
evokes the intertwined slaking of Penthesilea's sexual and blood lusts as
she kills and consumes Achilles:

> Sie schlägt, die Rüstung ihm vom Leibe reißend,
> Den Zahn schlägt sie in seine weiße Brust,
> Sie und die Hunde, die wetteifernden,
> Oxus und Sphinx den Zahn in seine rechte,
> In seine linke sie; als ich erschien,
> Troff Blut von Mund und Händen ihr herab.[21]

> [She sinks, tearing his armor from his body,
> She sinks her tooth into his white breast.
> She and the dogs, the contenders,
> Oxus and Sphinx into the right one,
> She into the left one; when I appeared
> Blood dripped from her mouth and hands.]

In this fleeting moment of all-encompassing gratification, Kleist performatively overcomes not only all strictures defining properly engendered
desire — the object of which here, in an obvious inversion of tradition, is a
man's white breast, not a woman's — in a manner that allows him briefly to
sublate not only those apparently hermaphroditic tendencies controversially
attributed to him by Wolf,[22] but also the prohibitions against enthusiasm
directed toward selfish ends by his spiritual nemesis, Kant. In her essay on
Penthesilea, Wolf claims the Amazon queen's deed signifies neither barbarism nor atavism, as it is committed in a state of "vollkommener Geistes-
abwesenheit" (complete absent-mindedness) and will, when she is roused
from this spiritually absent condition, forever separate her from her self
and her surroundings.[23] However, I would agree with Richter that Penthesilea does experience a moment of sublime contentment. Furthermore, the
transgression of orders from above in the heat of battle, orders intended to
channel enthusiasm and passion in a well-regulated, socially oriented course
much like Kant's hierarchical scheme in *Der Streit der Fakultäten*, can also
lead to a productive outcome when carried out in a semi-unconscious state;
this is the case with Prince Friedrich von Homburg's successful charge into
battle in Kleist's play of the same name. Kleist's works consistently reflect

the porous border between enthusiasm and fanaticism, and this ambiguity is also manifested in the persona of Wolf's Kleist in *Kein Ort. Nirgends.* Günderrode was a passionate devotee of the philosophy of Schelling. Indeed, her obsession with Schelling was so intense that it helped motivate Friedrich Creuzer, a married philologist with whom she carried on an affair after meeting him in August 1804 (two months after the narrative time of *Kein Ort. Nirgends*), to break off their relationship; she resisted his demand that she give up her study of Schelling, an occupation he and his friends felt to be unseemly for a potential housewife. Creuzer's termination of their relationship was a major factor in her suicide. In her essay on Günderrode, Wolf alludes to the couple's falling out over Schelling, indicating that Creuzer's circle primarily objected to Schelling's near atheism, and she quotes Günderrode's indignant response to the request she abandon the study of her favorite philosopher: "Es geht um Schellings Philosophie, die allerdings keinen persönlichen Gott glaubt. Da nimmt die Günderrode ihren Stolz zusammen: 'Soll ich mich entschuldigen über das, was ich vortrefflich in mir finde?'" (We are dealing with Schelling's philosophy, which indeed does not believe in a personal God. Here Günderrode shows her pride: 'Should I excuse myself for something that I find to be of excellence in myself?').[24] Schelling's principle text in the enthusiasm/fanaticism dispute is carried out, in the form of epistolary exchange, in the *Philosophische Briefe über Dogmatismus und Kritizismus* (Philosophical letters on dogmatism and criticism, 1795). As Peter Fenves notes, Schelling sought, contra Kant, not to eliminate fanaticism (*Schwärmerei*) but to find its middle point. Here Schelling and the friend to whom he addresses his letters can meet "at the point from which enthusiasm originates" and thereby stand beyond enthusiasm.[25] Spirit (*Geist*) sets the limits of reason, which fanaticism, by definition, attempts to overcome. Spirit as the possibility of self-intuition (*Anschauung*) is able by dint of endless reflection to poetically carry one over the "stream of representations" that sustains this activity (142–43). The constant struggle for freedom in the face of a fate that will overwhelm it is reflected in Greek tragedy, which honors human freedom by allowing the hero to battle fate's superior force.[26] These self-transcendent moments that Schelling articulates — the floating of the spirit above and through the representations carrying it along, images experienced by the spirit as fate in the poetic realm, the identification with the heroic thereby occurring in the soul — these are the moments that Günderrode regards as putting her into the domain of tragedy in *Die Günderrode*.[27] To be sure, this is Brentano's Günderrode, but the evocation of a nearly solipsistic fantasy, untouched by external "Bildung" and inappropriately characterized as fanatical or fantastical, is also central to Wolf's understanding of Günderrode's *poesis*, as enhanced by her reading of Brentano's correspondence.[28]

Schelling's articulation of the work of the spirit in its relation to poetic metaphor, as well as the relationship between freedom, tragedy, and fate as reflected within a resolutely interior domain, seems to have influenced Günderrode. It is Hölderlin, however, toward whom both correspondents express veneration in *Die Günderrode*, who articulates the form of enthusiasm most proximate to Günderrode's poetic purchase in her dramatic performance of violent contestation. In a prose fragment, Hölderlin describes the scale of enthusiasm as follows: "Von der Lustigkeit an, die wohl der unterste ist, bis zur Begeisterung des Feldherrn der mitten in der Schlacht unter Besonnenheit den Genius mächtig erhellt, giebt es eine unendliche Stufenleiter"[29] (From merriment, which is certainly the lowest, up to the enthusiasm of the general in the midst of the battle, powerfully illuminated by the circumspection of genius, there is an infinite hierarchy). Fenves is correct to note that even from the highest rung of the ladder, Hölderlin's general surveys only "a particular field: it opens onto the field of slaughter" where "from this, the highest perspective, life is seen to be lost" ("Scale," 152). However, the tone of detached concentration, sustained through a particularly rigid poetic diction as Günderrode narratively performs her bloodletting, obviates the need for the kind of third-person (and thus second-hand) representation employed in *Penthesilea*'s instantiation of slaughter and cannibalism. Günderrode's narrator seems to stand above the fray, like Hölderlin's general surveying the battle while controlling it, as in the following stanza from *Darthula nach Ossian* (Darthula after Ossian):

> Da ergrimmet Calibars finstre Seele,
> Und er winket, tausend Speere fliehn,
> Usnoths Söhne sinken wie drei Eichen,
> Die zur Erde ihre Wipfel neigen,
> Wenn des Nordens Stürme sie umziehen.[30]

> [Here Calibar's dark soul becomes infuriated
> And he beckons, a thousand spears flee,
> Usnoth's sons sink like three oaks,
> Which incline their tops to the earth,
> When the Northern storms swirl around them.]

The free-spirited, less self-repressed Brentano enacts a more uncontained and uncontrolled, more jovial enthusiasm on the Hölderlinian scale, as is evident in the following spontaneous, I-centered battle fantasy in *Die Günderrode*, which places her galloping horse next to Napoleon:

> Ach, ich denk mich schon in eine Schlacht auf einem Schimmel neben ihm herreitend zwischen allem Donner der Geschütze, Rauch und Pulverdampf, in der Verwirrung großer entscheidener

Momente, wie seinem sicheren Blick vertrauend ich alles glücklich
vollende, ich denk noch mehr, alles was glühender Ehrgeiz nur zu
unternehmen wagt, das fährt durch meine Seele, ich erleb's — ich
bin glücklich, freudig, jauchze im Gelingen, und alles Volk umringt
mich mitjauchzend und harrt meiner, daß ich ihm Labung zutröpfle
heiliger Freiheit. (375)

[Ah, I already think of myself in a battle on a white horse next to
him, riding between all the thunder of the artillery, smoke, and the
powder steam, in the confusion of great decisive moments, as, trust-
ing to his assured glance, I successfully achieve everything. I think of
even more, everything that glowing ambition only dares to undertake, that drives through my soul, I experience it — I am happy,
joyous, shout for joy in success, and all the people surround me
shouting joyfully along, and wait in anticipation of my dripping the
holy balsam of freedom upon them.]

Much of the correspondence in *Die Günderrode* reflects the eponymous
writer's attempt to reign in and depersonalize her friend's spirit through
education at the hands of tutors, a kind of control less tepidly and more
egotistically extended by Bettine Brentano's brother Clemens, as is evident
in another of her epistolary novels, *Clemens Brentanos Frühlingskranz*
(Clemens Brentano's spring wreath, 1844). That neither Günderrode nor
Clemens Brentano, nor, for that matter, Goethe and his mother, who also
attempt to channel the narrator Bettine Brentano's enthusiasm in a direction conducive to their own purposes in *Goethes Briefwechsel mit einem
Kinde*, completely succeed in shaping her as a writer for their own ends,
ultimately makes Bettine Brentano available as the subterranean utopian
voice of *Kein Ort. Nirgends.*

Narrative Structure and the Ideological
Origins of *Kein Ort. Nirgends*

The contrast between Brentano's spontaneity and Günderrode's externally imposed self-compunction is evident in both Wolf's essays on the
two women and in *Kein Ort. Nirgends*, which we will now address in a
more sustained manner. However, before examining how the articulation
of violent conflict, grounded in both the eighteenth-century debates on
enthusiasm inspired by the French Revolution and the individual circumstances of Kleist, Günderrode, and Brentano, inform Wolf's novel, we
must first briefly examine its narrative structure and the ideological scene
of its origin, for this inscription is only enabled by the unique deployment of voice in *Kein Ort. Nirgends*. Wolf's embrace of Seghers's position on Romanticism in the latter's debates with Lukács help explain why
and how violence is performatively instantiated in this work. Much critical

attention has already been focused on the ambiguity of narrative voice in *Kein Ort. Nirgends.* Julia Hell, for example, has underscored how "the novel opens with a passage which, thematizing voice and the possibility of speaking in an existential crisis, radically undermines any coherent speaking position."[31] In her book-length study of *Kein Ort. Nirgends*, Helga G. Braunbeck, drawing on such theorists as Jacques Lacan, Hélène Cixous, and Michel Foucault, shows that Wolf's destabilization and decentering of voice is grounded in a feminist refusal to establish and control her novel's narratological dimension. Most male authors, in Braunbeck's view, attempt to sustain one dominant narrative perspective, as well as absolute clarity concerning who is speaking to whom in their work, with the author's own voice at the top of a hierarchical chain. This rigid system of demarcation masks an attempt to oedipally vanquish the male author's predecessors, and is thus motivated by what Harold Bloom (whom Braunbeck does not cite) famously called "the anxiety of influence." Wolf's ambiguity, her refusal to suppress the egos of her literary predecessors by hierarchically controlling their voices, enacts throughout the course of *Kein Ort. Nirgends* a genuinely intersubjective dialogue.[32] Precisely such radical openness, such refusal to act like Hölderlin's general and constrictively deploy the voices of her characters, opens her novel to being performatively inscribed by a discourse of violence that the pacifist Wolf might consciously deplore.

To be sure, one should not exaggerate Wolf's passivity as the receptacle of her predecessors' voices; *Kein Ort. Nirgends* does not constitute an example of automatic writing. Rather, her openness to allowing characters like Kleist and Günderrode to speak "for themselves" simply enables the constellation of ideologies in the narrative without the usual (or usually "male," in Braunbeck's view) attempts at authorial counterpoint in a first- or third-person voice. Equally important for understanding why the predecessors' sublimation of violent conflict is allowed to manifest itself in the novel is Wolf's embrace of Seghers's views on Romanticism. Wolf's portrayal of Kleist and Günderrode as socially and politically marginalized writers is consistent with a number of imaginative and critical portrayals of Romantic authors in the 1970s German Democratic Republic, reflecting a general refutation of Lukács's orthodox Marxist view of Romanticism as decadent and solipsistic. Not only Wolf, but other GDR authors such as Günter de Bruyn, Franz Fühmann, and Wolf's husband Gerhard, in their positive literary treatments of Romantic authors, expressed solidarity with Seghers's view that the definition of acceptable literary realism should be expanded to include an author's internalized, imaginative assimilation of external experiences. The sympathetic identification with the Romantic author as outcast evident in Wolf's novel can therefore only be partially explained by her feelings of estrangement in the wake of Wolf Biermann's infamous expulsion from the GDR in 1976.[33] In a letter to Lukács dated 28 June 1938, Seghers argues that, like many geniuses guided by an overarching "great concept," Goethe was unable to perceive the enormous artistic talent of those, like Kleist and his generation of writers, who did not view life through the lens of this concept. Among this generation, which she contrasts with Goethe, are those who died insane (Hölderlin, Lenz, Gottfried August Bürger) and through suicide (Kleist and Günderrode). Goethe's rejection of all forms of disintegration or dissolution (*Auflösung*) is regarded by Seghers as directly linked to his antipathy toward the disharmonious Romantics. At this point in the letter, Seghers adds the following remark, seemingly extraneous and posed as an afterthought: "Ich vergaß noch, daß 1830 August Goethe starb: sein Vater hatte ihm nicht die Erlaubnis gegeben, in die Freiheitskriege zu gehen. Er wollte — 'seine irdische Existenz irdisch fortgeführt sehen'"[34] (I forgot to mention that August Goethe died in 1830; his father had not given him permission to go off to the wars of liberation. He wanted — 'to see his earthly existence continue to be conducted in an earthly manner').

What are we to make of this casual aside, a remark that stands out as an oddity in the context of a letter otherwise devoted to arguing for a definition of realism more inclusive than what her correspondent would allow? Given the date of its composition, as Nazi Germany was flexing its muscles and a continental war between communism and fascism seemed imminent, Goethe's decision to prevent August from participating in the "wars of liberation," and to root his son's being in a harmonious "earthbound" existence, places him in an unfavorable juxtaposition with the suicidal but martially disposed Kleist, whose own — albeit confused and disoriented — participation in precisely these wars is thematized in *Kein Ort. Nirgends*.[35] Lukács's response to Seghers — that Kleist embodied a mixture of the reactionary and the decadent and sided with Germany's reactionary wing in his opposition to Napoleon, and that *this* circumstance prompted Goethe's disinclination toward him[36] — became accepted GDR critical orthodoxy until the 1970s. As Hell has argued, "Wolf took over Seghers's literary-historical and political paradigm of an opposition between Goethe the classicist, on the one hand, and such authors of the Storm and Stress and the Romantic period as Hölderlin, Lenz, Kleist, Büchner, and Günderrode, on the other."[37] Hell makes this argument in the context of her broader thesis, namely, that Wolf consciously tried to identify herself with Seghers within the matrix of the GDR's narrative of heroic antifascism, whereby Wolf's battle against that nation's critical orthodoxies, which obfuscate the authenticity, rigor, and dynamism of this narrative, mirrors the earlier fight of her Marxist predecessor. In this context, the Kleist and Günderrode of *Kein Ort. Nirgends* must be seen as not only tragically marginalized literary outsiders, but as heroic figures of resistance whose literary sublation of violence therefore receives tacit valorization in the novel.

Contrary to Lukács's view that Kleist was a reactionary unequivocally opposed to Napoleon and the goals of the French Revolution, Wolf presents him in *Kein Ort. Nirgends* as thoroughly ambivalent, consistent with her treatment of him as deeply divided on all significant matters, including gender orientation. In the course of the teatime conversation at the home of merchant Joseph Merten, where most of the present timeframe narrative takes place, Kleist expresses hatred of the French, while reflecting that one hates whatever one has too deeply loved (54). Kleist is described as having engaged in a confused journey through France in search of the archenemy, Napoleon, to whom he wished to proffer his service in the hope such a treasonous military undertaking would result in his death. His hatred of Napoleon is conflated with his own self-hatred, and he is in despair that the Corsican had not provided him the "yearned-for battlefield" (70). Wolf's Kleist, in his love/hate relationship with revolutionary France in general and Napoleon in particular, is written into existence against the grain of Lukács's treatment of his political psychology. Thus, his express desire to die in battle for his archenemy, and his expression of hatred for Napoleon because this ambition has been frustrated, reveals not only the internal dividedness of this character, a dissonance at the heart of Wolf's characterization of Kleist, but serves two conflicted goals, one narrative and the other ideological. On the one hand, Kleist's reflection on a scuttled desire for a rather pointless death in combat enhances the novel's powerful foreshadowing of Kleist's real-life suicide, which took place some seven years after *Kein Ort. Nirgends'* 1804 timeframe. However, his wish to die heroically on the battlefield fighting for Napoleon is also a shot across the bow of the GDR orthodoxy's engagement with Kleist, a critical orthodoxy inaugurated by Lukács. Wolf's Kleist attains the ambience of tragic heroism through his vain wish to die in those "wars of liberation" in which Goethe refused to allow his son to participate, as Seghers notes in her, for Wolf, highly significant letter to Lukács. Although even the commentary to a critical edition of *Kein Ort. Nirgends* asserts that Kleist's decision in 1803 to travel to northern France to serve in Napoleon's army reflected a death wish,[38] one might also see in this endeavor a desire to overcome inner divisiveness and become part of a larger cause, to transgress one of the many Kantian limitations that plagued his spirit — in this case, the restriction of enthusiastic support of the French Revolution to passive spectatorship. While the suicidal Kleist in this episode of Wolf's novel serves her narratological needs, the transgressively enthusiastic Kleist of this tableau serves an ideological need, the wish to confront the GDR's critical orthodoxy. Later in *Kein Ort. Nirgends*, Wolf's Kleist expresses indifference toward military life, "dem Militärwesen" (81), but this only underscores the fierceness of his will to fight and die in the French cause.

War and Androgyny in
Wolf's Kleist and Günderrode

In Wolf's view, Kleist's feeling of hopelessness was not only tied to his lack of critical success as a writer, but also to his ambiguous sexuality. In her essay on *Penthesilea*, Wolf claims Kleist's penchant for "mystifications" stemmed from an eroticism that cut him off from typical liaisons with women, marginalizing him into a stance of proud isolation that clashed with an irresistible need to express himself: "Dieser Widerspruch regiert, wenn mich nicht alles täuscht, die geheimen Motive zur Ausarbeitung der 'Penthesilea': Kleists Ich in einer weiblichen Heldin" (668; Unless I am completely deceived, this contradiction governs the secret motives for carrying out the work on *Penthesilea*: Kleist's ego in a female heroine). Wolf, unlike the previously cited Richter, perceives no moment of self-transcendent ecstasy in the Amazon queen's frenetic murder and consumption of Achilles, only a feeling of utter hopelessness and a willingness to break a "Denk-Tabu" (thought-taboo) on cannibalism, a break shocking to that era's German classical veneration of a humane and noble ancient Greek culture (675). Nevertheless, in the most *Penthesilea*-like moment of *Kein Ort. Nirgends*, Kleist's dream of chasing a wild boar, vainly trying to force it into submission, and then shooting it to death, while also reflective of Kleist's sexual hopelessness (he told this tale to his fiancée Wilhelmine, bringing her to tears), constitutes a moment of self-sufficient ecstasy: "Wer sich an solche Blicke, an derartige Einsichten gewöhnt, verfällt keiner anderen Sucht, bedarf keines anderen Rauschmittels. Auch der Liebe nicht" (39; Whoever accustoms oneself to such glances, such insights, does not succumb to any other addiction, needs no other means of intoxication. Also not of love). Braunbeck claims the dream prefigures his suicide, and shows the hopeless dissonance of a man whose desires conflict with the expectations of a society whose approval he needs.[39] However, as with this fictive Kleist's suicidal wish to join the French forces and the tableau of murder/cannibalism in *Penthesilea*, the transgressive violence of Kleist's dream insinuates itself into Wolf's writing with a positive, indeed, transformative energy. It allows her Kleist to temporarily overcome the sexual and artistic fissures in his soul, propelling his art. In Wolf's Kleist — and this applies both to the fictive character of *Kein Ort. Nirgends* and the subject of her essay on Penthesilea — the collision of violence and androgyny leads to a personal tragedy that finds dramatic expression; at the same time, it is also invested with sublimation in the Hegelian sense, an ecstatic overcoming of duality in sensual form, whereby such ambiguity can only be resolved in death, and in the Freudian sense, as an enactment of cathexis, channeling Kleist's violent sexual energy into his art. As Wolf's novel prefigures, the societal pressure to overcome sexual ambiguity in a world where sexual rules were becoming increasingly rigidified ultimately drove Kleist to suicide. His androgyny, however, was initially a productive spur to his art. In a different register, the same can be said of Wolf's Günderrode.

As with Wolf's Kleist, it is helpful to understand the entwinement of transcendentally enthusiastic violence and artistic creativity by reading the fictive Günderrode in conjunction with Wolf's critical essay on this author. Unlike the essay on *Penthesilea*, "Der Schatten eines Traumes" (The shadow of a dream) treats its subject in a rather more exhaustive, multidimensional manner. However, the same preoccupation with sexual ambiguity in Wolf's essay on Kleist's drama is also profoundly reflected here. Indeed, it begins with a quote from Günderrode, dated 29 August 1801, in which she notes how her reading of Ossian's "Darthula" has reawakened her old wish to die a heroic death by throwing herself into the tumult of a battlefield (*Schlachtgetümmel*), bemoans her fate to have been born a woman, and expresses her aversion toward female virtues and happiness.[40] The reason this passage aroused Wolf's interest is not difficult to discern. In a 1973 interview with Hans Kaufmann, Wolf discussed her story "Selbstversuch" (Self-experiment), also published that year, in which a woman is medicinally transformed into a man. Wolf had undertaken this composition as a result of East Berlin–based editor Edith Anderson's challenge to a group of male and female authors to write stories based on the premise that a man or a woman is turned into the opposite gender. Wolf notes that she was very pleased with this notion, that it offered her the chance to enact "utopian mimicry," and that she generally enjoyed reading utopian books, even though most were of low quality[41] (the title *Kein Ort. Nirgends*, of course, translates the Greek term "utopia" — literally: no place). Although the novel's setting in the actual village Winkel am Rhein (where the actual Günderrode committed suicide and was buried) seems to belie the title, this work's deliberate obfuscation of narrative voice, as well as its investment of both Kleist and Günderrode with androgyny, represents a continuation of the "utopian mimicry" in the domain of gender that Wolf enacted in "Selbstversuch." As with her Kleist, the androgyny of Wolf's Günderrode is inextricably intertwined with violent battlefield conflict as the wellspring of self-overcoming, of the sublation of sexual difference.[42]

Günderrode, despite some erotically charged moments with Bettine Brentano that are reflected in *Die Günderrode*, seems to have been heterosexual, yet her enactment of gender reversal took place not simply through imaginative projection — in her blood-soaked mini-dramas, poetry, and short prose — but also as a correspondent. As Wolf notes, Günderrode wrote letters to two of her lovers, Creuzer and (earlier) the celebrated jurist Friedrich Carl von Savigny, as a man, "der Freund," to whom she would sometimes refer in the third person.[43] In *Kein Ort. Nirgends*, she teases Savigny with this sexual ambiguity, claiming that he knows nothing of his friend — "Ihrem Freund," echoing her real-life practice by not employing the feminine "in" ending — and that he seems too lazy to figure out who the real Günderrode is. She claims he does not know whether to trust appearances or believe rumors that fluctuate between treating her as a prude or a flirt, a "strongly male spirit" or "the incarnation of gentle womanhood" (76–77). Of course, precisely such ambiguity lies at the heart of Wolf's portrayal of Günderrode in both *Kein Ort. Nirgends* and "Der Schatten eines Traumes."

Needless to say, Günderrode's performance of gender confusion — and this applies to both Wolf's protagonist and the historical author — is not simply a coquettish game, but part of her desperate attempt to break free of the constricted role prescribed for women, even educated women, in her age. A number of women linked to German Romanticism's small coterie made this attempt. Patricia Herminghouse observes: "Wie Wolf bemerkt, ist Caroline von Günderrode eine dieser Frauen, und *Kein Ort. Nirgends* läßt erkennen, was jenen widerfahren kann, deren Ausbruchsversuch scheitert" (As Wolf notes, Caroline von Günderrode is one of these women, and *Kein Ort. Nirgends* allows one to recognize what can happen to those whose attempt at breaking out fails), and that this lesson begins with the novel's Kleist, who expresses disinclination toward women who write.[44] However, Wolf's Kleist shares both Günderrode's fate as a socially marginalized writer and her wish to transcend socially prescribed gender roles; this is the basis for their brief symbiotic bond in the novel. The strict division of the sexes is grounded in patriarchal thinking, which insists on clear borders in all domains of life, including the epistemological. Thus, the novel's Günderrode tells Kleist: "Savigny hat für alles ein Entweder-Oder. Sie müssen wissen, Kleist, er hat einen männlichen Kopf" (102; Savigny has an either-or for everything. You must know, Kleist, he has a male head). The historical Günderrode seems to have wished for such a resolute "male head," and she transposes this in her imaginative oeuvre into decisive females who never waver on the field of violent conflict. Thus, in the prose tale "Timur," Princess Thia acts without hesitation in the concluding scene to revenge her father's death at the hands of the eponymous protagonist, although he is her beloved: "Sie schlang ihren Arm um den König, und stürzte sich mit ihm die Felsen hinunter, daß ihr Blut sich mischte, und hinab rauchte zur wogenden See"[45] (She threw her arm around the king and plunged down the boulders with him so that their blood mixed and smoked down into the churning sea). As with Kleist's *Penthesilea*, the two genders become synthesized at the moment of death, although in Günderrode's tale this death must thereby claim both the royal heroine and her beloved. Wolf's Günderrode proclaims that "Wo ich zu Hause bin, gibt es die Liebe nur um den Preis des Todes" (Where I am at home, there is only love at the price of death), that she must hide this truth, like

plunder, in the lines of her poetry, and that those who would have the
courage to recognize this truth literally would learn fear (46–47). This
fear would seem to stem from the recognition, evident in the conclusion
to "Timur," that the division between the sexes can only be overcome
through an act of transcendent violence. In fact, the gender gap in Kleist
and Günderrode is frequently bridged through murder, suicide, cannibalism, and battlefield slaughter. This circumstance informs their utterances in *Kein Ort. Nirgends*. Toward its conclusion, Kleist claims that he
sometimes finds it unbearable that nature has rent man and woman asun-
der. Günderrode corrects him: "Das meinen Sie nicht, Kleist. Sie meinen,
daß in Ihnen selbst Mann und Frau einander feindlich gegenüberstehen.
Wie auch in mir" (133; You don't mean that, Kleist. You mean that in
you yourself man and woman are hostilely opposed to each other. Just
as in me). Wolf links their suppression of desire — caused both by their
androgynous tendencies and their marginalization, as socially and sexually unorthodox artists, by contemporary German society — to the absolute character (*Unbedingtheit*) of their poetry (126), which is to say, its
unadorned enactment of a brutality completely antithetical to the dominant Goethean ideal of ultimate harmony and this-worldly totality. Drawing on his own character and experience, Kleist proclaims the impossibility
of Goethe's idealism: "Daß er schier Unmögliches für wünschbar ausgibt,
dadurch für machbar" (126–27; That he serves up what is completely
impossible as desirable, thereby as achievable). Günderrode also adhered
to unrealizable ideals, ideals more appealing to Wolf than those of Goethe,
and Wolf's belief that they still cannot be realized in her day is evident
toward the conclusion of "Der Schatten eines Traumes." Citing Günderrode's famous remark that the earth never became her home,[46] Wolf proclaims that the striving for a holistic totality is too foreign an idea in our
time, that life and writing cannot be brought into harmony.[47] There is
no question that the parallels Wolf perceives in the treatment of the artist — who is at home neither in the rigidly controlled German society of
early Romanticism nor the GDR that attempted to silence the voice of
poet/singer Wolf Biermann and his intellectual supporters by forcing him
into permanent exile — caused her to embrace Seghers's defense of the
Romantics against Lukács, who preferred Goethe's vision of harmonious
totality and who, like Goethe, saw Romanticism as pathological. Perhaps
because Kleist and Günderrode were indeed plagued by an unendurable
sense of sexual androgyny, which they could only transcend in tableaus of
violent, gender-driven conflict in their imaginative writing, Wolf's identification with these authors could not be complete. When she concludes
her essay on Günderrode with the line: "Die Literatur der Deutschen als
ein Schlachtfeld — auch das wäre eine Weise, sie zu betrachten" (The literature of the Germans as a battlefield — that would also be a way to regard
it), the use of the conditional underscores not only her own reluctance to

equate literature with a battlefield, but also her concomitant sense that it is predominantly a battlefield in Günderrode's oeuvre. She concludes her essay by noting that poets are predestined to sacrifice, indeed to self-sacrifice.[48] She may have been thinking of her own sacrifices as a subversive writer in the GDR, but undoubtedly as well that, in Günderrode and Kleist, a literature strewn with victims to sexual antinomy is inextricably intertwined with the ultimate self-sacrifice, suicide. This is a key motif, albeit a tacit one, in *Kein Ort. Nirgends.*

Other Fictional Kleists

Wolf was not the only twentieth-century author to create a fictional portrait of Kleist. He constituted for German-language writers both early and late in the twentieth century a paradigmatic figure of the talented writer as an outsider. In his story "Kleist in Thun" (1907), the Swiss author Robert Walser uses the occasion of Kleist's sojourn near the Swiss village of Thun to narrate his extreme marginalization in and through the society in which he resides. His contact with the townspeople is always shown as indirect: He *hears*, for example, the laughter of women, but does not have any personal interaction with them; he *observes* people emerge from church on Sunday, but does not make contact with them. He spends most of his time unsuccessfully trying to write. Finally, his sister picks him up from the village and they depart. A marble plaque commemorates Kleist's visit, but people read it only uncomprehendingly: "Reisende mit Alpentourenabsichten können's lesen, Kinder aus Thun buchstabieren es, Ziffer für Ziffer, und schauen einander dann fragend in die Augen" (184; Travelers with the intention to tour the Alps can read it, children from Thun spell it, character for character, and then look questioningly into each other's eyes). Kleist's predicament in life and death reflects Walser's perception of the permanent isolation faced by the alienated author whose immersion in philosophical quandaries blocks spontaneous engagement with the populace at large, whose progeny continue existence in ignorance of a man whose literary genius means nothing to them.[49]

Günter Kunert was a citizen of the German Democratic Republic when he wrote his radio play *Ein anderer K.* (A Different K.), first broadcast in 1976 and first published in 1977. His engagement in the Biermann affair led to his emigration from the GDR some two years later. In 1976, he was involved in a polemic with the East German critic Peter Goldammer when Goldammer rejected his contribution to an essay collection for the two-hundredth anniversary of Kleist's birth. Among other things, Goldammer objected to Kunert's aspersions that Goethe bore responsibility for Kleist's lack of a just reception up to the present. Kunert saw Goldammer's approach as fundamentally bourgeois, attempting to smooth out the contradictions in the nation's classical literary heroes in order to make them seem like "one of us," undifferentiated digestible models for the present day.[50] The issue of Kleist himself as figure for emulation is the topic of Kunert's aptly titled essay "Heinrich von Kleist — Ein Modell" (Heinrich von Kleist — A model), where Kleist's melancholy, alienation, and (even for the present day) uncomfortable politics are underscored.[51]

In the radio play, Kleist and Henriette Vogel, the woman with whom he committed suicide in 1811, make a brief cheerful appearance as their voices emerge from a cacophony of recitations from diverse Kleist texts. They playfully discuss their quotidian plans for this day shortly before their suicide. Once their deaths are discovered, a search for their motivations is put into play by Prussian Chancellor Hardenberg. Reacting to his king's displeasure at the elegiac tribute to the suicide in a newspaper article, Hardenberg dispatches a spy to find out the real reason for Kleist's self-annihilation. The spy, Grollhammer, was a fellow inmate of Kleist's in a French military prison, and Hardenberg presses him into service in exchange for turning a blind eye to Grollhammer's embezzlement of government funds. Hardenberg's colleague, State Councilor Gruner, fears the suicide is being interpreted by the public as a former soldier's despairing attempt to awaken French-occupied Prussia from its lethargy.

The initially self-confident Grollhammer (the phonetic proximity of his name to that of Goldammer is not accidental) travels around Prussia interviewing the innkeepers who hosted Kleist and Vogel in their last hours: friends, family, former colleagues, and fellow writer Friedrich de la Motte Fouqué, as well as Vogel's widower. The Prussian government officials hope Grollhammer will find that the motivation for the murder-suicide is a typical star-crossed love affair between the victims, but as he discovers the tangled web of censorship, betrayal (by Goethe, among others), political suppression, and personal as well as professional exclusion suffered by Kleist, Grollhammer's confidence is gradually shattered. He fears even the guileless Fouqué has glimpsed his criminal soul. As in his essays, Kunert attempts to show in his radio play the ambiguous, complexly intertwined internal and external circumstances that propelled Kleist's work, superficially aberrant behavior, and suicide. He is literally given the last word by the narrator of *Ein anderer K.* before the cacophony of voices that marked the radio play's outset swallows up his speech at its conclusion. Kleist remarks that in the postlapsarian age, true knowledge (*Erkenntnis*) only appears in images and allegories, a condition that will last until the world is made whole again, a holism toward which the world must strive. Kunert's play, like his essays, attempts to counteract contemporary facile assimilations of Kleist into a classical pantheon and the frequent, concomitant attempts to portray his behavior and suicide as products of insanity.[52] Even more than Wolf, Kunert portrays Kleist in the totality of his complex, often contradictory persona by means of a fictionally retrospective look at his life by those who knew him.

Karin Reschke also offers an imaginative look at Kleist in her 1982 novel *Verfolgte des Glücks: Findebuch der Henriette Vogel* (A woman persecuted by happiness: The diary of Henriette Vogel). Very little is known about the historical Vogel, but it is clear that an extremely painful cancer of the uterus was the primary factor motivating her decision to end her life. Her only surviving writings are a few letters to her husband and friends as well as a note she wrote to Kleist just before their joint deed. Thus, *Findebuch* is almost entirely the product of the author's imagination. The term denotes a collocation of archival material, and the book presents Vogel's perspective through the immediacy of diary entries, journal jottings, and personal correspondence. It is an apt term with respect to the novel's formal construction. The relative anonymity in which Henriette Vogel lived her life allows Reschke to create an entirely fictitious persona reflecting her own proclivities, and her decision to create a woman possessed of a late twentieth-century, feminist, West German consciousness with respect to the oppression of her gender, but who goes through life as a fundamentally passive victim of a loveless marriage and sustains no positive agency or will to active resistance, has drawn harsh condemnation from critics.[53] Vogel's inner emptiness is symbolically filled by her cancer, but first pushes her into a fantasy world despite the encouragement of potential role models like Sophie Haza, who abandoned her secure marriage to pursue a relationship with Adam Müller, the publicist and political theorist who co-edited the periodical *Phoebus* with Kleist. Though Müller proves to be rather a chauvinist who believes women should be excluded from serious political discussion, Sophie is a liberated woman who encourages Vogel to live an independent life, and criticizes her passivity and self-pity by comparing her to Kleist: "Sie sind viel allein, sagte sie, vergraben sich, und wenn man Sie zu sehen bekommt, tragen Sie eine Leidensmiene zur Schau. Ganz wie unser Freund Kleist" (163; You are often alone, she said, bury yourself, and when one gets to see you, you display a suffering countenance. Just like our friend Kleist).

Though Henriette Vogel is known to posterity solely because of her tragic entwinement with Kleist, he only began to play a role in her life toward its conclusion. Thus, he makes only a relatively brief appearance at the outset of Reschke's novel, where the couple's initial aborted attempt at suicide after a journey to Auras is delineated, and then again near its conclusion, as Vogel meets him and they move toward their mutual destiny. Reschke uses her heroine to indulge in a proto-feminist critique of Kleist. For example, Vogel claims the figure of Penthesilea, the eponymous heroine of Kleist's tragedy, has no basis in life; only men are possessed of martial thinking and forging arms is an entirely male occupation (171). Reschke's casting of women as the pacifist sex in the early 1980s — when the arms race between the United States and the Soviet Union preoccupied Germans — appealed to feminists in the peace movement, but at the same time it denied the intersection between war and androgyny that scholars such as Simpson and Krimmer have come to regard as a core motif of *self*-liberation in writers such as Günderrode and Brentano, and that also links Kleist and Günderrode in *Kein Ort. Nirgends*. Reschke, unlike Wolf, characterizes Kleist as a somewhat conniving opportunist, evident when he and Müller rush around to listen to the eulogies devoted to the recently deceased Queen Louise of Prussia, despite Kleist's murmured disapproval of the pompous mourning (176).

Both Vogel and Kleist are portrayed as alienated, passive, depressed, and socially marginalized — character traits that are shown to forge their suicide bond. These elements are also evident in Wolf's treatment of Kleist and Günderrode, and Donna Hoffmeister accurately notes that "Reschke and Wolf arrive at similar conclusions about the loss of female emancipation, which also meant the loss of human emancipation, during the early nineteenth century."[54] Nevertheless, Reschke's Kleist and Vogel are cast as almost abject victims, while Wolf articulates a latent resistance to convention in her Günderrode and Kleist.

Bretano and Utopian Transcendence in Grass and Wolf

Bettine Brentano is only a minor protagonist in *Kein Ort. Nirgends*. The strongly masculine aspect of her spirit — an element that receives attention in Wolf's "Ein Brief über die Bettine" (A letter about Bettine) — is not touched upon in the novel. In contrast to this letter, and to the studies of Krimmer, Simpson, and others who stress Brentano's performative enactment of androgyny and cross-dressing, Wolf's novel depicts her as a teenager, still basically a child, more tempestuous and unruly (13) than informed by a masculine spirit. While she makes only brief appearances, she plays a key role in Günderrode's prophetic dream of her suicide. The two women are accompanied by Savigny on a walk in an area whose mix of strangeness and familiarity lend it the aura of the Romantic uncanny. Suddenly, Savigny spots a deer, raises his bow, and shoots it in the neck. Günderrode immediately bleeds from the corresponding spot on her own throat. Brentano is the first to perceive her catastrophe: "Lina! rief sie klagend. Die Wunde war an ihrem Hals, sie mußte nicht nachfühlen" (9; Lina! she cried out plaintively. The wound was on her throat, she did not have to feel around for it). The wound is cured by the hand and magic of Günderrode's erstwhile lover, Savigny (10). Nevertheless, Brentano's plaintive cry — "klagend" resonates as much with accusation as with despair — evokes the famous episode in *Goethes Briefwechsel mit einem Kinde* where Günderrode reveals the dagger, alluded to several times in *Kein Ort. Nirgends*, that will serve as her instrument of suicide, and Brentano, enraged at the material manifestation of her fears concerning her friend's intentions, takes the dagger and shreds Günderrode's armchair with it.[55] Brentano's employment of the epistolary genre, with its decentering of authorship and concomitant intersubjectivity, strongly impacted both the form and content of *Kein Ort. Nirgends*,[56] but the death scene with the deer specifically foregrounds her as the figure who, albeit vainly and almost alone, sought to win Günderrode for life.

A fictional Bettine Brentano also makes a brief appearance in Grass's *Der Butt*. Over a quarter of a century ago, Per Øhrgaard took note of this circumstance, and saw articulated in both Grass's novel and *Kein Ort. Nirgends* the perception that Romanticism encompassed the historical period of an attempt to overcome the gap between the genders, previously perceived as unbridgeable. However, he argues that these novels also show how this age ultimately witnessed the establishment of the foundations for the Western world's subsequent, and, as yet, predominant paternalism. In *Kein Ort. Nirgends*, Kleist and Günderrode evoke, in the course of their conversations, the vision of a genuinely holistic human being — this is the novel's positive utopian dimension — but Kleist's own inability to overcome his aversion toward dynamic creative women underscores the impossibility of their vision. In the panoramic sweep of *Der Butt*, Grass portrays the evolution of Pomeranian society from matriarchal to patriarchal governance. During the course of the novel's Romantic segment, a group of authors, including Achim von Arnim, the Brothers Grimm, Phillip Otto Runge, and Clemens and Bettine Brentano, meet in a forester's home in the Olivaer Forest. The men discuss two versions of the Pomeranian fairy tale *Von den Fischer un siene Fru* (The fisherman and his wife). In the more well-known tale, the fisherman's wife Ilsebill, granted wishes by the flounder whose life the fisherman spares, is so greedy for ever-greater power and possessions that the fish must, when her desires touch on divine privilege, return the couple to their original immiserated state. In the other version, also stemming from an old woman on the island of Oche who insists both takes are valid, it is the husband whose wishes are nullified when they reach blasphemous proportions. Runge wants to publish both versions, but Jacob Grimm, citing the need for an undivided truth that will unite Germany while it is enmeshed in the Napoleonic Wars, convinces Runge that only the misogynist variant should be printed. Given this fairy tale's significance as the novel's key intertextual thread — the flounder of the novel's title is the flounder of *Von den Fischer un siene Fru* — Runge's wish to publish both variants represents *Der Butt*'s utopian element, where, as in evanescent moments in the conversation between Kleist and Günderrode in *Kein Ort. Nirgends*, a transcendent vision of humanity truly balanced between the antipodes of gender is evoked. Both Wolf and Grass drew upon early Romanticism's idealistic valorization of androgyny in composing their novels.[57]

Employing the technique of character iteration in the comprehensive historical landscape of *Der Butt*, Grass imaginatively radicalizes Judith

Butler's proposal for performing gender-switching in the actual public sphere by having Swedish marauders of the Thirty Years War reincarnated as butch lesbians in the novel's contemporary 1970s timeframe. However, it is Wolf who performs Brentano's voice throughout the course of *Kein Ort. Nirgends* by mining her three epistolary novels — *Clemens Brentanos Frühlingskranz*, *Goethes Briefwechsel mit einem Kinde*, and, most importantly, *Die Günderrode* — for material on Brentano's beloved mentor and creatively employing it for her own purposes, much as Brentano blended truth and fiction in the above-mentioned works. Grass's version of her not only defends Napoleon, but briefly succeeds in sustaining Runge's holistic vision. While the painter hesitantly discourses on artistic coincidence and primeval forces, Brentano, whose voice is filtered through the indirect discourse subjunctive, tries to use her powers of persuasion to unite the disputing Romantics behind the comprehensive publication of *Von den Fischer un siene Fru*'s two variants: "Sie alle, die Freunde, seien herrlich. Ein jeder habe recht. Jede Idee finde Platz. So sei ja die Natur in ihrer schönen Unordnung: geräumig. Man möge das alles in seinem Wildwuchs und nur mäßig geordnet dem Leser übereignen. Der werde schon seinen Gebrauch machen" (442; All of you, the friends, are wonderful. Everyone is right. There is a place for every idea. This is the way nature is in its beautiful lack of order: spacious. One may transmit all of that in its untamed growth and only moderately ordered to the reader. He will certainly make his use of it).[58]

Brentano's presence in *Kein Ort. Nirgends* as the voice for a utopian holistic androgyny is entirely covert, and is only actualized when we consider her significance not only as a genuine authorial source for much of the novel's form and content, but also for Wolf's idealization of her in a key passage in "Ein Brief über die Bettine": "Sachte zieht Bettine die Günderrode auf die Seite ihres Gegen-Entwurfs, ihrer Weiberphilosophie, ihrer 'Schwebe-Religion,' die, hätte sie nur eine geringe Chance gehabt, verwirklicht zu werden, die Männerkult der Aggressionen nicht an den Rand der Selbstvernichtung getrieben hätte"[59] (Gently Bettine draws Günderrode to the side of her counter-design, her female philosophy, her 'floating-religion,' which, if it had only had the slightest chance to be realized, would not have been driven by the male cult of aggression to the brink of self-destruction). For Wolf, Brentano personified the Romantic desideratum of synthesizing Enlightenment rationality with the enhanced power to perceive and act on the basis of emotional sensibility.[60] After the loss of this epistemological plenitude subsequent to the dissolution of early Romanticism, the possibility for actualizing such feminine sensibility was dashed, and instrumental reason was given free reign, leading to an ends/means perspective as well as the exploitation of nature.[61] The "Schwebe-Religion" proposed by Brentano was indeed holistic and dynamic, advocating a Spinozistic oneness with God and an equally harmonious interaction between the individual and the wider world.[62] While

Grass presents her totalistic thinking, with its transcendence of gender-based antinomies, in a brief passage that occludes her agency by mediating it via indirect discourse, Wolf actualizes it by performing it in both the structure of *Kein Ort. Nirgends* and in its tragically unrealizable utopian thread. Brentano's spiritual presence is unable to overcome the violent conflict inherent in the lives of the novel's two chief protagonists, Kleist and Günderrode, a violence deeply inscribed into the novel.

Conclusion

The East German turn to Romanticism emerged in the wake of the Biermann affair. When this poet and singer/songwriter was barred from reentering the GDR after his tour in the West, the hope of GDR intellectuals placed in the liberalization enacted during the early years of the Erich Honecker regime years was dashed, and they began to see in German Romantics kindred victims of state suppression. The most significant work to emerge from the Romantic turn was Wolf's *Kein Ort. Nirgends*, whose protagonists Kleist and Günderrode are constituted as figures marginalized not only by their society's political hierarchy, but also by their androgynous sexuality. Wolf came to see early Romanticism as an idealistic age in which gender and social antinomies could be sublated and overcome, but her protagonists' suicides, subtly alluded to in the novel and foregrounded in essays on these figures, materially manifests the collapse of the Romantic movement's ideals. Other fictional treatments by East German authors such as Kunert refute Kleist's supposed membership in the German classical pantheon, while Western feminists such as Reschke treat both Kleist and his co-suicide Henriette Vogel as largely passive casualties of the conservative, manipulative forces highlighted by Wolf and Kunert.

Both Grass and Wolf saw in Bettine Brentano a manifestation of positive Romantic holism that, despite her energy (in Wolf) and conciliatory engagement (in Grass), was doomed to failure due to the ingrained prejudices of the age. These prejudices, it is suggested, continue into the present day. Particularly in Wolf, the violence inherent in Romantic narratives is articulated as a cathartic response to the conservative, regressive forces shaping the politics and constraining the holistic idealism of their day and of divided Germany in the 1970s.

Notes

[1] Christa Wolf, *Kein Ort. Nirgends*, 2nd ed. (Darmstadt: Luchterhand, 1979).

[2] To cite just a few examples: Linda Dietrick, "Appropriating Romantic Consciousness: Narrative Mode in Christa Wolf's *Kein Ort. Nirgends*," in *Echoes and Influences of German Romanticism: Essays in Honour of Hans Eichner*, ed. Michael S. Batts, Anthony W. Riley, and Heinz Wetzel (New York: Peter Lang, 1987),

211–23; Gizela Kurpanik-Malinowska, "Stil und Traditionsbezüge gehören zusammen: Zu Christa Wolfs Aufarbeitung der deutschen Romanik," in *Romantik — Eine lebenskräftige Krankheit: Ihre literarischen Nachwirkungen in der Moderne*, ed. Erika Tunner (Amsterdam: Rodopi, 1991), 135–44; Edith Waldstein, "Christa Wolf's *Kein Ort. Nirgends*: A Dialogic Re-Vision," in *The Enlightenment and Its Legacy: Studies in German Literature in Honor of Helga Slessarev*, ed. Sara Friedrichsmeyer and Barbara Becker-Cantarino (Bonn: Bouvier, 1990), 181–93.

[3] Judith Butler, "Performative Acts and Gender Constitution: An Essay in Phenomenology and Feminist Theory," in *Performing Feminisms: Feminist Critical Theory and Theater*, ed. Sue-Ellen Case (Baltimore, MD: Johns Hopkins UP, 1990), 270–82.

[4] Karin Reschke, *Verfolgte des Glücks: Findebuch der Henriette Vogel* (1982; Hamburg: Rotbuch, 1996).

[5] Robert Walser, "Kleist in Thun," in *Das Gesamtwerk*, ed. Jochen Greven, vol. 1 (Geneva: Helmut Kossodo, 1972), 174–85.

[6] Günter Kunert, *Ein anderer K.* (Stuttgart: Philipp Reclam, 1977).

[7] Günter Grass, *Der Butt*, 6th ed. (Darmstadt: Luchterhand, 1978).

[8] Elisabeth Krimmer, *In the Company of Men: Cross-Dressed Women around 1800* (Detroit, MI: Wayne State UP, 2004).

[9] Patricia Anne Simpson, *The Erotics of War in German Romanticism* (Lewisburg, PA: Bucknell UP, 2006).

[10] A trenchant and concise overview of these themes in Kleist is provided by Seán Allan, "'Mein ist die Rache spricht der Herr': Violence and Revenge in the Works of Heinrich von Kleist," in *A Companion to the Works of Heinrich von Kleist*, ed. Bernd Fischer (Rochester, NY: Camden House, 2003), 227–48.

[11] Krimmer, *In the Company of Men*, 134.

[12] Simpson, *The Erotics of War*, 214.

[13] On this aspect of Kant's engagement with enthusiasm, see Peter Fenves, "The Scale of Enthusiasm," in *Enthusiasm and Enlightenment in Europe 1650–1850*, ed. Lawrence E. Klein and Anthony J. La Vopa (San Marino, CA: Huntington Library, 1998), 122–23.

[14] Christa Wolf, "Der Schatten eines Traumes: Karoline von Günderrode — ein Entwurf," *Die Dimension des Autors: Essays und Aufsätze, Reden und Gespräche 1959–1985* (Darmstadt: Luchterhand, 1987), 571.

[15] On these points, see Andreas Gailus, *Passions of the Sign: Revolution and Language in Kant, Goethe, and Kleist* (Baltimore, MD: Johns Hopkins UP, 2006), 28–73.

[16] Immanuel Kant, "Der Streit der Fakultäten," in *Gesammelte Schriften*, ed. Königlich Preußischen Akademie der Wissenschaften, vol. 7 (Berlin: Georg Reimer, 1907), 93. Somewhat contradictorily, Kant also associated war with the sublime. See Simpson, *The Erotics of* War, 39–41 and Krimmer, "The Gender of Terror: War as (Im)Moral Institution in Kleist's *Hermannschlacht* and *Penthesilea*," *German Quarterly* 81.1 (2008): 68–69.

[17] See Anthony La Vopa, "The Philosopher and the *Schwärmer*: On the Career of a German Epithet from Luther to Kant," in *Enthusiasm and Enlightenment*, 85–115.

[18] Gailus, *Passions of the Sign*, 6, 8.

[19] A concise summary of the novel's temporal and geographical frame is provided by Eva-Maria Schulz-Jander, "'Das Gegenteil von Gebrechlichkeit ist Überein-kunft': Christa Wolf's *Kein Ort. Nirgends*," in *The Age of Goethe Today: Critical Reexamination and Literary Reflection*, ed. Gertrud Bauer Pickar and Sabine Cramer (Munich: Wilhelm Fink, 1990), 232–33.

[20] Simon Richter, *Missing the Breast: Gender, Fantasy, and the Body in the German Enlightenment* (Seattle: U of Washington P, 2006), 241. In Richter's reading, Penthesilea's act is primarily regarded as the attempt to satisfy a breast fixation.

[21] Heinrich von Kleist, "Penthesilea," in *Werke und Briefe in vier Bänden*, ed. Siegfried Streller (Berlin: Aufbau, 1978), 2:105.

[22] In an interview with Frauke Meyer-Gosau conducted in 1982, Wolf summarized a general male rejection of her treatment of Kleist as follows: "Die richtet sich manchmal ausgesprochen gegen die 'weibischen' Züge bei Kleist! Neulich hat mir jemand gesagt, Kleist sei der Autor des Kohlhaas, ein entschlossener, mutiger, zupackender Autor, und ich würde ihn mit 'weibischen' Zügen ausstatten und daher verzeichnen" (Sometimes it is unequivocally directed against the 'feminine' traits in Kleist's work. Recently someone told me Kleist was the author of 'Kohlhaas,' a decisive, courageous, vigorous author and I supposedly imbued him with 'feminine' traits and therefore misrepresented him). In: "Projektionsraum Romantik: Gespräch mit Frauke Meyer-Gosau," *Die Dimension des Autors*, 894.

[23] Wolf, "Kleists 'Penthesilea,'" in *Die Dimension des Autors*, 675.

[24] Wolf, "Der Schatten eines Traumes," 556.

[25] Fenves, "The Scale of Enthusiasm," 136.

[26] Friedrich Schelling, "Philosophische Briefe über Dogmatismus und Kritizismus (1795)," in *Werke*, ed. Manfred Schröter (Munich: C. H. Beck and R. Oldenbourg, 1927), 1:260.

[27] Bettine [Brentano] von Arnim, *Die Günderrode*, in *Werke und Briefe*, ed. Gustav Konrad (Frechen: Bartmann, 1959), 1:467.

[28] Wolf, "Der Schatten eines Traumes," 518–19.

[29] Friedrich Hölderlin, "Reflexion," *Sämtliche Werke*, ed. Friedrich Beissner (Stuttgart: W. Kohlhammer, 1961), 4:233.

[30] Karoline von Günderrode, "Darthula nach Ossian," *Gesammelte Werke*, ed. Leopold Hirschberg (1920–1922; Bern: Herbert Lang, 1970), 1:9.

[31] Julia Hell, *Post-Fascist Fantasies: Psychoanalysis, History, and the Literature of East Germany* (Durham, NC: Duke UP, 1997), 250.

[32] Helga G. Braunbeck, *Autorschaft und Subjektgenese: Christa Wolfs Kein Ort, Nirgends* (Vienna: Passagen, 1992).

[33] See Dietrick, "Appropriating Romantic Consciousness," 211–12.

[34] This letter was published, along with several others exchanged by these two leading Marxists at the end of the 1930s, in Georg Lukács, "Ein Briefwechsel zwischen Anna Seghers and Georg Lukács," *Probleme des Realismus* (Berlin: Aufbau, 1955), 241.

[35] A rather different image of Goethe is intended by Thomas Mann when he brings up the father's refusal to allow his son to go to war in *Lotte in Weimar*. Goethe is shown to exert all his influence to prevent this from happening. While August complains that this circumstance has alienated him from his friends who went off to war, Mann seems to want to present the elder Goethe as a concerned father willing to pull out all the stops to keep his son alive, though he seems to regard this son more as an indispensable employee rather than as his truly beloved offspring ("Lotte in Weimar," 538–42).

[36] Lukács, "Ein Briefwechsel," 254.

[37] Hell, *Post-Fascist Fantasies*, 185. The validity of her position is substantiated by Wolf, who in "Der Schatten eines Traumes" criticizes the German academic veneration of the Classical German authors and, citing the example of Lukács, the concomitant casual dismissal of Kleist and the Romantics as "unvollendet" (512; incomplete).

[38] Wolf, *Kein Ort. Nirgends: Mit einem Kommentar von Sonja Hilzinger* (Frankfurt am Main: Suhrkamp, 2006), 140–41.

[39] Braunbeck, *Autorschaft und Subjektgenese*, 89.

[40] Wolf, "Der Schatten eines Traumes," 511.

[41] Wolf, "Subjektive Authentizität: Gespräch mit Hans Kaufmann," *Die Dimension des Autors*, 797–98.

[42] For an analysis that treats the motif of androgyny in Wolf's novel by focusing on its mystical elements and employing a broadly Jungian methodology, while ignoring the dimension of Romantic violence I am highlighting in the present essay, see Edith Borchardt and Jennifer Wright, "Androgyny: The Search for Wholeness in Karoline von Günderrode and Heinrich von Kleist. Christa Wolf's Novel *Kein Ort. Nirgends*," *Journal of the Fantastic in the Arts* 11.2 (2001): 245–56.

[43] Wolf, "Der Schatten eines Traumes," 554.

[44] Patricia Herminghouse, "Die Wiederentdeckung der Romantik: Zur Funktion der Dichterfiguren in der neueren DDR-Literatur," trans. Reinhart Jost, in *DDR-Roman und Literaturgesellschaft*, ed. Jos Hoogeveen and Gerd Labroisse (Amsterdam: Rodopi, 1981), 244.

[45] Günderrode, "Timur," *Gesammelte Werke*, 1:21.

[46] This utterance constitutes the title of a recent biography of Günderrode, Dagmar von Gersdorff's *"Die Erde ist mir Heimat nicht geworden": Das Leben der Karoline von Günderrode* (Frankfurt am Main: Insel, 2006).

[47] Wolf, "Der Schatten eines Traumes," 568.

[48] Wolf, "Der Schatten eines Traumes," 571.

[49] Menke, *Lenz-Erzählungen in der deutschen Literatur*, 99–101.

[50] Kunert, "Pamphlet für K.," in *Die Schreie der Fledermäuse*, ed. Dieter E. Zimmer (Munich: Carl Hanser, 1979), 337–38.

[51] Kunert, "Heinrich von Kleist — Ein Modell," in *Diesseits des Erinnerns* (Munich: Carl Hanser, 1982), 36–62.

[52] For a fuller discussion of these points, see Jacques Lajarrige, "Wahnsinn mit Gänsefüßchen: Zur Rehabilitierung Heinrich von Kleists in Günter Kunerts *Ein anderer K.*," in Tunner, *Romantik — Eine lebenskräftige Krankheit*, 145–58.

[53] See, for example, Ernst Osterkamp, "Karin Reschke *Verfolgte des Glücks: Findebuch der Henriette Vogel*," *Kleist-Jahrbuch* (1984): 163–75, and Stephanie Bird, *Recasting Historical Women: Female Identity in German Biographical Fiction* (Oxford: Berg, 1998), 26–43.

[54] Donna L. Hoffmeister, "Rewriting Literary History through Fiction: Karin Reschke and Christa Wolf," *South Atlantic Review* 49 (1984): 14.

[55] Von Arnim, "Goethes Briefwechsel mit einem Kinde," *Werke und Briefe*, ed. Gustav Konrad (Frechen: Bartmann, 1959), 2:55.

[56] See Braunbeck, *Autorschaft und Subjektgenese*, 93–125.

[57] Per Øhrgaard, "He, Butt! Das ist deine andere Wahrheit: Die Romantik als Bezugspunkt in der deutschen Gegenwartsliteratur," *Text & Kontext*: 18 (Supp.: 1983): 128–45.

[58] Brentano's brief speech does conclude with an exclamation spoken in the first person: "'Forschen könnt ihr dann immer noch!'" (442; You can still keep on researching!). This suggestion evokes her own self-distancing from scholarly research as a detached, impersonal activity, a disinclination reflected in the historical Bettine Brentano's epistolary novels and, from a Lacanian perspective, articulated by Friedrich Kittler in "Writing into the Wind, Bettina," trans. Marilyn Wyatt, *Glyph* 7 (1980): 32–69.

[59] Wolf, "Nun ja! Das nächste Leben geht aber heute an: Ein Brief über die Bettine," *Die Dimension des Autors*, 603.

[60] Wolf's association of early German Romanticism with the search for holistic plenitude, and her view that the social rejection during this temporal period of those invested in such a search created a dissatisfaction with life among women continuing into the present day, is underscored in a 1979 interview. See "Ich bin schon für eine gewisse Maßlosigkeit: Gespräch mit Wilfried F. Schoeller," *Die Dimension des Autors*, 874.

[61] Wolf, "Ein Brief über die Bettine," 605.

[62] See Gersdorff, "*Die Erde ist mir Heimat nicht geworden*," 132.

2: Hölderlins East and West

IN A BRIEF ESSAY EXAMINING the rediscovery of German Romanticism in
the German Democratic Republic, published shortly after the dissolution of that nation, Sonja Hilzinger concisely describes the circumstances
inspiring this rediscovery and the sort of imaginative and critical writing
to which it gave rise. She opens with a long quotation from a 1982 interview in which Christa Wolf describes the origins of *Kein Ort. Nirgends*,
noting the centrality of the expulsion of Wolf Biermann in polarizing the
GDR's intellectual elite. Hilzinger's choice of Wolf's voice as the vehicle
for commencing her essay is appropriate, as *Kein Ort. Nirgends* continues to be the most canonic work to emerge from the brief flowering,
in the wake of the Biermann affair, of GDR literature that imaginatively
brought to life leading figures of Romanticism. Hilzinger argues that East
German writers took recourse to the earlier generation of poets because
of the Romantics' conflict with Classicist aesthetic norms in a conservative restoration society, which produced an existential crisis stemming
from the feeling of being trapped — much like their GDR counterparts
were — in a political dead end. Both the German Romantics and East
German authors thus felt forced into the kind of exclusive recourse to
literature that Wolf describes in the interview. For Hilzinger, the GDR
engagement with German Romanticism manifested a desire to escape the
desultory reality that confronted that nation's cultural elite with a sense
of political impotence; at the same time, it also provided that elite with
a means to protest the reactionary ambience instilled by Honecker and
his allies in the GDR leadership following Biermann's expulsion. Hilzinger also notes that, by imaginatively and critically engaging with German Romanticism's outcast authors, intellectuals such as Wolf, Christoph
Hein, Günter Kunert, Günter de Bruyn, and Sigrid Damm were consciously following in the footsteps of Anna Seghers's defense of Romantic
authors against Lukács's denigration of them, as discussed in the previous
chapter. Specifically, Hilzinger notes near the conclusion of her essay that
an engagement with the poet Friedrich Hölderlin constituted a clear focal
point for GDR writers' rediscovery of Romanticism. Even though Kleist
was the Romantic writer most frequently treated in essays, both he and
Hölderlin were configured as authors whose lives were destroyed by the
circumstances prevailing in Germany in their age. Again, the Romantics
were seen to mirror the experience of GDR authors in being unheard by
their society and in despair at their invisibility.[1]

Hilzinger's essay confirms a number of the central arguments of the previous chapter: the cardinal significance of Christa Wolf's *Kein Ort. Nirgends* among the profusion of GDR texts that imaginatively reconfigured the lives of leading German Romantics; the Biermann episode and its consequences as the trigger for the revival of interest in Romanticism in East Germany[2]; and the centrality of Seghers for the turn to Romanticism. Hilzinger argues that Seghers was the most authoritative figure among the GDR's intellectual pioneers to be drawn upon by later writers to legitimate their positive reception of the Romantics. However, while Hilzinger and the critics cited in the previous chapter are correct in noting Lukács's role as an agonistic figure for Wolf and her colleagues, an important caveat must be introduced here with respect to Hölderlin. Hölderlin was the most popular object of imaginative encounters by novelists, dramatists, and short-story writers in the German-speaking world in the 1970s, both in the GDR and in the Federal Republic of Germany as well. In the case of Hölderlin, however, Lukács wrote a groundbreaking essay arguing that the Swabian poet was an ardent revolutionary, a Jacobin sympathizer whose political proclivities were occluded — first, in the nineteenth century, by nationalist reactionaries who distorted and simplified his work to transform him into a vanguard patriot (a misappropriation continued by the National Socialists), and then, in the early twentieth century, by the obscurantist elites of the Stefan George Circle. Lukács's essay "Hölderlins *Hyperion*" was published in 1934, but it was not until the late 1960s that Hölderlin began to emerge, in both imaginative and critical works, as a committed leftist radical who could serve as an inspiration to European insurrectionists seeking to overthrow the established order during that turbulent time. In this chapter, I will examine the four most significant imaginative engagements with Hölderlin in the 1970s: two from the GDR and two from the FRG. We will see that the four authors who wrote these works had different priorities, which were not exclusively political. The two GDR works are Stephan Hermlin's radio play *Scardanelli* (1970)[3] and the nineteen sketches published by Gerhard Wolf under the title *Der arme Hölderlin* (1972)[4]; from the West, I will analyze Peter Weiss's lengthy drama *Hölderlin* (1971)[5] and Peter Härtling's expansive novel *Hölderlin* (1976).[6]

Marxist Orthodoxy: Lukács's View of Hölderlin

For the sake of continuity with the previous chapter, the texts of Hermlin and Wolf will be discussed before those of Wolf and Weiss. However, given Lukács's position as both the oppositional figure for the GDR's Romantic renaissance and also the thinker who made Hölderlin a key figure in German political debates in the West, I will first look at his 1934 essay on the poet. At the outset, it should be noted that the popularization of

Hölderlin as a Jacobin revolutionary who might plausibly serve as a role model for contemporary radicals — a view that finds expression in Weiss's play — cannot be directly attributed to Lukács. Instead, the chief inspirer of this image was the French scholar Pierre Bertaux, who made a dramatic, well-publicized presentation to the Hölderlin Society in 1968 on the occasion of the 125th anniversary of the poet's death. Bertaux rather brazenly claimed in this address that Germans could not adequately comprehend Hölderlin, as they lacked the intimate knowledge of the French Revolution possessed by Frenchmen such as himself. Bertaux's cudgel was taken up by German leftists at the 1970 Hölderlin jubilee, where, for example, the then-young and rebellious Martin Walser furthered the image of Hölderlin as a radical. These leftists refuted what they saw as Hölderlin's institutionalization as an innocuous aesthete at the hands of scholars such as Friedrich Beißner, editor of the still most widely cited edition of the poet's works.[7] Nevertheless, Lukács, as the progenitor of GDR critical orthodoxy, exercised a direct influence on the Hölderlins of Weiss and Härtling, and seems ironically to have steered the unhappy East German intellectuals Gerhard Wolf and Hermlin *away* from creating an image of Hölderlin as revolutionary, an image that would have confirmed Lukács's view.

Lukács opens his essay by acknowledging the centrality of Hölderlin's Graecophilia for an understanding of the poet and his works, but finds his reception of ancient Greece darker and more anguished than the utopian treatment evident in the Renaissance and the Enlightenment. He could have added the names of Goethe and Schiller — whom Lukács upheld in his correspondence with Seghers as heroic counterweights to Romanticism's putative reactionary tendencies — as purveyors of an idealized Greece. In comparison with Hölderlin, Goethe and particularly Schiller held rather sanguine views concerning the Hellenic Age. More importantly, however, Lukács contrasts Hölderlin's reception of the French Revolution with that of "reactionary" German Romanticism. Citing Marx, Lukács takes the position that because the circumstances necessary for opposing Napoleon's occupation of Germany by means of a middle-class revolution were lacking, the desire for national liberation through a revolutionary emancipation movement was stymied. This gave rise to a reactionary Romanticism, which was resisted by both Hölderlin and Hegel, though Hölderlin did not accept his former Tübingen seminary roommate's view that the German "misery" attendant to the reaction was an inevitable and necessary phase in the historical dialectic. While Hölderlin, in Lukács's view, neglected the capitalist contradictions that sustained that era's malaise, the utopian element of the epistolary novel *Hyperion* offers a vision, albeit somewhat mystified, of the regenerative revolutionary social transformation advocated by Marxists in Lukács's age. He characterizes Hölderlin as consistently Republican in his inclinations, finding that the poet's sympathies lay with an Athenian vision of the ideal state rather than with the ascetic, Sparta-oriented principles of the Jacobins. This view puts Lukács somewhat at odds with Bertaux and Weiss. However, later in the essay, Lukács, anticipating Hölderlin's later reception by Western leftist intellectuals such as Walser, Bertaux and Weiss, places the Tübingen poet decisively on the path of Robespierre and the Jacobins, albeit with a mystic-Romantic tinge redolent with yearning for heroic, sacrificial death. Nevertheless, Lukács locates the ground of Hölderlin's somewhat obscurantist elegiac perspective in a mourning for the loss of a democratic ancient Greece, and finds Hölderlin advocated the reattainment of such democracy through revolutionary means. Lukács characterizes *Hyperion* as a lyric-elegiac "citoyen" novel that manifests a yearning, as opposed to a concrete call, for revolutionary action. Hölderlin's idealistic embrace of a heroic refusal to compromise is contrasted by Lukács with the accommodation to reactionary circumstances made by Hegel and Goethe — an accommodation that, though bereft of Hölderlin's idealism, constituted the soundest foundation for the development of bourgeois thought according to Lukács. Hölderlin's failure to make this kind of accommodation, while bringing about the sort of poetic revolutionary public vision Lukács admired, also led Hölderlin into a dead end, so that he remained truly unique and had no successors.[8]

Stephan Hermlin's Depoliticized Victim of Insanity

There is an obvious contrast between the brief celebration, foreshadowed in Lukács's essay, of Hölderlin as a revolutionary by Bertaux and the German Left on the one hand, and Hermlin's treatment of the poet on the other. Thus, Robert Savage — after noting how the Hölderlin scholar Günther Deicke saw revolutionary continuity in the coincidence that the two-hundredth birthdays of Beethoven, Hegel, and Hölderlin were observed in the same year (1970) as Lenin's hundredth — opens his cursory look at the East German's configuration of the poet by noting: "Stephan Hermlin's radio play *Scardanelli*, broadcast in the same year, was concerned less with celebrating Hölderlin as a patron saint of the worker's state than with piecing together the stages of his descent into madness."[9] While Lukács's essay may have instigated the chain of events leading to Hölderlin's celebration as a revolutionary, Hermlin helps inaugurate the orientation of East German writers toward Romanticism by creating a relatively depoliticized Hölderlin, at a time when GDR authors were starting to turn away from Lukács as an intellectual father figure. The artist as madman is, after all, a key Romantic topos, and, as we saw, Seghers had placed Hölderlin within the Romantic pantheon of writers who went mad.

To be sure, Hermlin's play, which contains fifteen rather disparate scenes intended to illustrate Hölderlin's fall into insanity, and intersperses these flashback scenes with tableaus of the already insane poet in his tower, does not ignore how the thwarting of Hölderlin's political visions contributed to his unfortunate condition. In the second scene, when the Duke of Württemberg visits the seminary because of reports that the students are sympathetic to the French insurrection — a moment in Hölderlin's life that receives extensive treatment in Härtling's novel — the young poet protests he will not submit to arbitrary, senseless laws. Hermlin inserted a number of anonymous voices into the radio play, and after one of them proclaims that the seminary's young people have been infected by the "freedom nonsense" (*Freiheitsschwindel*), Hölderlin responds, in a subdued tone: "Der Mißbrauch fürstlicher Gewalt wird schrecklich werden. Bete für die Franzosen, die Verfechter der menschlichen Rechte" (13; the misuse of royal violence will become horrible. Pray for the French, the champions of human rights).

The anonymous voices in this radio play, such as this one denouncing the revolutionary sympathies of the Tübingen seminary students, are effective in establishing an atmosphere of fear — indeed, paranoia — contributing to Hölderlin's ultimately incurable dementia, although not all of these voices betray a reactionary sensibility. After Hölderlin complains to fellow student and poet Christian Neuffer about the violent suppression of their youthful hopes, one voice claims that his position was the most advanced, contrasting it with the stance of progressive civil servants and ministers in Weimar and Jena who, while in despair at current circumstances, saw no other path than the one they were taking (28–29). Hermlin would seem to be adopting a stance here akin to that of Lukács in "Hölderlins *Hyperion*," where Hegel's and Goethe's accommodation is contrasted with Hölderlin's revolutionary utopianism. However, in noting Hölderlin's most advanced political standing, the above-cited voice adds a caveat: "Aber dort vermochte er nicht zu stehen" (28; But he was unable to remain abiding there). As the title of Hermlin's play itself indicates, the focus of the play is on the nuances of Hölderlin's madness, and less on the political circumstances that may have contributed to this condition: "Scardanelli" is one of the names and identities adopted by the mad Hölderlin in his tower, where much of the play takes place. The radio audience hears a broken man, who alternates between manic outbursts, servile obsequiousness, and a catatonic stupor that must be evinced through the words of others, as when Wilhelm Waiblinger, another student, responds to an anonymous voice's question concerning Hölderlin's condition by simply noting: "Er ist abwesend. Nicht hier" (37; He is absent. Not here). Helen Fehervary has accurately noted that *Scardanelli* was the first work in the GDR to intentionally create an image of Hölderlin contrary to his orthodox reception in that country, and finds in Hermlin's Hölderlin far more of the languid, introverted Western antihero than the eloquent, ardent, ultimately communist soldier Johannes Hörder, who supposedly embodies the sensibilities of the historical Hölderlin in Johannes R. Becher's play *Schlacht um Moskau* (Battle for Moscow, 1942).[10]

The East German government's revocation of Wolf Biermann's citizenship and its concomitant refusal to allow him to reenter the country from the Federal Republic occurred in 1976, so that this event, of key significance for the turn toward German Romanticism, was too late to have influenced Hermlin's radio play. Nevertheless, the play was innovative enough in the GDR to be termed a prototype for later East German engagements with writers whose heroic and lonely crusades in the realm of poetry, love, life, and indeed politics drove them to madness or suicide. Thus, Silvia Schlenstedt is fully justified in her claim that Hermlin was the first GDR writer to imaginatively appropriate Seghers's defense of those Romantic writers who, as Seghers put it, "rubbed their foreheads raw" on the "social wall of their country," and were essentially expelled from life after strenuous exertions in defense of their ideals. This defense was buttressed by a condemnation of the way nonconformist poetic visionaries were being marginalized in that country.[11] In the 1982 interview cited by Hilzinger, Wolf points to 1976 as the year when many GDR writers were faced with an existential crisis, having been marginalized by a government that made it clear that their participation in the political and social life of the country was no longer desired.[12] Hermlin's Hölderlin can also be regarded as the prototypically marginalized author, the sort of Romantic visionary with whom Christa Wolf and other GDR writers would come to identify in the wake of the Biermann affair when they were made to feel like a Hölderlin, Kleist, or Günderrode in their country. Schlenstedt notes that Hermlin wanted to make one of the Romantic writers championed by Seghers relevant to the contemporary, socialist context of the GDR in order to demonstrate how vitally important it was to a poet to feel needed and useful.[13] The despair Hermlin's Hölderlin experiences at his sense of utter exclusion would be experienced by Wolf and her colleagues some five years later, leading to the full flowering of imaginative and critical works focused on Romantic writers.

In a speech delivered at the Hölderlin conference in 1982 and first published in the prominent GDR critical venue *Sinn und Form* in that year, Hermlin spoke out against the political instrumentalization of the Tübingen poet. Thus, he reversed the direction taken by Bertaux and the German Left at the Hölderlin Society conferences in 1968 and 1970. To be sure, his denunciation primarily focuses on the use of Hölderlin for propaganda purposes during war in general and World War II in particular. Having noted that Hölderlin is a favored author of Germans when they are engaged in martial conflict, he wonders how they regard him: as a lonely, mad descendant of those who gathered at the Champs de Mars, or as a messenger of the future Third Reich. His *Scardanelli* evoked this first image of Hölderlin, while the Nazis, particularly their followers in the Hölderlin Society during Hitler's reign, ardently promoted the latter vision. Hermlin then goes on to gently criticize Lukács's 1934 essay on Hölderlin, even though he says this work provided him a lightening-like moment of illumination at that dark time. Nevertheless, Hermlin recounts in his 1982 speech that, during one of his frequent meetings with Lukács after the war, he damned the Hungarian with faint praise, pointing out that Lukács had achieved the singular feat of writing a major work on Hölderlin without once mentioning Hölderlin's poems. With bemusement, Lukács concurred.[14]

Obviously, Hermlin was more distressed by the Nazis' political use of Hölderlin than he was by Lukács's lack of attention to Hölderlin's poetry, and yet what he found most notable in Lukács's essay was its characterization of Hölderlin as a "belated Jacobin."[15] Hermlin's mention of this in the same paragraph as his reference to the popular wartime perception of Hölderlin as a prophet for the Third Reich indicates a generalized dissatisfaction with the treatment of this figure by both the Left and the Right, despite Hermlin's own commitment to the Left at that time. His essay also mentions how he wrote an essay on Hölderlin while hiding from the Nazis in France, and his attempts to convince his comrades that Hölderlin was their secret, invisible ally. However, he felt a kinship with Hölderlin primarily because of the mutually dangerous, confusing path both were forced to take in life and not because of any overt political affiliations across the centuries.[16] Therefore, it is not surprising that in *Scardanelli*, Hölderlin's loneliness and isolation are highlighted at the cost of any nuanced exploration of his political views, which remain, before his lapse into insanity, vaguely democratic and utopian, supportive of the French Revolution, but not sharply defined. The following passage may serve as an example of this tendency:

> Dies ist meine seligste Hoffnung, die mich stark erhält und tätig, unsere Enkel werden besser sein als wir, die Freiheit muß einmal kommen, und die Tugend wird besser gedeihen in der Freiheit heiligem erwärmenden Lichte als unter der eiskalten Zone des Despotismus. (30)

> [This is my most fervent hope, that keeps me strong and active, our grandchildren will be better than we are, freedom must finally come, and virtue will flourish better in the holy warming light of freedom than in the ice-cold zone of despotism.]

Though at the conclusion of the 1982 speech he disavowed the essay he wrote while hiding from the Nazis,[17] this earlier effort, written to mark the hundredth anniversary of Hölderlin's death, also focuses to a great extent on the mature Hölderlin's madness, as well as on the isolation, lack of recognition, and tragic experiences in his love life that pushed him into this condition.[18] These are also the central themes of *Scardanelli*, and it is likely the essay's remarkably flowery style[19] (not a hallmark of Hermlin's mature work), rather than its perspective, that led him to refute this early effort. Indeed, Hermlin's vision of Hölderlin remained consistent throughout his life, and this constancy sustained the powerful vision of the poet that was to prove influential on later East German literary treatments of the German Romantics.

The Fusion of Art and Politics in Gerhard Wolf's Hölderlin

In a 1975 conversation with his wife Christa, first published as a coda to a collection of Hermlin's essays in 1995, Gerhard Wolf expresses the view that Hermlin enjoyed an advantage that was becoming increasingly rare — namely, that the political and the artistic are not only experienced by this author with the same level of intensity, but are fused together (*verschmolzen*) within his personality.[20] Lukács's failure to treat Hölderlin with an awareness that these two domains were deeply intertwined in the world view of the Tübingen poet undoubtedly lay behind Hermlin's good-natured but sincere criticism that his friend had written a lengthy treatise on Hölderlin completely lacking in an engagement with the latter's poetry. As we have noted with respect to Hermlin, Schlenstedt has argued persuasively that *Scardanelli* shows a fundamental accord with Seghers's position on Hölderlin and the Romantics.[21] It is therefore not surprising that *Scardanelli* itself shows how politics and art were fully blended in Hölderlin's works, and how his lack of recognition as an artist was coeval with the frustration of his political vision. *Scardanelli* shows how the thwarting of his relationship with Suzette Gontard, combined with the dashing of his political hopes, brought about Hölderlin's isolation, alienation, and ultimate madness. Gerhard Wolf's *Der arme Hölderlin* has a rather different focus and purport. Fehervary has argued that this collection of nineteen numbered, somewhat disconnected episodes — which she, noting this work's structural affinity with his wife's *Nachdenken über Christa T.* (1968), terms a novel — reverses the chronology of Hermlin's radio play. While Hermlin more or less observed the historical timeline of events leading to Hölderlin's insanity, this is the point at which Wolf's narrative begins. In Fehervary's view, this turnabout of temporal order challenges Hermlin's intention to show how alienation leads to madness. Fehervary finds that *Scardanelli*'s attempt to elicit a "sentimental response" gives way, in Wolf's novel, to a more cause-and-effect oriented exploration of how the antinomies in the poet's life led to the condition he suffers at the outset of *Der arme Hölderlin*. Fehervary argues that the philosophical orientation of this novel is rooted in Ernst

Bloch's *Das Prinzip Hoffnung* (The principle of hope, 1938–47) and its style (as opposed to its structure) is based upon Johannes Bobrowski's brief narrative "Boehlendorff" (1965), which concerns Casimir Böhlendorff, Hölderlin's friend, fellow poet, and recipient of a famous letter from Hölderlin on the relationship between Germany and Greece. Böhlendorff went mad and committed suicide after years of wandering the Baltic homeland of his youth. Fehervary strongly suggests that by demystifying the conditions leading to Hölderlin's insanity, revealing the concrete contradictions leading to this state of mind through the reverse chronology, and anchoring this approach in the firm historical ground of the French Revolution, Wolf's Hölderlin is a less Romantic figure than Hermlin's Hölderlin, even though she does not use this term.[22]

Fehervary argues her positions convincingly and well, especially with respect to the works and authors primary to influencing the style, structure, philosophy, as well as the general purport of *Der arme Hölderlin*. However, she seems to suggest that the reasons Wolf does not portray Hölderlin as a fundamentally Romantic figure derive from his apparently objective, "historical-materialistic" (albeit dialectically bound to "private-psychological factors"[23]) approach to portraying the circumstances of Hölderlin's mental illness. While *Der arme Hölderlin*, like *Scardanelli*, was published prior to the Biermann affair and the more decisive turn of GDR intellectuals toward German Romanticism, Wolf's decision to republish his novel in a collection of fictional works and critical essays written by both Wolf and his wife Christa (a collection also including *Kein Ort. Nirgends*) entitled *Ins Ungebundene gehet eine Sehnsucht: Gesprächsraum Romantik* (A yearning goes into the unbound: Conversational space romanticism, 1985), indicates that Gerhard Wolf, at least in retrospect, saw his novel as belonging to the East German Romantic turn. Whether or not Hermlin influenced him in this regard, the Hölderlin of his novel embodies the ideal Wolf found incorporated in the personality of his GDR colleague: the absolute fusion of the artistic and the political.

Like Hermlin (and, for that matter, Weiss and Härtling), Wolf drew on extensive reading and research in order to intersperse his narrative with quotes from Hölderlin and those with whom the poet interacted. However, one of the elements that make his narrative somewhat less objective and realistic than Fehervary's interpretation would lead us to believe is the employment in the opening episode of an imaginative encounter, delineated in the first-person plural, between the narrator and the mad poet at his home in the residence of the carpenter Zimmer, who took him in: "Wir sagen, verwirrt, einige einleitende Worte, die mit den verbindlichsten Verbeugungen und einem Widerschwall von Worten empfangen werden, teils unverständlich und mit Französisch durchworfen" (In confusion, we utter a few introductory words, which are received with the most friendly bows and a cascade of words, partly incomprehensible and interspersed with French). Like Hermlin's Hölderlin at the conclusion of the play (and underscored by the play's title), the poet in the initial gambit of Wolf's novel is obsequious and refuses to accept his former identity, signified by the name Hölderlin (9). This use of the first-person narrative voice gives way to the employment of a third-person narrator frequently interspersed, without transition, with the first-person perspective of Hölderlin himself (for example, 85). This deliberate oscillation of voices is also present in *Kein Ort. Nirgends*, as we noted, with the difference that one can always discern with relative ease who is speaking in *Der arme Hölderlin*, but with the added complication, at the outset, of an intrusive narrator.

The tone for this shuttling between the personal and the historical is set by the epigraphs that preface the novel. The first is an observation by Hölderlin's friend Waiblinger on the enormous gap between Hölderlin and the rest of humanity, and the second a quote from Anatolij Lunacharsky concerning how conditions obtaining during the Napoleonic era in Germany rendered Hölderlin's adjustment to bourgeois life in that country impossible, and his madness inevitable. A third epigraph from Hölderlin himself expresses how previous failed attempts to express the joyful in a joyful manner come to final fruition in his articulation of such joy in sorrow.[24] As in the novel itself, there is a transition from personal observation and experience to a detachment from the immediacy of intimate acquaintance through the abyss of history, culminating in the fusion of the personal and the historical in Hölderlin's verse. Expressing the joyful through the sorrow of the discrete poetic voice strikes the balance between perspectives grounded in the subjective immediacy of friendship (Waiblinger) and the objective but disjunctive lens of a historically distant observer (Lunacharsky). Hölderlin's distich also anticipates the novel's concluding verse:

> Weh mir!
> Und sag ich gleich,
> ich sei genaht, die Himmlischen zu schauen,
> sie selbst, sie werfen mich tief unter die Lebenden,
> den falschen Priester, ins Dunkel, daß ich
> das warnende Lied den Gelehrigen singe.
> Dort[25]

> [Woe is me!
> And even if I say,
> I have drawn near to see the heavenly hosts,
> they themselves, they cast me deep among the living,
> the false priest, into the darkness, that I
> sing to the learned the warning song.
> There]

Here the prophetic task of warning those supposedly possessed of objective knowledge — the learned — is completely imbricated with the voice of the personal poetic ego. The vision of heaven to be mediated to all those standing outside the poet's nimbus blends with his individuated being and the emotional, subjectively oriented genre — the song — by which he would deliver his message. This choice of citations allows Wolf's Hölderlin to seem a Romantic, because whether in the philosophies of Fichte and Schelling, or the poetic utterances of Novalis and Günderrode, the personal and the prophetic, subject and object, are inextricably intertwined. In both the distich of the novel's third epigraph and in this closing verse, one can find as well the thwarted yearning to be part of a collective — the "many" who try to express the joyful in a joyful way, "the living" into whose midst the poet is cast — from which he must remain detached. Indeed, all three epigraphs express this detachment.

A characteristic difference between Hermlin and Wolf in their treatment of Hölderlin may be seen in their respective contextualizations of an identical citation from the poet, the passage quoted earlier from *Scardanelli* when Hölderlin enunciates his most fervent hope as the feeling that freedom must eventually be realized, virtue will better thrive in the warm light of freedom than in the frozen domain of despotism, and that his time was marked by a striving for better days. As noted, this seemingly vague prophecy is not informed by concrete political contours in the play. One of Hermlin's voices asks laconically if the poet has no hope, a second voice responds that indeed he does (a signification compactly encapsulated within the simple word "Doch" that he employs). Then follows the citation that concludes with the sentence: "Ich möchte ins Allgemeine wirken" (30; I would like to have a general influence). In Wolf's novel, the quoted snippet follows the narrator's observation that Hölderlin is closely following the events in Paris, where the question of whether France will perish or become a great nation hangs in a very precarious balance. The vague sentence about striving for a broad or general (*Allgemeine*) effect is absent in Wolf's novel, although it is contained in the letter of Hölderlin to his brother Karl from which the rest of the passage is derived.[26]

By anchoring this epistolary passage within the context of Hölderlin's sympathetic efforts to track, from Tübingen, the events in the French Republic (72), Wolf presents a more resolutely political Hölderlin than does Hermlin. Indeed, just prior to the passage, the narrator describes the young Hölderlin, together with his seminary classmate Hegel, as deemed to be supporters of the Jacobins (71). Gerhart Hoffmeister has argued against the tendency of leftists like Bertaux to characterize Hölderlin as a Jacobin. He finds that, for Hölderlin and other major writers whom he situates within West European Romanticism, such as Jean Paul, "it was never a question of political involvement but rather of transforming the impulses released by the French events to revolutionary ideas on the moral, philosophical, educational, and poetical plane."[27] This image of Hölderlin is somewhat better reflected in Hermlin's configuration of the poet than in Wolf's. Nevertheless, Wolf's many citations of Hölderlin's poetry show he does not neglect the "poetical plane."[28] Though *Der arme Hölderlin* does not fuse art and politics into quite the seamless whole Wolf described as an inherent aspect of Hermlin's very being, these domains, along with the tragic circumstances of Hölderlin's personal life, are fully evident in Wolf's novel, which creates an imaginative vision of the author closer to the tragic visionary of *Scardanelli* than to the rather unpoetic poet that Hermlin discerned in Lukács's essay. Both *Scardanelli* and *Der arme Hölderlin* thereby anticipate the Romantic turn in GDR literature, when the imaginative treatment of this period's poetic luminaries reaches its apogee, culminating in *Kein Ort. Nirgends.*

Peter Weiss's Political Radical

In her treatise on East German cinema, Daniela Berghahn has noted the shift of interest from Weimar Classicism to Romanticism in the GDR of the 1970s and early 1980s was also reflected in that nation's cinema. With reference to *Scardanelli* and *Der arme Hölderlin*, she remarks that the "reassessment of Hölderlin, which emphasizes the poet's pathological side and asserts his affinity with the Romantics, enhanced his identificatory potential and explains the considerable number of books and films dedicated to him since the 1970s." By "identificatory potential," Berghahn seems to signify a desire by intellectuals at that time to identify with Hölderlin. This emphasis and this empathy come at the cost of Goethe, whose adherence to the Restoration leads to a dearth of films and fictional literature about him, except as an object of derision.[29] This situation also applied in the West, where Weiss's play and Härtling's novel sympathetically treated Hölderlin as a tragic Romantic visionary who fell victim to mistreatment at the hands of Goethe.

Hermlin and Wolf also allude to Hölderlin's strained relationship with Goethe and Schiller. In the third scene of *Scardanelli*, Hölderlin fails to remember either of Weimar's leading luminaries despite Waiblinger's prompting. Painful associations with these figures have caused the poet to repress his memory of them, and the rest of the scene shows why: Schiller tells Goethe he finds his friend and protégé talented but labile and overly subjective, while Goethe offers tepid praise for his efforts. Hölderlin's pleas for Schiller's engagement on his behalf are intoned in a monologue, which shows that they are ignored until Schiller finally claims he is too busy to submit his own work to Hölderlin's new journal (15–18). Episode fourteen of *Der arme Hölderlin* recollects, in Hölderlin's first-person account, the famous episode when the Tübingen poet failed to recognize the privy counselor in Schiller's study, as well as their later unhappy encounters and Schiller's somewhat half-hearted attempts to provide advice and promote Hölderlin's work (73–75). While these brief imaginative evocations of Goethe and Schiller paint them in less-than-flattering hues — thereby beginning the GDR trend away from the orthodox hagiographic treatment of Weimar Classicism as a fundamentally progressive movement that built a seamless continuity with the socialist state, and indeed constituted its spiritual and intellectual inheritance — Weiss sketched Goethe in particular in far more condemnatory fashion in his play. Weiss's Goethe, along with the figures of Schelling, Hegel, and Fichte, come across as restorationist toadies willing to accommodate the reactionary forces arrayed against the French Revolution in order to further their own careers. Despite his leftist sympathies, most of Weiss's plays were premiered in West Germany, which awarded him a number of literary prizes, and in Stockholm, his primary place of residence. *Hölderlin*'s premiere took place in 1971 in Stuttgart. The initial performance of the play in the GDR occurred in 1973 in Rostock. The delay was necessitated by that nation's displeasure at the way Goethe, Schiller, and Hegel were portrayed, so that Weiss had to somewhat modify his play for its initial East German performances.[30]

Robert Cohen has noted that Weiss was indebted to both Bertaux and Lukács for the image of Hölderlin presented in his drama, and Bertaux's essay was certainly consistent with his portrayal to the Hölderlin Society of the poet as a passionate adherent of the Jacobins. Cohen's belief, however, that Bertaux's groundbreaking treatment of Hölderlin would have remained largely irrelevant in the Federal Republic without Weiss's play has been called into question by Robert Savage's account of Bertaux's notoriety; nonetheless, Cohen is correct in pointing out the significant effect Lukács's essay had on Weiss.[31] However, Lukács goes to some length to mitigate Hegel's "accommodation" and seemingly opportunistic betrayal of revolutionary Republicanism by underscoring the "world historical" significance of the Hegelian dialectic in which this accommodation comes to expression.[32] With respect to Goethe, Lukács is content to contrast, without expressing any preference, *Wilhelm Meisters Lehrjahre* (Wilhelm Meister's apprenticeship) as a novel of education (*Erziehungsroman*) calling for adaptation (*Anpassung*) to contemporary capitalist realities, with *Hyperion* as a novel of education calling for heroic resistance to this reality.[33] However, in Weiss's play, both Hegel and Goethe are cast in a highly disparaging light. At the outset of *Hölderlin*, Hegel's revolutionary sympathies as a Tübingen seminary student come to the fore, as he proclaims that God's empire — not itself established by God, but by humanity — will be democratically realized in a reason-grounded free state (273). Nevertheless, contra Lukács, Hegel's later accommodation is not presented as a dialectically grounded attempt to view reality as necessity in the teleological progression of the world spirit, but as a sycophant's attempt to curry favor with his wealthy employer when he, like Hölderlin, finds work as a private tutor in a bourgeois household. At the conclusion to the play's first act, Hölderlin, Hegel, and Goethe join the wealthy bourgeois who employ the former Tübingen classmates in a discussion. The merchants praise the power of money to flow and circulate in the financial world like blood coursing through the body, and underscore the need for the strong to become stronger and the power of wealth to elevate taste, understanding, and friendship, bemoaning only Germany's inability to rival the British and the Dutch as a colonial force. Hegel agrees that colonial expansion is a precondition for the flourishing of the modern industrial state, and argues that a minimal subsistence level is sufficient for the masses. Goethe offers an optimistic vision of Germany's future unification through the import of the steam locomotive, recently developed in England, into the German lands in concert with an evolutionary pedagogy.[34] Later in this scene, with the appearance of the revolutionary poet Siegfried Schmid, Goethe expresses to Hegel — in tones derived from an actual letter Goethe had written to Schiller but with a clear allusion to 1960s and 1970s unkempt student leftists[35] — his disapproval of the shaggy hair, dissolute appearance, and primitive, aesthetically unrefined language of Schmid, Hölderlin, and other radicals who live at the margins of society rather than compromise their ideals. In language almost identical to that of Schiller in the third scene of Hermlin's *Scardanelli*, Weiss's Goethe condemns Schmid and Hölderlin for an extreme subjectivity, and wonders if it is the empirical world in which they are forced to live that is responsible for their "Romantic inclination."[36] However, Hölderlin's invective in this scene, prompted by Goethe's faint praise of *Hyperion*, is more extreme in its unmediated rage against a Germany that is crushing his revolutionary hopes than can be found in any passage from *Scardanelli*, *Der arme Hölderlin*, or other fictionalizations of the Tübingen poet. After claiming his instantiation of Greece in *Hyperion* was intended to rally his own country to destroy the miserable state framework in which its citizens are being "degraded" — prompting Goethe to raise his hands as a plea to Hölderlin to stop his tirade — the poet condemns his nation with a bluntness and coarseness more reminiscent of the tirades to be found in Weiss's most famous play, *Marat/Sade* (1965)[37]:

Dies Land es ist ein DungHauffen
Ausschütten will ich
meinen Hass
auf die Stubenheizer Speichelleker
und Schmarozzer unsrer Fürsten
die im AasGestank
all des verronnenen LebensBluths
sich räkeln (347)

[This land
it is a pile of dung
I would pour out
my hate
on those who heat their rooms, lick spittle
and are freeloaders of our princes
who luxuriate
in the corpse-stink
of all the life blood that has been gushed out]

The extreme hyperbole employed here is purely the product of the play-wright's imagination. Even Bertaux, who found in Hölderlin's essays a highly encrypted embrace of the Revolution's goals and was more overt than Lukács in underscoring Hölderlin's strong political sympathies,[38] could not have been the main impetus for the kind of invective the poet enunciates in this passage. Weiss was less interested than Hermlin and Wolf in creating a Hölderlin relatively faithful to the historical figure, although it is clear this was also not the priority of the two East German writers. Instead, Hölderlin becomes in Weiss's drama a cipher for the angry alienation the exile writer Weiss experienced. As Roger Ellis has noted: "Weiss encouraged the audience to regard history from a contemporary, politically based standpoint. The crisis in Hölderlin's life thus became the result of 'future shock,' of political shock, because Hölderlin was shown in possession of a modern historical consciousness which his contemporaries did not share." This modernization of Hölderlin's consciousness, as Ellis notes, includes the entirely fictitious encounter between Marx and Hölderlin in the play's final scene.[39] It also included the use of violent, rabble-rousing rhetoric, a rhetoric of which the historical Hölderlin would have been constitutionally incapable.

One of the most powerful scenes in the play is the episode in which Hölderlin fails to recognize Goethe in Schiller's study. In Wolf's version, Hölderlin uses the first-person voice that occurs with some frequency in *Der arme Hölderlin* to give a rather emotionless, objective account of their meeting. He notes the presence of a stranger — "Der Fremde" — who only makes a few insignificant comments on the subjects of the Weimar Theater and of Frau von Kalb; thus, the stranger is obviously aware of the Tübingen poet's role as her son's tutor. While Schiller greets Hölderlin warmly and discusses an issue of the journal *Thalia*, to which Hölderlin had contributed a poem and a fragment from *Hyperion*, the stranger remains cold and aloof, prompting Hölderlin to address him in a cursory, monosyllabic manner. Hölderlin claims he was completely unaware the stranger was Goethe, and the only technique Wolf uses to allude to the significance of this misrecognition is a switch to the third-person narrative voice, in a single-sentence paragraph, to underscore Hölderlin's surprise, also expressed in the previous paragraph, at the stranger's identity: "Er hat ihn nicht erkannt" (73–74; He didn't recognize him).

In Weiss's play, an emotional Hölderlin argues with Schiller over the proper role of Hellenic Greece for contemporary literature. While Schiller asserts that the confluence of the ideal and the real was only fulfilled in antiquity, and that only an aesthetic education can eventually achieve such harmony in the current age, Hölderlin claims his recourse to Greece was designed to create effective symbols (*SinnBilder*) inspirational for the present day, and that the French Revolution employed Greek art to create a vision of the future imbued with clarity and greatness. This presentation of Hölderlin's Graecophilia — traditionally attributed by scholarship to an apolitical, otherworldly idealism on the part of the poet — as a political instrumentalization of antiquity is probably derived from Bertaux, who took this novel position in his work on Hölderlin and the French Revolution. However, it is the unrecognized Goethe who inspires the poet's real passion; responding to the stranger's position that art must be modest, dispassionate, and objective, and that current revolutionary writers are fleeting figures (*IrrLichter*), egotists cut off from society, Hölderlin argues there can be no modesty and contentment until radical change can make its claims. Authors are only relevant with respect to their engagement with their age, and a willingness to tarry within prevailing conditions will someday cause deep shame to such disengaged writers. This prompts Goethe to leave, whereupon Schiller reveals the identity of the stranger. The scene ends with Hölderlin's emitting a donkey-like scream upon hearing this revelation (305–16).

In an interview conducted in Swedish in 1972, Weiss acknowledged that his reading of Bertaux confirmed his perspective of Hölderlin. However, Bertaux underscored Hölderlin's caution in proclaiming his embrace of the Revolution. Bertaux emphasizes that Hölderlin, in both his letters and in his poetic work, employed an elusive, encoded language to mask his political views, a language only his allies and friends could decipher.[40] Weiss's incautious Hölderlin, who has no qualms about airing his radical views to a stranger, and then later, in one of the play's invented scenes, to a Goethe he now recognizes, is a distortion of the historical individual in the service of Weiss's desire to create an overtly committed, engaged author-hero who could serve as an inspiration for his contemporary audience. Just as his Hölderlin utilizes the Greeks for political ends, so Weiss utilizes the figure of Hölderlin. In the 1972 interview, Weiss claims his understanding of Hölderlin derived entirely from his reading of the poet's letters, including the letter to Neuffer in which the encounter with the unrecognized Goethe is described.[41] However, while Wolf's enactment of the encounter is exceptionally faithful to the account given in the letter, even quoting it mostly verbatim,[42] Weiss, consistent with the purport of his play, sensationalizes the meeting in order to create a Hölderlin unwaveringly committed to the Jacobin cause.

Weiss had a penchant for drawing on tragically marginalized men of letters who were also political visionaries and were doomed for their devotion to their ideals. Jean-Paul Marat, portrayed somewhat sympathetically in *Marat/Sade*, and Leon Trotsky, who was also characterized as a martyr — much to the displeasure of GDR officials — in *Trotzki im Exil* (Trotsky in exile, 1970), along with Hölderlin, were all inflected by Weiss's tendency toward, as Olaf Berwald puts it, "staging writers as outcasts."[43] Certainly, Hölderlin, Marat, and Trotsky are treated by Weiss as untimely heroes who suffered death or madness in the cause of a revolution that cannot yet be realized, and in the penultimate scene Weiss portrays Hölderlin gagged and straitjacketed in a madhouse, being treated — like Georg Büchner's famous Woyzeck in the play of the same name — as an odd human specimen, an object of detached clinical interest (381–94). Yet the play's concluding scene (there is also an epilogue) is optimistic, offering the inspiring, albeit entirely fictitious, spectacle of Marx visiting the poet in his tower. This Marx claims that reading *Hyperion* dashed his own ambitions as a creative writer and forced him to take the path leading to an "Analyse der konkreten historischen Situation" (analysis of the concrete historical situation), while his description of the other path, "die visionäre Formung tiefster persönlicher Erfahrung" (410; the visionary forming of the most deeply personal experience) is obviously intended to signify the journey — tragic but inspirational — taken by Hölderlin. More than was the case with Marat or Trotsky, who actively pursued political careers, Weiss could identify with a fellow creative writer who tried to sustain the revolution through his poetic visions. As Peter Hanenberg has noted, Weiss instrumentalizes Hölderlin not so much in the service of the purely political as in fixing the positionality of the author; Hölderlin functions as a navigational star by which the writer can thematize and situate his role between politics and art.[44] Few other postwar German authors who wrote fictional accounts of writers from the Age of Goethe identified so closely with their subject.

Indeed, there is an autobiographical dimension to Weiss's sympathetic attachment to Hölderlin. In 1928, his mother, baffled as to the best way of dealing with her recalcitrant young son, sent Weiss to live with her sister and the sister's husband in Tübingen, where he spent nearly five months. This husband was Dr. Eugen Authenrieth, a descendent of the Eugen Authenrieth who invented the gagging mask Hölderlin was forced to wear in an effort to "cure" him.[45] It is this earlier Authenrieth who subjects Hölderlin to a cruel interrogation in the seventh scene of *Hölderlin*. In a 1978 interview, Weiss indicated that he found his sojourn at the Authenrieth house unrelentingly stressful, as the couple tried — with an obvious lack of success — to educate him to be a good bourgeois (*Bürger*). He felt as though he were in prison. However, only during the research phase of *Hölderlin* did Weiss learn that his uncle was a scion of Hölderlin's tormentor. Perhaps it was, at least in part, the shock of recognition that caused Weiss to viscerally experience the description of Authenrieth's brutal treatment of the "desperate" poet.[46] Savage has noted the persistent autobiographical element in Martin Heidegger's obsession with Hölderlin, posing the question: "What are we to make of these repeated attempts to interweave private genealogy and Occidental heritage, physical proximity and spiritual affinity, biographical coincidence and historical fate, Hölderlin's poetry and Heidegger's thinking, against the background of a shared topography?"[47] If unhappy dormant childhood memories rekindled by the stunning revelation of familial ties between his uncle and the Tübingen doctor who mistreated Hölderlin played a role in motivating *Hölderlin*'s nightmarish seventh scene, and Swabian kinship helped shape Heidegger's antithetical, mystically autochthonous engagement with the poet, the significance of a sense of space-grounded kinship with Hölderlin — a carceral space for Weiss, a utopian topography for Heidegger — is nevertheless far greater in the case of Peter Härtling than for either the dramatist or the philosopher.

The Historical Author as Alter Ego: Peter Härtling's Autobiographical Interventions

Härtling was born in Chemnitz in 1933, but after the war resettled as an adolescent in the Swabian town of Nürtingen, where Hölderlin had lived for ten years as a young boy. In his novel *Hölderlin*, third-person accounts of Hölderlin's life are persistently interspersed with the narrator's first-person recollections of his own youthful years in Nürtingen and its environs. When Hölderlin is shown walking down an alley or past a building familiar to the narrator, this narrator will frequently interject his own experiences of the alley or building. While this employment of temporally intercalated episodes shuttling between the eighteenth and twentieth centuries with their concomitant third- and first-person perspectives grounded in a mutual spatial plane is most persistent in *Hölderlin*, Härtling composed a number of other historical novels whose eponymous protagonists were, like the Tübingen poet, late eighteenth- and early nineteenth-century authors associated with southwest Germany. For example, *Niembsch oder Der Stillstand* (Niembsch or the standstill, 1964) is an account of the poet Nikolaus Lenau (the pen name of Nikolaus Franz Niembsch) after he returned to Germany in 1833 from his unhappy sojourn in America and settled, for a time, near Stuttgart; the Stuttgart period is the primary focus of the narrative. The novel *Waiblingers Augen* (Waiblinger's eyes, 1987) is focused on the title figure, Hölderlin's friend and fellow Swabian poet, whose 1827–28 essay on Hölderlin's "poetry and madness" continues to be a source of biographical information for Hölderlin scholars. Like Härtling's Hölderlin, Lenau and Waiblinger are shown to suffer extreme self-alienation, enhanced in the case of Niembsch by his reception as an exotic foreigner by the Swabians among whom he resides.[48] In these three novels, the grounding of the narrative in a distinct southwest German regionalism is enhanced by the frequent interjection of Swabian dialect. Albeit with a somewhat narrow focus, this is also the case with another, rather brief, novel by Härtling concerning a Swabian author, *Die dreifache Maria* (The threefold Maria, 1982), which concerns an episode in the life of Eduard Mörike when he became infatuated with the mysterious Maria Meyer.

To be sure, the prolific Härtling has written artist novels on historical figures without a strong affiliation with Swabia, such as Franz Schubert in *Schubert: Zwölf Moments musicaux und ein Roman* (Schubert: Twelve moments musicaux and a novel, 1992), Robert Schumann in *Schumanns Schatten: Variationen über mehrere Personen* (Schumann's shadow: Variations on a number of people, 1996), and E. T. A. Hoffmann in *Hoffmann oder Die vielfältige Liebe: eine Romanze* (Hoffmann or the manifold love: A romance, 2001).[49] However, the frequent employment of Swabian dialect in the novels on Hölderlin, Lenau, Waiblinger, and Mörike, along with the strong, concrete evocation of region and place in three of these four works (*Die dreifache Maria* is an exception), imbue them with the ambience of the *Heimat* (homeland) novel, where a discrete topographic fixation and the frequent or exclusive use of the regional idiom suggest the author's strong kinship with the territory in which the novel takes place, even if an overt autobiographical dimension is lacking. To be sure, traditional *Heimat* novels tend to be informed by a conservative, autochthonous anti-cosmopolitan element[50] that is lacking in the Left-oriented Härtling's oeuvre. Pithily paraphrasing Härtling's views concerning the ideal nature of the relationship between historical fiction and putatively objective historiography, Stefana Sabin notes: "Ohne die Subjektivität von Geschichtenerzählern gäbe es auch die Objektivität der Geschichtsschreiber nicht"[51] (Without the subjectivity of the narrators of stories, the objectivity of history writers would be lacking). This idea that historiographers should learn from the historical novel, particularly from the novelists' attempt to subjectively evoke the sensual ambience, the "'feel' for life in the past" without concern for the objective reliability of informational content, has been echoed by the noted historiographer Dominick LaCapra.[52] And if, thanks to the attributes they share with the *Heimat* novel, Härtling's Swabia-based historical fictions are informed by a more "subjective" perspective than is usually the case with his other works, Härtling's use of first-person narrative intrusions directly derived from his own life experiences makes *Hölderlin* unquestionably the most subjective of the four Swabian novels.

In an essay entitled "Das Ende der Geschichte: Über die Arbeit an einem 'historischen Roman'" (The End of History: Concerning Work on a 'Historical Novel'), Härtling claims that psychology and sociology have taught us to question the validity of the subjective retrospective glance. We therefore mistrust language's ability to reconstruct the past. We learn to be extremely cautious about such an undertaking and therefore proceed carefully in our examination of history, with an awareness of its multidimensionality. Such awareness and such uncertainty somewhat constrict those who would narrate the past, but this caution is helpful in prompting the writer to weigh his or her options carefully with respect to source material and methodology. Ultimately, however, Härtling takes umbrage at the historiographer's insistence on facts, ordered chronology and objectivity. Subjective memory (*das eigene Gedächtnis*) resists the arguments of the historians, and Härtling announces the decision to pursue his own history: "Ich mißtraue den Geschichtsschreibern und gehe meiner eigenen Geschichte nach"[53] (I mistrust the writers of history and pursue my own history). This essay, first published in 1968, addresses Härtling's work on *Niembsch* and another historical novel from which Härtling derived the title of his essay: *Das Familienfest oder Das Ende der Geschichte* (The family festival or the end of history, 1969), where Härtling already alternates between third- and first-person narrative voices. In researching this novel concerning a Nürtingen family, Härtling reflected on how Schelling and Hölderlin attended the town's Latin school. This circumstance inspired Härtling to reread Hölderlin's letters.[54] *Das Familienfest* begins in the year 1857 with the return from exile of the entirely fictional figure Georg Lauterbach, a professor of history and philosophy, but Härtling's research for the book clearly stimulated a renewed interest in the figure of Hölderlin. More importantly, the principle enunciated in the essay on the historical novel — that those who work in this genre have to mistrust historians and their obsession with objective facts, not fret over findings of psychologists and sociologists concerning the reliability of human memory, and make the engagement with history their own quest, even if it becomes rooted in subjectivity — is most emphatically and creatively realized in *Hölderlin*.

Härtling reenacts the competing discourses of the historiographer oriented toward objectivity and of the historical novelist, the novelist who has decided to pursue his "own history" and thus employs a more subjective approach, in the opening sequence of *Hölderlin*:

Am 20. März 1770 wurde Johann Christian Friedrich Hölderlin in Lauffen am Neckar geboren —
— ich schreibe keine Biographie. Ich schreibe vielleicht eine Annäherung. Ich schreibe von jemandem, den ich nur aus seinen

Gedichten, Briefen, aus seiner Prosa, aus vielen anderen Zeugnissen kenne. Und von Bildnissen, die ich mit Sätzen zu beleben versuche. Er ist in meiner Schilderung sicher ein anderer. (7)

[On the 20th of March 1770 Johann Christian Friedrich Hölderlin was born in Lauffen on the Neckar —
— I am not writing a biography. I am writing, perhaps, an approach. I am writing about someone whom I only know from his poetry, letters, from his prose, from many other documents. And from images that I attempt to animate through sentences. In my portrayal he is certainly another.]

While Gerhard Wolf's narrative begins with a plural first-person visit to the Zimmer residence for a personal encounter with the poet, there is no narrative admission that the pursuit of Hölderlin is a private, subjective adventure, and such personal intrusion does not extend beyond this opening gambit. Hermlin and Weiss employ the dramatic genre in their imaginative engagement with Hölderlin, and since they do not employ the technique of parabasis frequently favored in theatrical works by Romantics such as the young Ludwig Tieck, a self-conscious narrator is lacking in their treatment of the poet. While in the novel *Hölderlin*, first-person interventions are to be seen as the act of the author, Härtling, and thus not to be associated with the often-unreliable independent agency favored in Romantic parabasis, the term "Annäherung" is manifestly evocative of that period, reminiscent of Friedrich Schlegel's ideal of endless approximation toward the narrative object. The term "Annäherung" can be translated as both "approach" and "approximation." The idea of writing an "Annäherung" is consistent with the principle adumbrated in "Das Ende der Geschichte" that history itself is irreducibly multiple and ambiguous, so that one may indeed attempt to approach, to approximate, the historical object, but will never truly reach or achieve it in an epistemological sense. Thus, a subjective, indeed a Romantically subjective approach, must be available to the historical novelist.

To be sure, Härtling's idiosyncratic personalization of his encounter with Hölderlin across the ages goes beyond mere subjectivity. It may be assumed that Weiss drew upon the painful experiences of the months spent as a boy in the Authenrieth household in Tübingen when he created the powerful seventh scene featuring his uncle's brutal namesake and ancestor, but he did not inject his own person into the foreground of that scene. When Härtling's narrator, who, one can assume, faithfully represents the author's voice, places himself into the novel, "Annäherung" as approach is enacted. The narrator approaches Hölderlin across time by comparing his life experiences to that of the eighteenth-century poet via the bridge of a mutual spatial-cultural topography. He wonders who Hölderlin's pastor might have been, noting at least two possibilities. Then he speaks of the pastor whom he himself knew as a young man, and how he didn't respond to this man's letter as an adult because he found it difficult to write to his childhood (*an seine Kindheit zu schreiben*), and followed the same path as Hölderlin behind his pastor (39). Thus, in this brief passage, "Annäherung" is actually instantiated in both nuances of the German term. The narrator approaches Hölderlin through the ages by alluding to the shared experience of having a Swabian pastor, and treading behind his pastor on the path Hölderlin had tread some two hundred years earlier. "Annäherung" as approximation takes place through the revelation of multiple possibilities with respect to the identity of Hölderlin's reverend. Historical fact cannot be firmly established, and historiographic closure, rooted in objectivity, is thwarted. Even through this relatively simple passage, Härtling reveals a central aim of his historical novels as adumbrated in "Das Ende der Geschichte," namely, that the book of history remains open when subjective history is allowed free reign and the novelist does not have to assume the role of historian, psychologist, or sociologist.

This liberation from the constraints of historical objectivity and reliable memory also allows a direct narrative identification with the historical subject, even the narrator's admission that he wishes to frame his Hölderlin in a manner in accord with his own proclivities. Thus, after elucidating in a rather freewheeling style the teenage Hölderlin's first erotic experiences, the narrator proclaims: "ich will ihn nicht als Helden und dennoch ist er eine Ausnahme. Deshalb kümmere ich mich so nachdrücklich um seinen Alltag" (103; I don't want him as a hero and he is nevertheless an exception. This is why I am concerning myself so emphatically with his daily routine). More often than not, imaginative writers create protagonists not associated with known historical personalities. Often these protagonists are based on individuals directly or indirectly familiar to the authors, who need feel no constraint in shaping them according to the requirements of the narrative. Those who compose historical fiction with well-known figures must seek a balance between sticking to the accepted facts about their characters on the one hand, and keeping in mind the telos of the narrative on the other — regardless of their own political, social, aesthetic, or even market-driven tendencies. Rarely, however, does an author of historical fiction bring this dilemma into the foreground of his or her work, and *Hölderlin* is a rarity in its immediate conveyance of Härtling's ruminations in this regard, even in comparison with his other historically based works. For example, his recent novel on the adult life of E. T. A. Hoffmann has only a few first-person references to the research undertaken for its composition. Härtling's frequent use of parabasis in *Hölderlin*, therefore, inclines the reader to assume that his emotional investment in the eighteenth-century poet was particularly intense and complex.

Härtling's retrospective essay on the composition of the novel, "Mein Hölderlin" (My Hölderlin, 1984) — the very title reveals an obviously personalized, possessive link to this subject — confirms this assumption. This brief essay reveals Härtling's ambivalent attitude toward Hölderlin. As a young man in Nürtingen, he initially refused to read the poet and retrospectively surmises that this rejection was tied to a disinclination toward the city itself. Eventually, however, he was unable to leave Hölderlin's books unread, and he found that Hölderlin's verse — shaped as it was by his Swabian homeland experiences — accompanied him in his peregrinations through the town. This spiritual/geographic companionship became a key theme in *Hölderlin*. The revolutionary year 1968 witnessed the emergence of a leftist Hölderlin in the works of Weiss and, to a lesser extent, Wolf and Hermlin. Härtling's rereading of Hölderlin in that year inspired a hopeful vision of the future as well, though it was a vision he came to recognize as illusory. While he expresses in his essay an appreciation for Bertaux's daring discovery of a political Hölderlin, "Mein Hölderlin" makes it clear that this political Hölderlin was not the focus of Härtling's novelistic interest, and the novel's presentation of a Hölderlin less preoccupied with politics than was the case with Weiss may be linked to the circumstance that Härtling was still working on the book after the revolutionary hopes of the late 1960s and early 1970s had been dashed. Instead, as this brief treatise indicates, the poet's relationship to his mother, his erotic liaisons, and his evocation of Greece as a counterweight to the pedagogical constrictions he experienced as a seminarian were as significant in the novel's composition as his friendship-inspired revolutionary sentiments. The ambivalent attitude the essay displays toward its subject also informs the novel and contributes to its parabasis: Härtling asks how he can claim Hölderlin as his own when the poet is unattainable, incapable of being possessed. Härtling dares to make this appropriation only because Hölderlin has also taken possession of him. His relationship to the poet across time is marked by alternating repulsion and attraction, alienation and a yearning for those moments when Hölderlin's "gentle but stubborn" nature takes possession of him.[55]

A greater sense of where Härtling's portrait of Hölderlin's converges with that of Hermlin, Wolf, and Weiss, and where it takes a different direction characteristic of the uniquely subjectivist approach outlined above, becomes apparent in an episode in Hölderlin's life discussed above in Gerhard Wolf's and Weiss's works — namely, the poet's fateful first encounter with Goethe. Like Wolf, Härtling quotes a large portion of Hölderlin's letter to Neuffer describing this unfortunate episode, a missive written in a relatively factual tone yet still betraying the poet's foreboding at the meeting's potentially negative consequences; quoted by neither Wolf nor Härtling, however, is the conclusion of the letter where Hölderlin describes the event as an "Unheil," a catastrophe. Also left out of their citations is Hölderlin's mention of how Schiller comforted him through his cheerfulness and conversation.[56] Härtling quotes one more line than does Wolf from the Neuffer letter: After the sentence indicating that Hölderlin has learned of Goethe's appearance at Schiller's home that day, Hölderlin entreats heaven to help him make good his unfortunate faux pas when he goes to Weimar. Whereas Wolf concludes his citation with the letter's previous sentence about Goethe's midday presence at the Schiller residence — thereupon proclaiming in the third person that Hölderlin didn't recognize him — Härtling adds laconically after his lengthy citation from the letter that heaven did not help the Tübingen poet. Wolf's approach in this regard is thus more suggestive and open-ended than Härtling's, merely hinting at the consequences of Hölderlin's misrecognition. More importantly, and characteristic of Härtling's approach to his novel, a series of questions and surmises follow his comment on Hölderlin's unanswered prayers, as well as the observation that Schiller tried but failed to bring about a reconciliation between the two men of letters (a circumstance unmentioned by Weiss and Wolf):

> Wie muß Hölderlin auf Schiller fixiert gewesen sein! Mit welcher Hingabe muß er jedes Wort seines Protektors aufgenommen haben. Neben dem galt keiner. Und selbst ein Bedeutender wurde offenbar unscheinbar in Schillers Nähe. Kannte er kein Bild von Goethe? War ihm nicht aufgefallen, wie würdevoll der Mann auftrat, wie ostentativ bedeutend er sprach? Vielleicht ärgerte ihn gerade das. Daß sich einer bei seinem Schiller so aufblies.

> [How Hölderlin must have been fixated on Schiller! With what devotion he must have taken in every word of his protector. Next to him no one counted. And even a significant personage clearly became inconspicuous in Schiller's proximity. Wasn't he familiar with some picture of Goethe? Wasn't it obvious to him with what dignity the man made his entrance, with what ostentatious significance he spoke? Maybe he was irritated precisely by that. That someone would puff himself up so much in the presence of his Schiller.]

This intrusion of the narrator asking himself how such a monumental oversight was possible on the part of the poet is followed by the revelation that the grotesque episode spares the writer the necessity of bringing Goethe into his narrative, even though he could find suitable citations allowing Goethe to speak (314–15). Whereas Wolf portrays the episode as simply one more step along the path of alienation leading to Hölderlin's madness, and Weiss's scene shows a defiant Hölderlin who angrily refutes the unrecognized Goethe's tacit equation of engaged literature with egotism, Härtling shows once again his belief that a novelist should not foreclose the multiple possibilities latent in significant historical events, should not exclude the open-ended nature of history by attempting to record what the historiographer prioritizes as unambiguous, objective fact. This leads Härtling not only to interject himself frequently into his narrative, but to pose questions he refuses to answer. The episode with the unrecognized Goethe in Schiller's study is paradigmatic in this regard.

In their respective portrayals of Hölderlin, Wolf and Weiss are quite clear in showing how the poet's insanity was centrally tied to the demise of the French Revolution in Germany. While portraying Hölderlin as a Romantic in his alienation and idiosyncrasy, in his configuration as an antihero, Hermlin nevertheless linked Hölderlin's lapse into madness to his radical political views and to the final defeat of political Jacobinism in his homeland, as Fehervary suggests.[57] Although Hermlin, Wolf, and Weiss show how Hölderlin's political views were shaped by his association with young progressive Swabian intellectuals, they nevertheless tend to underscore a certain defiant individualism that set him apart from his friends and led to the configuration, in his works, of similarly individualist figures like Hyperion and Empedocles who are forced to choose a lonely path separate from, though ideally inspiring to, the collective. This is particularly the case with Weiss, who strongly associated Hölderlin with that most popular of 1960s revolutionary leftist heroes, Che Guevara.[58] In "Mein Hölderlin," Härtling emphasizes the circumstance that the poet's visionary political perspective, his hopes as a seminarian for a future grounded in present-day revolutionary ideals, were spurred through his friendships (*beflügelt von Freundschaft*),[59] an emphasis also reflected in the novel. Thus, when Hölderlin argues for a rigorous, uncompromising approach to the revolution, he is responding to the ardor of Friedrich Muhrbeck and refuting the diplomatic, negotiation-oriented approach of the mature Isaak Sinclair (483–84). Later, when Hölderlin is already somewhat given over to madness, it is Sinclair who inspires a brief flickering moment of coherence, an insight into the masses' embrace of the king out of fear and ignorance: No one had taught them to think differently (560–61). When Sinclair is arrested and Hölderlin is absolutely bereft of all former politically oriented friends, and thus of all revolutionary hopes, he screams out that he does not want to be a Jacobin and "Vive le roi" (568–69). When he enunciates these lines in *Der arme Hölderlin*, what is stressed is the danger he faces from reactionary political authorities rather than his isolation from Sinclair and others (23). Again, Härtling's somewhat unique treatment of Hölderlin's political life was partially shaped by the time in which he wrote, when accommodation and resignation had set in after the dying out of the revolutionary fires that had once burned in West Germany and France, fires buring brightly when the other three works were composed. Härtling was certainly aware of how political solidarity drove mass insurrectionary political movements,[60] whether these movements took place in the 1960s or 1790s. Regardless of the century, the fragmentation of the collective meant the end of revolutionary political engagement.

In later imaginative configurations of figures associated with Hölderlin, Härtling largely abandoned the political dimension altogether. In *Die dreifache Maria*, Neuffer, the recipient of Hölderlin's letter on the fateful encounter with Goethe and a prominent member of Hölderlin's leftist inner circle as a young man (and who functions as such in *Hölderlin*), appears as the mature, married pastor of his later years. He is the father of Mörike's childhood sweetheart, and when it becomes obvious that this neurasthenic poet has no real professional prospects, he and his wife convince their daughter to break off with him.[61] In the novel *Waiblingers Augen*, Hölderlin's fellow poet and author of the most influential first-hand account of his life is portrayed as deeply self-alienated, consistent with Härtling's fictional treatment of Lenau, Hölderlin, and Mörike. This portrait of the writer as detached from his inner being culminates in Härtling's fictional biography of Hoffmann, where the motif of the double (*Doppelgänger*) is enacted multiple times to show how this Romantic's manic eroticism leads to a split self essential to his creativity.[62] Unlike his future biographical subject, Waiblinger is shown to be rather apolitical in the novel about him: When he resolves to write an account of Hölderlin, it is the poet's love life, in which he sees parallels with his own, that is shown to be the focus of his interest.[63]

In Weiss's play, right-wing nationalist students are seen to instrumentalize Hölderlin for their own nefarious purposes in a manner designed to foreshadow National Socialist tendencies some 130 years later (398–400). However, such instrumentalization was commonplace in the twentieth century on the part of many leading German intellectuals, at least up to 1976, as Fehervary has demonstrated in *Hölderlin and the Left*. All four of the fictionalizations of Hölderlin discussed in this chapter, which constitute the most substantive imaginative treatments of him in the second half of the twentieth century, participate in Hölderlin's recuperation from his role during the Third Reich as an inspiration for battlefield self-sacrifice, a treatment embraced even by the Hölderlin Society during the war years.[64] For Hermlin and Wolf, however, the poet — in opposition to his valorization by Lukács — is deployed in a manner anticipating the embrace of the Romantics in the battle against GDR literary/historical orthodoxy, while in Weiss's play he becomes a conflicted yet ardent proponent of revolution. In Härtling's novel, the personal and the political, the autobiographical and the biographical, become inextricably intertwined. Härtling's later novelistic accounts of the Swabian poets Waiblinger and Mörike, as well as his earlier treatment of Lenau, tend to exclude the political domain almost entirely. Particularly in *Die dreifache Maria* and *Waiblingers Augen*, and later in *Hoffmann oder Die vielfältige Liebe*, Härtling focuses on how familial, intimate, and erotic aspects of the poets' personal lives combine with music (particularly, in the case of Waiblinger and Mörike, and to some degree with Hoffmann, an obsession with Mozart's *Don Giovanni*) to shape their writing. As we will see in the following chapter, Renate Feyl has an altogether different set of priorities, at variance with those of the four authors we have just examined and with Christa Wolf's historical fiction.

Conclusion

Like Kleist, Hölderlin was a central and somewhat anticipatory figure in the turn to Romanticism seen in Age-of-Goethe fiction published in the GDR in the 1970s, even though both men are considered by many scholars not to belong to the small coterie of writers and philosophers who constituted early German Romanticism's core. However, precisely their extreme marginalization made them compelling protagonists for GDR authors. Hermlin's treatment of Hölderlin, while groundbreaking in its refusal to embrace Lukács's orthodox image of the poet as a precocious revolutionary, generally steers clear of the political realm in portraying him as an introverted, isolated antihero who descends into madness. Gerhard Wolf's experimental shuttling between first- and third-person narrative allows him to alternate his focus between the personal, introspective aspects of the poet's life and the historical, social, and political forces that brought about the tragedy of the second half of his existence.

In the West, Weiss's radical leftist politics resulted in Hölderlin's transformation into a committed revolutionary ideologue on the stage, a Jacobin whose political fervor is represented as almost entirely the cause of his downfall. In his novel, Härtling dramatically enhanced the autobiographical dimension of Hölderlin fiction evident in Gerhard Wolf and Weiss by creating a first-person narrator who, like Härtling himself, literally follows the poet's footsteps in Swabia. While making Hölderlin's encounter with Goethe and his political views central elements in his narrative, as is common in Hölderlin fiction, Härtling's first-person interjections blunt narrative closure and one-sidedness, and prevent the appearance of using Hölderlin for contemporary political ends. Härtling deliberately leaves open the question of final causes concerning the poet's madness, an openness with respect to plot resolution extended even to historical fiction that anticipates later postmodern trends.

Notes

[1] Sonja Hilzinger, "'Avantgarde ohne Hinterland': Zur Wiederentdeckung des Romantischen in Prosa und Essayistik der DDR," *Text + Kritik, Sonderband: Literatur in der DDR: Rückblicke*, ed. Heinz Ludwig Arnold (1991): 93–100.

[2] An interesting counterexample with respect to the GDR's turn to Romanticism is provided by the author Gisela Kraft. She actually moved *to* East Germany in 1984, where she later wrote a novelistic trilogy on the Romantic poet Novalis. Particularly in the first of these, *Prolog zu Novalis* (Prologue to Novalis, 1990), Kraft symbolically mourns the demise of poetic life and the failure of utopian hope in the GDR, a country nearing, at that time, the end of its existence; she allegorically links this national/political death to the death of Novalis's young fiancée Sophie von Kühn. The other novels in the trilogy were composed after the GDR was formally dissolved, but deal with some of the same issues. See Birgit Tautz, "Paths of Orientation: Gisela Kraft's turn to Romanticism circa 1990," *Colloquia Germanica* 38 (2005): 175–94.

[3] Stephan Hermlin, *Scardanelli* (Berlin: Klaus Wagenbach, 1970).

[4] Gerhard Wolf, *Der arme Hölderlin* (Darmstadt: Hermann Luchterhand, 1982).

[5] Peter Weiss, "Hölderlin," in *Stücke vol. 2/2* (Frankfurt am Main: Suhrkamp, 1977), 265–416.

[6] Peter Härtling, *Hölderlin* (Darmstadt: Hermann Luchterhand, 1976).

[7] See the discussion of this leftist reception of Hölderlin in the late 1960s and early 1970s by Robert Savage, *Hölderlin after the Catastrophe: Heidegger — Adorno — Brecht* (Rochester, NY: Camden House, 2008), 195–200.

[8] Georg Lukács, "Hölderlins *Hyperion*," in *Der andere Hölderlin: Materialien zum "Hölderlin" Stück von Peter Weiss*, 2nd ed., ed. Thomas Beckermann and Volker Canaris (Frankfurt am Main: Suhrkamp, 1979), 19–47.

[9] Savage, *Hölderlin after the Catastrophe*, 203.

[10] Helen Fehervary, *Hölderlin and the Left: The Search for a Dialectic of Art and Life* (Heidelberg: Carl Winter, 1977), 132–33. On Becher's play, see 73–75.

[11] Silvia Schlenstedt, *Stephan Hermlin: Leben und Werk* (West Berlin: deb, 1985), 211.

[12] Wolf, cited in Hilzinger, "'Avantgarde ohne Hinterland,'" 93.

[13] Schlenstedt, *Hermlin*, 211.

[14] Hermlin, "Hölderlin 1944," in *Äußerungen 1944–1982*, ed. Ulrich Dietzel (Berlin: Aufbau, 1983), 436–37.

[15] Hermlin, "Hölderlin 1944," 437.

[16] Hermlin, "Hölderlin 1944," 436–40.

[17] Hermlin, "Hölderlin 1944," 440.

[18] Hermlin, "Gesang vom Künftigen: Zum hundertsten Todestag Friedrich Hölderlins," *Neue Schweizer Rundschau* 7 (1944): 390–401. For a brief discussion of this essay, see Schlenstedt, *Stephan Hermlin*, 41–42.

[19] What follows is an example of this flowery, ornate style in a passage describing Hölderlin's love affair with Suzette Gontard: "Vom Strahle des Gottes durchschüttert, begreifen die Liebenden ihre Einzigartigkeit, und während von Hölderlins bewußtlosen Lippen der Dämon immer süßer tönt, tritt Diotima für die Ewigkeit, neben Marianna Alcoforcado und Louise Labbé, in die Reihe der Großen Liebenden ein" ("Gesang," 393; Profoundly shaken by God's ray, the

lovers comprehend their singularity, and while the daemon sounds ever more sweetly from Hölderlin's unconscious lips, Diotima enters eternally, next to Marianna Alcoforcado and Louise Labbé, into the ranks of the great lovers). Diotima was Hölderlin's name for Gontard, as well as the beloved of Hyperion in the eponymous novel.

[20] Christa and Gerhard Wolf, "Nicht beendetes Gespräch: Zum 60. Geburtstag Stephan Hermlins 1975," in Hermlin, *In den Kämpfen dieser Zeit* (Berlin: Klaus Wagenbach, 1995), 105.

[21] Schlenstedt, *Stephan Hermlin*, 211.

[22] Fehervary, *Hölderlin and the Left*, 142–53.

[23] Fehervary, *Hölderlin and the Left*, 151.

[24] Wolf, *Der arme Hölderlin*, 5, 7. Fehervary interprets these three mottos as indicative of the novel's dialectical structure (*Hölderlin and the Left*, 144–45).

[25] Wolf, *Der arme Hölderlin*, 107.

[26] Friedrich Hölderlin, *Sämtliche Werke*, 6.1: 92–93.

[27] Gerhart Hoffmeister, "Rhetorics of Revolution in West European Romanticism," in *The French Revolution and the Age of Goethe*, ed. Gerhart Hoffmeister (Hildesheim: Georg Olms, 1989), 93.

[28] Indeed, immediately following the citation from the September 1793 letter, Wolf quotes the following stanza from "Das Schicksal": "Wohl ist Arkadien entflohen; / des Lebens bessre Frucht gedeiht / durch sie, die Mutter der Heroen, / die eherne Notwendigkeit" (73; Truly Arcadia has fled / life's better fruit prospers / through her, the mother of heroes, / iron necessity).

[29] Daniela Berghahn, *Hollywood behind the Wall: The Cinema of East Germany* (Manchester: Manchester UP, 2005), 112–14. Though she does not mention it as an example of a derisive literary approach to Goethe, a paradigmatic instance of such treatment is provided by Peter Hacks's play *Ein Gespräch im Hause Stein über den abwesenden Herrn von Goethe* (A conversation in the house of Stein on the absent Mr. Goethe, 1974). With respect to literature, she cites instead Ulrich Plenzdorf's *Die neuen Leiden des jungen W.* (The new sorrows of young W., 1972), which is an ironic reworking of Goethe's novel *Die Leiden des jungen Werthers* (The sorrows of young Werther, 1774/1787), rather than a parody of Goethe himself. See Berghahn, 132n14.

[30] See Jens-Fietje Dwars, *Und dennoch Hoffnung: Peter Weiss: Eine Biographie* (Berlin: Aufbau, 2007), 237–38.

[31] Robert Cohen, *Peter Weiss in seiner Zeit: Leben und Werk* (Stuttgart: J. B. Metzler, 1992), 216–17.

[32] Lukács, "Hölderlins *Hyperion*," 22, 23.

[33] Lukács, "Hölderlins *Hyperion*," 45.

[34] On Goethe's prophetic vision of the railway as, literally, the engine of German unification, see Todd Samuel Presner, *Mobile Modernity: Germans, Jews, Trains* (New York: Columbia UP, 2007), 89.

[35] See Disa Håstad, "*Hölderlin* beginnt mit Marats Tod: Gespräch mit Peter Weiss. Ende 1972," trans. Michael Kanning, in *Peter Weiss im Gespräch*, ed. Rai-

ner Gerlach and Matthias Richter (Frankfurt am Main: Suhrkamp, 1986). Weiss describes his adoption of Goethe's letter to Schiller, and its topicality for the current age, as follows: "Goethe klagt in einem Brief an Schiller über die langhaarigen, ungepflegten Umstürzler, die wild rumglotzen würden. Gewisse Phänomene scheinen sich über Generationen hinweg zu erhalten" (197–98; Goethe complains in a letter to Schiller about the longhaired, unkempt subversives, who stare wildly about them. Certain phenomena appear to sustain themselves over the course of generations).

[36] The two passages resemble each other so closely that it seems likely Weiss transferred Schiller's words in *Scardanelli* to Goethe's character in *Hölderlin*. See *Scardanelli*, 18 and *Hölderlin*, 348. Fehervary has found other notable parallels between the two works and assumes that Hermlin's radio play influenced Weiss's drama (*Hölderlin and the Left*, 270–71n115).

[37] See Olaf Berwald, who quotes and discusses one such tirade — that of Charlotte Corday — in *An Introduction to the Works of Peter Weiss* (Rochester, NY: Camden House, 2003), 35.

[38] Pierre Bertaux, "Hölderlin und die Französische Revolution," in *Der andere Hölderlin*, 65–100.

[39] Roger Ellis, *Peter Weiss in Exile: A Critical Study of his Works* (Ann Arbor: UMI Research Press, 1987), 108.

[40] Bertaux, "Hölderlin und die Französische Revolution," esp. 99–100.

[41] Håstad, "*Hölderlin* beginnt mit Marats Tod," 197.

[42] Hölderlin, *Sämtliche Werke*, 6.1:140 and Wolf, *Der arme Hölderlin*, 73–74.

[43] This is the title of Berwald's chapter on *Marat/Sade, Trotzki im Exil, Hölderlin, Der Prozess* (The trial, 1975) and *Der neue Prozess* (The new trial, 1982). See Berwald, *An Introduction to the Works of Peter Weiss*, 33–68.

[44] Peter Hanenberg, *Peter Weiss: Vom Nutzen und Nachteil der Historie für das Schreiben* (Berlin: Eric Schmidt, 1993), 105.

[45] See Dwars, *Und dennoch Hoffnung*, 23.

[46] Peter Roos, "[Gespräch mit] Peter Weiss. [1978]," in *Peter Weiss im Gespräch*, 230.

[47] Savage, *Hölderlin after the Catastrophe*, 75.

[48] Nevertheless, on the surface, Niembsch is not bothered by his reputation in Swabia as an exotic. See Härtling, *Niembsch oder Der Stillstand: Eine Suite* (Stuttgart: Henry Goverts, 1964), 65–66.

[49] For a discussion of these three books as "artist novels," as well as an opening analysis of Härtling's *Hölderlin*, see Sjaak Onderdelinden, "'So kann es gewesen sein': Peter Härtlings Künstlerromane," in *Künstler-Bilder: Zur Produktiven Auseinandersetzung mit der schöpferischen Persönlichkeit*, 129–48.

[50] See Elizabeth Boa and Rachel Palfreyman, *Heimat — A German Dream: Regional Loyalties and National Identity in German Culture 1890–1900* (Oxford: Oxford UP, 2000). Härtling's articulation of "Heimat" as a deeply personal space devoid of politically autochthonous instrumentalization is evident in his brief treatise *Über Heimat*. He explains here that he conceptualized dialect as his means of

resisting, as a newcomer to Swabia, the arrogant reprimanding tone of the standard language (Ludwigsburg: Verlag der Buchhandlung Aigner, 1982).

[51] Stefana Sabin, "Im Schatten des Objekts: Über Peter Härtlings literaturhistorische Figuren in den Romanen *Niembsch oder Der Stillstand*, *Hölderlin* und *Die dreifache Maria*," in *Peter Härtling: Auskunft für Leser*, ed. Martin Lüdke (Darmstadt: Luchterhand, 1988), 53.

[52] Dominick LaCapra, *History and Criticism* (Ithaca: Cornell UP, 1985), 115–34, esp. 126.

[53] Härtling, "Das Ende der Geschichte: Über die Arbeit an einem 'historischen Roman,'" in *Meine Lektüre: Literatur als Widerstand*, ed. Klas Siblewski (Darmstadt: Hermann Luchterhand, 1981), 113–14.

[54] Härtling, "Das Ende der Geschichte," 114–23.

[55] Härtling, "Mein Hölderlin," in *Zwischen Untergang und Aufbruch: Aufsätze, Reden, Gespräche* (Berlin: Aufbau, 1990), 301–5.

[56] Hölderlin, *Sämtliche Werke*, 6.1:140–41.

[57] Fehervary, *Hölderlin and the Left*, 135.

[58] See Ellis, *Peter Weiss in Exile*, 99, 138.

[59] Härtling, "Mein Hölderlin," 304.

[60] In *Über Heimat*, Härtling remarks on how the rebellious youth of the 1960s and 1970s ceased their striving for solidarity and went their own ways. He finds that politics lost its visionary character and was replaced by an approach informed by short-term thinking and pragmatism (20).

[61] See Härtling, *Die dreifache Maria: Eine Geschichte* (Darmstadt: Hermann Luchterhand, 1982), 30–50.

[62] This is especially the case with Härtling's portrayal of Hoffmann's relationship to Julia Mark, a primary focus of the novel. See Härtling, *Hoffmann oder Die vielfältige Liebe: Eine Romanze* (Cologne: Kiepenheuer & Witsch, 2001), 70–222.

[63] Härtling, *Waiblingers Augen* (Darmstadt: Hermann Luchterhand, 1987), 174–75.

[64] Savage, *Hölderlin after the Catastrophe*, 5–13.

3: Between Feminism and National Identity: The Historical Novels of Renate Feyl

IN THE INTRODUCTION TO A COLLECTION of essays exploring the somewhat discordant relationship between feminism and cultural studies, Sue Thornham lists a series of issues explored by a woman she sees as a forerunner for those working at the intersection of these two areas — Mary Wollstonecraft. Thornham's list includes "questions about women's relation to (the dominant) culture, to power, to discourse, to identity, to lived experience, to cultural production and to representation."[1] In novels written both during the existence and subsequent to the demise of the East German state where she resided, Renate Feyl pursues precisely these issues, and can thus be characterized as a writer at the nexus of cultural studies and feminism. Her historical fiction foregrounds the struggle of Age-of-Goethe female authors against dominant patriarchal power structures at home, in the literary marketplace, and in the political domain. These women overcome seemingly insurmountable obstacles in the spheres of cultural production, self-representation, and authorial identity as female authors. Their "lived experience" at both the personal and professional level is vividly rendered through Feyl's minute attention to the ambience and material details of the period. What makes Feyl stand out among the writers whom Thornham would place at the uneasy juncture between feminist theory and cultural studies is her pursuit of the vexed issue of German national identity in the GDR (in her first novel) and in the Berlin Republic (in her subsequent historical fiction), as refracted through her eighteenth- and early nineteenth-century settings.

Though not as prolific an author as Härtling, Feyl has also written both historical and contemporary novels,[2] and if she has attracted less critical attention than Härtling or Christa Wolf, this is most likely due to her relative lack of formal experimentation. Unlike the Härtling of *Hölderlin* and Gerhard Wolf in *Der arme Hölderlin*, she eschews narrative intrusion, generally adopting an omniscient third-person stance devoid of parabasis or the kind of occluded voice characteristic of Wolf's *Kein Ort. Nirgends.* Born in Prague but a resident of the German Democratic Republic throughout that nation's entire existence, her only work to have attracted much critical attention is *Idylle mit Professor* (Idyll with professor, 1986), but she has published three other significant historical novels.[3]

Idylle mit Professor is an account of the life of Luise Adelgunde Victoria Kulmus's career as author and translator under the stifling tutelage of her philandering husband, the noted reformer of German language and literature Johann Christoph Gottsched. It has been evaluated as both a significant example of late GDR feminism and as a veiled critique of that nation's treatment of its authors. In this reading, Gottsched's straitjacket of rules and regulations for German-language authors, and his paternalistic, opportunistic use of his wife's fame and talent for his own ends, can be seen to reflect the GDR's manipulation and censorship of its own imaginative writers. Seen in this way, *Idylle mit Professor* belongs to the body of historical novels written in the GDR that use an earlier period in German history to allusively polemicize against East Germany's cultural politics, although, as we have seen, these works tend to be set in the Romantic age, while *Idylle mit Professor* commences in 1735, when Luise Kulmus married Johann Christoph Gottsched.

Feyl's other historical novels were written subsequent to the GDR's dissolution in 1990 and have been largely ignored by Germanists. They include *Die profanen Stunden des Glücks* (The profane hours of happiness, 1996), *Das sanfte Joch der Vortrefflichkeit* (The gentle yoke of exemplarity, 1999), and *Aussicht auf bleibende Helle: Die Königin und der Philosoph* (Prospect for enduring luminosity: The queen and the philosopher, 2006). With the exception of this last work, which treats the late seventeenth century relationship between Prussia's first queen, Sophie Charlotte, and the philosopher Gottfried Wilhelm Leibniz as an intellectually sublimated secret love, Feyl's historical novels are focused on eighteenth- and early nineteenth-century women writers. *Die profanen Stunden des Glücks* examines the mature life of Sophie La Roche, the first German-language woman writer to attain renown through her fiction, and *Das sanfte Joch der Vortrefflichkeit* deals with Caroline von Wolzogen, whose fame until recent times was largely based upon her status as Friedrich Schiller's sister-in-law and the author of the first significant biography of the dramatist, but whose initial celebrity was based on her novel *Agnes von Lilien* (1798), and whose imaginative literature has been the subject of renewed critical interest today. Among contemporary German-language novelists, Härtling and Feyl have exhibited the most sustained imaginative engagement with the authors and philosophers of eighteenth and early nineteenth-century Germany. However, while Härtling's historical novels are primarily linked by means of the southwestern German provenance of the writers he examines, as well as by their engaging eccentricity (also present in the works to be examined in chapter 5) and the often related problem of social alienation, Feyl's period pieces are unique in both treating their protagonists in relation to feminism and framing them within the boundaries of German national identity. That is to say, Feyl not only wants to portray her female writers as valiant figures whose success was achieved

despite the restrictions imposed upon them by familial and social patriarchy, but also to evoke the distinctly German context of their careers.
This unique dual trajectory is what justifies this chapter being devoted
almost entirely to her historical works. In order to more fully elucidate
the singularity of Feyl's technique of steering between the poles of feminism and German national identity, I will conclude by briefly contrasting
her approach with that of another GDR novel about a well-known Age-
of-Goethe figure: Caroline Böhmer-Schlegel-Schelling, the protagonist of
Brigitte Struzyk's *Caroline unterm Freiheitsbaum: Ansichtssachen*[4] (Caroline under the freedom tree: Perspectival matters, 1988).

The feminist dimension in Feyl's historical novels is relatively easy to
discern, although it contains some unique elements necessitating explica-
tion. Its formal contours are distinct, for example, from those exhibited
by Christa Wolf in the anti-patriarchal nuances of *Kein Ort. Nirgends* and
the essays linked to that novel's composition. As with Wolf, Feyl's commitment to the struggle against the patriarchal order in East Germany
and the world at large is clearly evident not only in her novels, but in her
nonfictional works as well. In 1984, she published a collection of state-
ments by prominent thinkers that exposes historical sexism, as is evident
in the title, which quotes the nineteenth-century materialist philosopher
Ludwig Feuerbach: *Sein ist das Weib, Denken der Mann: Ansichten für
und wider die gelehrten Frauen* (Being is woman, thinking is man: Views
for and against the educated women). She also published her own collection of essays on women who, not unlike the subjects of her historical fiction, successfully struggled against male domination to become
renowned scientists and critical thinkers: *Der lautlose Aufbruch: Frauen
in der Wissenschaft* (The silent beginning: Women in science, 1981). It
is more difficult to perceive the elucidation of national identity in Feyl's
novels, and one might overlook this dimension entirely were it not for a
programmatic statement issued in the course of an interview and included
as "bonus material" in an afterword to *Aussicht auf bleibende Helle*. This
statement led me to pose a question to Feyl in the course of an interview I
had with her in August 2008, and her response helped clarify her attitude
toward instilling a feeling for national identity in contemporary German
readers. In the interview in *Aussicht auf bleibende Helle*, Feyl was asked to
explain the current popularity of historical novels. Her answer was somewhat surprising:

> Ich kann hier nur aus meinen Erfahrungen sprechen, denn in den
> vielen Diskussionen mit Lesern spüre ich immer wieder: Je mehr es
> auf Europa zugeht, desto größer wird das Bedürfnis, etwas aus der
> eigenen Geschichte zu erfahren, von den eigenen Traditionen und
> eigenen Wurzeln. Die Leser wollen wissen, wo kommen wir her, um
> klarer sehen zu können, wo geht es hin. Die Kenntnis der eigenen

Geschichte gibt im Prozeß fortgesetzter Veränderungen einen Halt, ist ein Stück Heimat und Identität.[5]

[I can only speak here from my own experiences, because in the many discussions with readers I sense again and again: the more we are moving toward Europe, the greater the need is becoming to experience something from one's own history, from one's own traditions and roots. The readers want to know where we come from, in order to be able to see where things are going. Knowledge of one's own history gives one a foundation, is a piece of homeland and identity.]

In the case of a novel like Daniel Kehlmann's *Die Vermessung der Welt* (Measuring the world, 2005) — the most successful German historical novel focused on the nation's eighteenth-century intellectual lineage — it's likely that neither a readerly interest in the specifics of German national history, nor a yearning for the roots and traditions of homeland (*Heimat*) inspired its large readership, as we will see in chapter 5. However, these factors may help to explain Feyl's own, more modest popularity. In my interview with her, she confirmed her view that reading novels rooted in Germany's past helps to sustain German identity in an age of globalization. Furthermore, she insisted that one cannot know and appreciate foreign cultures without knowledge of one's own, and that those with contempt for one's own homeland inevitably harbor contempt for lands outside their borders. Most of her novels are set in periods prior to the dawning of nationalist sentiment in the Napoleonic age (although precisely such nascent nationalism is thematized in *Das sanfte Joch der Vortrefflichkeit*), and Feyl presents not just her chosen protagonists, but also Schiller, Goethe, and even the otherwise rather negatively portrayed Gottsched, in a positive light with respect to their contributions to German culture. While many of his contemporaries and subsequent generations of Germanists saw in Gottsched a slavish adherent to Aristotelian poetic rules and French Neoclassicism, he emerges in *Idylle mit Professor* as a unifier of German language and culture, as one who sought to establish German literature as a viable, discrete domain worthy of comparison to French and English letters. In addition, historically transcendent themes such as writer's block and marital discord are filtered through a language often marked by eighteenth-century turns of phrase and, to modify Clifford Geertz's well-known phrase, a thicker description of eighteenth- and early nineteenth-century milieus than is typical of most historical fiction. In his introduction to M. M. Bakhtin's *The Dialogic Imagination*, Michael Holquist refers to the Russian theorist's attunement to how language is used within "the dense particularity of our everyday lives," "the power of the particular context" in which language utterances are made, and Bakhtin's "extraordinary sensitivity to the immense plurality of experience" in which language is grounded.[6]

Through rooting her antiquated circumlocutions in such particularity by painting vivid, detailed historical tableaus, usually in everyday contexts, Feyl convincingly conjures the period settings of her novels across the expanse of the late seventeenth through early nineteenth centuries. However, as we will see, one of Feyl's techniques undercuts this successful evocation of historical context and imbues the Germany of the period with a globalized, twenty-first-century aura, even though the author's intention was precisely the opposite of this effect. Particularly evident in *Das sanfte Joch der Vortrefflichkeit,* the technique involves using English-language turns of phrase and nicknames for German personages of the time.

A Subtle Critique of GDR Patriarchy: Feyl's Luise Gottsched

Because *Idylle mit Professor* is Feyl's only historical novel written prior to the dissolution of the GDR, and thus prior to the contemporary age of full-blown economic globalization, Anglophone hegemony, cultural transnationalism, and a homogenizing European Union, Feyl was at that time undoubtedly not as concerned with those trends as she was later, in the above-cited interviews. Instead, as Helen Bridge has pointed out, Feyl's novel is written against the grain of a different kind of homogenizing discourse, namely, the tendency of GDR historiographers to treat "the term 'women' as an unproblematic universal category." Feyl calls into question such abstract generalized theorization concerning women by focusing on the particularity of one historical life, and tacitly juxtaposing Luise Gottsched's "lived experience" with the GDR's undifferentiated "theoretical models" concerning women.[7] As Bridge goes on to note, *Idylle mit Professor* and Sigrid Damm's *Cornelia Goethe* (discussed in the following chapter) "differ from GDR historiography in relating individual lives to a history of gender notions and female oppression, rather than to a narrative of social progress," thereby calling into question the efficacy of East German socialism.[8] Thus, one can speak of two quite distinct motivations for Feyl's use of a thick description highly attuned to particular context and to the discrete, plurivocal character of eighteenth- and early nineteenth-century German life in her historical novels. In the GDR phase of her career, this formal approach was undertaken in order to challenge official state historiography's abstract, unrealistic teleology of irreversible improvement in the life of women under real existing socialism. She was also focused, as she made clear in my interview with her, on addressing themes (such as pre-twentieth-century German literary history) of broad national interests, interests that transcended the inter-German border, in order to counter East German parochialism. Her post-GDR works employ the same technique in order to instill in her readers a feeling for Germany's historically rooted national context and to provide them a reassuring foundation (*Halt*), a sense of German identity and feeling for *Heimat* in an age of globalized culture and EU standardization. In my interview with her, Feyl indicated she writes in opposition to what she referred to as contemporary "Nivellierung," a leveling process that tends to reduce many aspects of life to a universal sameness.

With reference to *Idylle mit Professor*, J. H. Reid has argued that "much of the attraction of Feyl's narrative is its cool and understated style," noting that "Feyl lets events speak almost entirely for themselves." He contrasts this approach with Irmtraud Morgner's use of strong irony and Christa Wolf's high degree of stylization.[9] As noted, Feyl's light hand with respect to parabasis, irony, occluded narrative voice, and other techniques, a direct approach that creates an almost reportage-like ambience in her narratives, is the likely cause of her relative critical neglect. However, precisely this approach allows one to perceive history as a densely "lived experience" through the lucid filter of her narrative accounts of significant individuals in Germany's past. Her rather realistic style also allows her to portray, in a straightforward manner, her leading female protagonists as women of great achievement; in her interview with me, Feyl stressed that she has always focused in her writing on prominent women who can serve as inspiring models for contemporary German women.

Idylle mit Professor traces the trajectory of a marriage between two highly gifted intellectuals at a time when a wife was expected to subordinate her ambitions to those of her husband. Because Gottsched at first encourages and promotes his wife's literary career when she is unknown and her writing and translating serve his own agenda, but tries to stifle her when she achieves a measure of success rivaling — indeed, exceeding — his own, the second strand of the novel, the delineation of Luise's[10] writing career, is completely intertwined with the story of her relationship to her husband. Gottsched's growing animosity toward Luise also stems from her increasing rejection of his core literary principles, namely, that literature must be composed according to rigid formal codes and must serve to enhance the spread of reason and other Enlightenment values among readers and spectators of theatrical performances. Feyl portrays the young Luise as an admiring, even adoring, wife when Gottsched's erudition, oratorical skills, and charisma make him one of Germany's most influential professors, college administrators, and cultural arbiters. However, her increasing independence of thought and concomitant success as an author instill in her an admiration for the spontaneity and emotionality of contemporary poets like Friedrich Klopstock and Albrecht Haller, as well as for the views of theorists like Johann Jakob Bodmer that "Der wahre Dichter ist ein Seher und Prophet" (106; the true poet is a seer and prophet). Luise's increasing refutation of her husband's literary values is linked not only to his transformation in public opinion from a bold reformer to a laughably fanatic adherent of stale orthodoxy, but to his increasing coldness toward her, his aggressive attempts to employ her literary skills for his own purposes, his suggestions that their inability to produce offspring (a circumstance deeply painful to both of them) is entirely her fault, and, ultimately, the discovery of his infidelity. As with Feyl's novels on Sophie La Roche and Caroline von Wolzogen, *Idylle mit Professor* presents a history of German literature inextricably linked to the personal and intimate life of its chief protagonist, and both dimensions are shown to be completely imbricated with the moral, material, and intellectual milieu of the period. Feyl's greatest success lies in creating a convincing dialectical relationship between universal themes such as marriage, career, and martial conflict (part of the novel takes place during the Seven Years' War) with the particularities of the novel's temporal and geographical aspects.

As Reid has noted, the pivotal moment in Luise's relationship to Gottsched in the novel, the point when she ceases to be primarily a loving helpmate to her husband and their marriage becomes irreparably strained, occurs with the appearance of the German translation of Pierre Bayle's *Dictionnaire*, edited by her husband, and her name is not included among the translators.[11] Feyl makes use of free indirect style, a technique to which she frequently resorts, to describe this omission and Luise's emotional response to it:

> Alle anderen, die an diesem Werk beteiligt waren, hat Gottsched im Vorwort genannt: den gelehrten Herrn Schwabe, Herrn Königslöwen, den Herrn Müller, den Herrn Gärtner, den Herrn Ibbeken, den Herrn Gellert. Nur sie ist als 'seine Gehilfin' erwähnt. Ohne Vornamen. Ohne Zunamen. Die gute Fee, der treue Beistand, die zärtliche Mutmacherin im Hintergrunde. (126)

> [Gottsched mentioned all the others who participated in this work in the foreword: the learned Mr. Schwabe, Mr. Königslöwen, Mr. Müller, Mr. Gärtner, Mr. Ibbeken, Mr. Gellert. Only she is mentioned as 'his assistant.' Without first name. Without surname. The good fairy, the faithful assistant, the gentle encourager in the background.]

The circumlocution "learned" in front of Schwabe's name, the sheer accumulation of long-forgotten eighteenth-century scholars, and the use of antiquated terms like "good fairy" and "gentle encourager" as free-floating signifiers revealing Luise's dawning awareness of how Gottsched really regards her, constitute a paradigmatic example of adroitly using period-specific figures and language, as well as a small detail of eighteenth-century German literary history, to instantiate a universal theme: marital crisis brought on by a wife's awareness that she has been abused in some manner by her husband. This is the point at which Luise realizes, to quote Lorna Martens, that "Gottsched loves her only when she works for him, when she helps him enhance his public image."[12] The filtering of this recognition through a uniquely eighteenth-century linguistic and literary register grounding the novel's turning point enhances the evocation of the period's milieu.

Though Luise's crushing disappointment at Gottsched's failure to mention her among the translators marks the point when her marriage enters into an irreversibly downward spiral, it also marks her beginning liberation from her husband's control of her own self-perception. Through the powerful agency of free indirect style, Feyl shows how Luise recognizes herself as the good fairy and faithful assistant, realizes that this is Gottsched's image of her, and sees that she has faithfully adhered to this destructive ideal. In discussing the reworking of the Clytemnestra motif by the German writers Christa Reinig and Christine Brückner, Kathleen Komar, citing Sigrid Weigel, argues that these authors undertake in their "re-visions of a female archetype" the activity of "erasing those images of women painted by the male hand on the mirror of representation, which is then held up for women to see themselves in." Whereas Clytemnestra was regarded by men in antiquity primarily as the brutal murderer of her husband Agamemnon, she is transformed in contemporary feminist writing into a liberated, liberating figure who challenges the exclusivity of patriarchal authority.[13] A German feminist like Reinig and Brückner, Feyl turns the pivotal incident of Gottsched's slighting of his wife in the Bayle translation into the moment when Luise begins to "erase" her husband's image of her, an erasure instantiated through her initial shock of recognition, and then has Luise substitute Gottsched's "mirror of representation" with an empowered, autonomous self-image. Myra Jehlen has noted that women must recognize they are always distorted through the appropriating vision of others into a "kind of fiction,"[14] and this recognition comes for the fictionalized Luise Gottsched when she finally realizes how her husband envisions and uses her. Whether or not the real-life Luise experienced her feminist epiphany as a result of Gottsched's failure to include her among those credited in the *Dictionnaire* is difficult to discern, but her commitment to empowering women by supporting their autonomous rights to "authority and authorship" are consciously expressed in one of her mature comedies, *Das Testament* (The testament, 1745), as an insightful study of this work has shown.[15]

Another universal motif that comes to expression in *Idylle mit Professor* through a powerful evocation of the novel's eighteenth-century context is war. Toward the conclusion of the novel, and indeed not long before Luise's death in 1762, the Prussians marched into Leipzig, where Gottsched held his professorial chair. This eruption of the Seven Years' War into their lives is introduced when Luise rushes into Gottsched's room with the "horrible news" that hussars are roaming the city. The commotion caused the by Prussian invasion is marked by incidents common to wars both then and now (the flight of citizens to places of worship, urban destruction) and mostly particular to an earlier age (the arrest of the city magistrate, the confiscation of merchants' goods and the sealing of their houses). Gottsched responds rather laconically, claiming that, as a native Prussian, he has nothing to fear from the Prussian ruler, Friedrich the Great, whom he greatly admires (238–39). Indeed, the cultivated Friedrich demands an immediate audience with the professor, who is irritated that the monarch's first question concerns his wife's work. Nevertheless, after passing what amounts to a translation test (he is requested to render a stanza of Baptiste Rousseau into German), Gottsched gains Friedrich's favor in the form of a poetic ode to his successful ability to force "a language of barbarians" to resonate more melodiously in his own songs. Gottsched is delighted at the king's positive response (244–48), and the episode illustrates both Gottsched's servility and the service he rendered to German language and literature in Friedrich's Francophile age. Indeed, earlier in the novel he is shown to be a patriotic defender of German poets such as Martin Opitz and Paul Fleming against the Swiss critic Bodmer's rejection of German writers in favor of John Milton, whom Bodmer had translated and whom Gottsched (contra Luise) loathed (102–3). This image of Gottsched as a defender of the country's poetry runs counter to the widespread image of the critic as himself a fanatic Francophile, a view made popular by Gotthold Ephraim Lessing (who is mentioned several times in the book as one of Gottsched's enemies), although Feyl's image of Gottsched as a German patriot[16] is mitigated in the account of his fawning treatment of Voltaire when the French writer, who held German letters in contempt, pays a visit to Leipzig.

The appearance of servility toward those with power and influence is enhanced by Gottsched's obsequious behavior toward Friedrich. He goes so far as to praise the Prussian occupation of Leipzig as a "turbulentes und doch zugleich soviel geordnetes Treiben" (242; turbulent and yet at the same time quite well-ordered activity), even though he, a native Prussian, had originally come to Saxon Leipzig in order to avoid being conscripted into the Prussian army. As Reid notes, Luise, who comes from the free city of Danzig, takes the opposite view, regarding the Prussians as narrow-minded militarists who value the force of arms over friendship.[17] Just as her correspondence was first read by her husband, so her epistolary exchange with Dorothea Runckel, a primary source for Feyl in the composition of *Idylle mit Professor*, is subject to interception by the Prussians during the Seven Years' War. In this issue of epistolary censorship on the part of both an overbearing husband and a dictatorial state, Feyl's feminist sensibility intersects with her critique of the GDR's repressive political apparatus.[18] The contemporary political thrust of Feyl's first historical novel is evident when one considers how such censorship and oppression in the GDR state are thematized in her novel *Ausharren im Paradies* (Enduring in paradise, 1992), published just after reunification. Here Feyl's critique of the communist state's interference in its citizens' private lives and intellectual endeavors, its creation of what she termed a "Gefängnis der Lügen" (prison of lies) in my interview with her, no longer needed to be filtered through the veil of a fictional biography set in the past.

Fame and Struggle: A Novel Look at Sophie La Roche

Feyl's next historical novel, *Die profanen Stunden des Glücks*, was composed after reunification, and the issues of state censorship and the patriarchal control of women are not imbricated in this work. Feyl's Sophie La Roche suffers from neither of these impediments, in contrast to Luise Gottsched, who toils anonymously for years in the service of her husband before gaining recognition as an independent writer — a recognition that contributes to the destruction of her marriage to the envious Gottsched. Sophie La Roche gains immediate fame with her first book, the *Geschichte des Fräuleins von Sternheim* (The history of Lady Sophia Sternheim, 1771), described by Todd Kontje as "probably the single most influential work for the next several generations of German women writers,"[19] while Luise — despite being recognized along with her husband by the most illustrious figure of the Holy Roman Empire, Empress Maria Theresa, in an episode in Feyl's first historical novel that reveals all the royal pomp of the period (158–63) — does not significantly influence subsequent German literary history. Also distinguishing the two women is the circumstance that Sophie's husband, the court official Georg Michael Franck von La Roche, makes no attempt to control his wife's writing. Feyl portrays him as a charming and graceful workaholic with no interest in imaginative literature, who does not deign to read his wife's work and regards her sudden belletristic success with bemused detachment. However, a career that began as a hobby for the relatively well-to-do wife of a privy counselor to the Elector of Trier, a husband whose reputation and largesse were enhanced when he was ennobled, becomes a matter of necessity when La Roche is dismissed from service through an intrigue enabled by his enlightened religious views. He falls into a depression and their financial circumstances force Sophie to turn her hobby into the couple's chief source of income. Feyl's Luise Gottsched lives at a time when royal patronage, rather than the sale of books in an emerging capitalist economy, was dominant in spurring the production of elevated literature, and Gottsched's academic position secures the couple's financial stability. To be sure, Luise strives to be as independent as possible of her husband after their estrangement, and given Gottsched's embrace of Prussian military governance in Leipzig during the Seven Years' War, a regime marked by censorship and coercive control, Luise's struggle for personal freedom in her life and writing is certainly intended as an expression of feminist principles against the GDR's paternal orthodoxy in its treatment of its writers. Her failure to find a publisher for her *Geschichte der lyrischen Dichtkunst der Deutschen* (History of the lyric art of the Germans) during the war makes her feel as though she has been beheaded. She finds writing a book that remains unprinted is like death for the author and is angry that publishers are only concerned about a secure profit (271–72).

Nevertheless, Feyl never implies that this blow late in Luise's life affects her pecuniary circumstances. Living and writing in a unified Germany that allows its authors autonomy, but forces them in large measure to compete in the marketplace for sales like any entrepreneur, Feyl's second fictional biography focuses on an author whose later life reflected her own post-GDR condition as an independent writer. The shift in Sophie's career from novelist to editor of the journal *Pomona* mirrors her transformation from a housewife with a writing hobby to a profit-oriented capitalist: "Aber bislang war sie ja auch nur die Dichterin von Romanen gewesen. Jetzt aber war sie literarischer Produzent, Unternehmer und Kaufmann in einer Person" (152; But until now she was only the author of novels. But now she was a literary producer, entrepreneur and salesman in one person), one who stands, like all entrepreneurs, under strong deadline pressures (155). In the *Author, Art, and the Market: Rereading the History of Aesthetics*, Martha Woodmansee suggests La Roche's prolific productivity as author and journal editor truly began in earnest "when the collapse of her husband's diplomatic career and then his death caused real financial need."[20] After the GDR's collapse, many of East Germany's intellectuals, no longer enjoying state patronage, faced real financial need as well, and this circumstance probably helped to inspire Feyl's selection of Sophie as the subject of her second historical novel.

One trait shared by Feyl's Luise and Sophie is an assertive will in their dealings with leading men in their lives, a trait that allows them to maintain independence and autonomy in a profession, writing, that is almost completely controlled by men. This image of two leading German women of letters in, respectively, the first and second halves of the eighteenth century is somewhat contested by scholarship. In her study *Luise Gottsched: A Reconsideration*, Veronica Richel notes that "critics since Lessing have tended to dismiss her work as an uninteresting implementation of Gottsched's theories,"[21] though more recent scholars such as Arnd Bohm and Susanne Kord have persuasively contested this view.[22] A more interesting contrast between scholarly analysis and imaginative biography is provided by comparing Woodmansee's examination of the relationship between Sophie and Christoph Martin Wieland in *The Author, Art, and the Market* and Feyl's portrayal of their liaison in *Die profanen Stunden des Glücks*.

Woodmansee's study focuses to a large extent on the realm of aesthetics under the sign of the nascent literary mass market in the late eighteenth century — and the historical circumstances governing literary production at that time — as a means of calling into question the Kantian axiom that art must be viewed and evaluated through the prism of an atemporal, disinterested pleasure. In composing a second novel that, in contrast to *Idylle mit Professor*, highlights the material and economic elements of the late eighteenth-century literary marketplace, Feyl has created a work that frequently recalls Woodmansee's groundbreaking analysis. However, contrary to Woodmansee, Feyl highlights the intimacy of the La Roche-Wieland relationship. As *Die Profanen Stunden des Glücks* opens, Sophie is already the forty-year-old author of the *Fräulein von Sternheim*, but almost immediately experiences a reminiscence of her youthful love affair with Wieland when he announces his impending visit. The two cousins had been passionately in love, but he traveled to Switzerland and, after two failed engagements, she married Georg La Roche (18–21). Their reunion after eighteen years brings to the surface long-suppressed feelings. Wieland praises *Sternheim* as an epoch-making event (25–26). They remain in epistolary contact, and Wieland urges her to send her further literary contributions to him as editor of the *Teutschen Merkur*. Learning from Wieland of *Merkur*'s many female subscribers inspires Sophie to found *Pomona* as a literary journal devoted exclusively to women. Through her careful logistical and financial planning, the response to her journal is overwhelmingly positive, and Wieland agrees to take care of its distribution and marketing (*Vertrieb*) in Thuringia (131). Only La Roche is unhappy with the project, as it shames him to no longer play the role of breadwinner, but Sophie explains in detail why the couple's savings are insufficient to support them and their still somewhat dependent progeny (134–35). She is shown to be in firm financial control of *Pomona* throughout the course of its brief existence. However, the tastes of the masses have begun to dictate the direction of the literary marketplace, as she reflects after a visit with a discouraged young Friedrich Schiller. She is angry that authors are expected to earn less than those who edit, produce, and review their work, and agrees with Wieland that authors deserve to enjoy a secure middle-class existence (163–65). Sophie's experiences and reflections in this regard undoubtedly mirror the perspectives of Feyl, living as an independent author in the Berlin Republic, but also show Sophie to be a feminist role model for contemporary women who seek autonomy and control in their financial and personal lives. Late in life she pays a final visit to Wieland, and the novel concludes with her correspondence with him regarding the publication of what will be her last novel, *Melusinens Sommerabende* (Melusine's summer evenings, 1806). She becomes impatient after having to wait some time for his response, but is deeply moved when it finally arrives, as he claims he would never have become a poet had their early, failed relationship not taken place. She is also overjoyed that Wieland agrees to publish her novel. He only requests a brief autobiography that will enhance the book's sales. *Die profanen Stunden des Glücks* concludes with the expression of her reserved assent; she finds this addendum unnecessary, but follows his advice, which had been consistently advantageous for her (298–300).

Woodmansee cites Wieland's preface to *Sternheim*, a novel originally published anonymously, to argue that Wieland exercised a strategy of occluding female authorship. In Wieland's preface, the author of the novel is defined through a description of her status as a writer of interest only to women, as an amateur rather than a true artist. Wieland emphasized the book's practical educational value to housewives and mothers, denying its aesthetic merit (again reflecting the Kantian dictum that practical lessons in a work of art are inimical to such aesthetic merit). Woodmansee believes this strategy effectively guaranteed Sophie's exclusion from the literary history of her age and her transformation from an author into "Wieland's muse."[23] As an introductory epigraph to her chapter on Sophie, she cites the same passage of Wieland's letter to his former lover, proclaiming he would never have become an artist without "fate" having brought them together, that Feyl incorporates near the conclusion of her novel.[24] Woodmansee's view is partially shaped by her reading of Silvia Bovenschen, who claims Sophie always remained the "Fräulein von Sternheim" while Goethe successfully outgrew his conflation with the figure of Werther from his early eponymous novel.[25] In his brief preface to *Melusinens Sommerabende*, Wieland does cast Sophie as an author "for Germany's daughters," as though her book were not suitable for male readers, but he also consistently describes her as an author (*Schriftstellerin*), not an amateur, and emphasizes his very light hand in editing her manuscript.[26] Feyl's Sophie is a strong feminist role model from an earlier period in German literature, while Woodmansee tries to show how and why she was excluded from the literary histories of that period. This does not mean Feyl would disagree with Woodmansee and Bovenschen, but rather that she seeks to recuperate authors such as Luise Gottsched and Sophie La Roche from such exclusion. Nevertheless, Wieland's preface to *Melusinens Sommerabende* shows Woodmansee's treatment of his editorial relationship to Sophie La Roche is rather incomplete.

There is a dual strategy at work in Feyl's post-unification goal of imbuing her German readership with a sense of national identity. One component is the portrayal of Sophie's interactions with the literary luminaries of the age: Not only Wieland, Goethe (as well as his mother and sister, who are all friends of the La Roche family), and Schiller, but also Lenz, who tried to gain support for his dramas through his ardent letters to her (75–78), Klopstock, and others are shown to enjoy her friendship and occasional support. The birth and youth of her famous grandchildren, Bettine and Clemens

Brentano, are also delineated in the narrative. A focus on this aspect of Sophie's life is undoubtedly intended to promote her importance for German letters in its "golden age," but also to simply reawaken an interest in the period among German readers by bringing its leading figures to imaginative life. There is little interest today among young Germans for the literature of the Age of Goethe, and authors such as Feyl and Rafik Schami, who wrote *Der geheime Bericht über den Dichter Goethe, der eine Prüfung auf einer arabischen Insel bestand* (The secret report on the poet Goethe, who passed a test on an Arabian island, 1999), wish to counteract this circumstance with their historical fiction. Secondly, Feyl weaves the thread of feminism together with her intent to awaken national consciousness by focusing on Sophie's role in bringing into being a German literature that is distinct from its counterparts in France and England, countries that nevertheless exercised a strong influence on its development. Kontje has argued that *Sternheim* appeared at precisely the time when German writers were trying to liberate themselves from such foreign models, and that La Roche's pioneering efforts were as significant as those of as Herder, Lessing, and Goethe with respect to adapting foreign exemplars "to a German context."[27] *Die Profanen Stunden des Glücks* is not a hagiography of Sophie and her literary contemporaries; their prejudices and blind spots are on full display. For example, Sophie fails to predict the brilliant literary career of the young Goethe, and feels he is a poor candidate, given his limited future prospects, for marriage to her daughter Maximiliane (35). However, by showing these individuals as vibrant human beings in their vividly evoked milieu, Feyl attempts to reawaken a sense for German literary history among a post-unification populace that has had little exposure to it outside the classroom.

Schiller's Independent Sister-in-Law Caroline von Wolzogen

In *Die profanen Stunden des Glücks,* Sophie tries to win Caroline von Wolzogen as a contributor to *Pomona* (155), and Feyl made her the central protagonist of her next novel, *Das sanfte Joch der Vortrefflichkeit*. If Feyl was partly motivated to write *Die profanen Stunden des Glücks* in order to show that Sophie La Roche was much more than "Wieland's muse," she was undoubtedly interested in showing that Caroline von Wolzogen had a significance far beyond her normative status as Schiller's sister-in-law and first important biographer, though these roles are also central to her makeup in Feyl's novel about her. Indeed, at first glance, it would seem ironic that Caroline's role as Schiller's muse is a far more significant thread in *Das sanfte Joch der Vortrefflichkeit* than was the case with Sophie's relationship to Wieland in the earlier novel. This circumstance is reflected on the back-cover blurbs of the two novels; Wieland is not even mentioned in the description of *Die profanen Stunden des Glücks*, which stresses instead Sophie's role as grandmother of the Brentano siblings and the sudden fame she attained as the author of *Sternheim*. The blurb for *Das sanfte Joch der Vortrefflichkeit* begins by mentioning that Caroline first met the impoverished Schiller while she was working on a novel, and that despite their mutual attraction, Schiller nevertheless married her younger sister, Lotte. However, Caroline is portrayed as equally strong, resilient, and independent as Sophie was in the previous novel, and it is a historical fact that Caroline and Schiller consistently lived in closer physical proximity than did Sophie and Wieland. Feyl's historical novels accurately reflect this circumstance.

The Schiller portrayed at the outset of *Das sanfte Joch der Vortrefflichkeit* makes the same first impression on Caroline as he had made on Sophie La Roche in Feyl's earlier novel. In *Die profanen Stunden des Glücks*, Sophie is surprised when she meets the author of the scandalous play *Die Räuber* (The robbers, 1782) because she expected to find in Schiller the sort of bold, impudent, impetuous young man lionized in his early drama. Instead, she meets a pale, modest young man with excellent manners (141–42). Caroline's expectations concerning Schiller are identical to those of Sophie, but where the already middle-aged author of *Sternheim* is pleased by the figure Schiller cuts, the young Caroline, trapped in a loveless marriage to the dreary courtier Friedrich Wilhelm Ludwig von Beulwitz, is a bit disappointed. Schiller is accompanied by his friend Wilhelm von Wolzogen, whom Caroline marries years later after divorcing Beulwitz, and Wolzogen had described the dramatist to her as entertaining and amusing (15–17). Caroline soon finds Wolzogen was correct, and a mutual attraction develops. Ultimately, Schiller marries her younger sister Charlotte, but is revealed to be a boundless egotist in continuously pressing Caroline to live in a triangulated relationship with the couple. He imagines his physical needs being met by his wife and his literary and spiritual development being furthered by her more intellectually gifted sister.[28] Much of the novel revolves around Caroline's efforts to manage this difficult triad, and Feyl's ability to imbue Caroline with the same positive attributes, the same exemplary proto-feminist traits evident in Luise Gottsched and Sophie La Roche, derive from the portrayal of how Caroline — like Sophie after her husband's fall from grace — not only adroitly copes with sudden poverty after her marriage to the initially impecunious Wolzogen, but also skillfully manages her difficult, demanding, unstable, and often ill brother-in-law. After his death, she helps to ameliorate her sister's precarious financial circumstances by helping to pave the way for the publication of Goethe's correspondence with Schiller, largely through adroit negotiations with the self-serving privy counselor. Indeed, as in her novel on Sophie La Roche, Feyl brings the most prominent figures of Weimar Classicism into continuous contact with a prominent woman of letters, once again linking the portrayal of a nascent historical feminist role model with the (for Feyl) equally important goal of enhancing contemporary German national consciousness by revivifying the most illustrious figures of Germany's most celebrated literary age. However, again as with *Die profanen Stunden des Glücks, Das sanfte Joch der Vortrefflichkeit* is no exercise in hagiography. Even putatively lofty disputes such as the debate between Schiller and Herder on the viability of Kantian philosophy are shown to degenerate into petty egotistical bickering in small-town Weimar, a milieu revealed to be narrow minded in its inability to accept Goethe's common-law relationship to the plebian Christiane Vulpius (204–7).

Feyl's desire to actualize German literary history in her novels in order to promote her feminist ideals and also enhance a distinct national consciousness in a homogenizing global age would have aroused strong opposition in orthodox GDR circles. In his essay on the function of the historical novel in East German literature, Jay Rosellini notes that the theory of this genre established by Lukács in *Der historische Roman* (1955) went largely unchallenged in the communist state. Among the trends disapproved of by Lukács and his followers was the attempt to make historical novels directly relevant to the present day and to draw obvious analogies between past events and present circumstances. Thus, Lion Feuchtwanger, an author otherwise praised in the GDR for his humanism and antifascism, was obliquely criticized for thinking of his historical fiction as a "costume" and as a stylistic means for creating the illusion of reality.[29] Feyl's attack in *Idylle mit Professor* against GDR paternalism and critical orthodoxy was rather veiled, and did not arouse ire in that country, but her more obvious intention to establish Sophie La Roche and Caroline von Wolzogen as feminist role models after German reunification shows a clear break with Lukács's views on the historical novel, as do the obvious allusions to her personal circumstances in Sophie's tirades about the unjust financial treatment of the writing class and Caroline's contemporizing complaints about writer's block and the distress to serious authors caused by those who search for a source of money before they begin to compose (265–66 and 307–8). When she reflects on the sudden patriotic fervor of the Germans as the tide of the Napoleonic War turns and liberation from the French occupation appears possible, this seems less an appeal to the German national consciousness Feyl is otherwise at pains to arouse than an allusion to Germany at the moment of the fall of the Berlin Wall: "Es schien nur noch ein Thema und ein Ziel zu geben: das Vaterland von der Herrschaft Napoleons zu befreien. Die Jugend, noch vor wenigen Wochen auf nichts als Anspruch und Versorgung aus, drängte ins Feld" (267; There seemed to be only one theme and one goal remaining: the liberation of the fatherland from Napoleon's rule. The youth, concerned only with personal demands and needs a few weeks ago, pressed toward the battlefield). There seems little doubt that Feyl intends here, through synchronic parallelism, to evoke that moment late in 1989 when Germans on both sides of the Wall put aside their personal concerns and ambitions, became newly minted German patriots, and the term "fatherland" once again acquired inspiring nationalist overtones. Caroline is quite skeptical about the sudden anti-Napoleonic fervor despite her antipathy to the "world ruler" (268), and this ambivalence also reflects that of the East and West German intelligentsia toward reunification.[30] Feyl's stated goal of imbuing her readers with a sense of *Heimat* is more closely approximated when she engages in dense, "thick" descriptions of customs unique to Germany at that time, such as her detailed portrait of the marksmen's festival in the context of Schiller's discomfort at having been commanded to participate, in uniform, at such an event (45–47). Here, too, Feyl's narrative practice runs contrary to the dictums of Lukács, who eschewed such dense, static description as a retardant to the development of narrative action.[31]

One technique, however, that Feyl employs to evoke the eighteenth- and early nineteenth-century milieu in *Das sanfte Joch der Vortrefflichkeit* as a means of creating a richly described atmosphere so her readers will gain a heightened, particularized German national consciousness, has the opposite effect. In her conversation with me, Feyl noted that her research revealed the frequent use of English-language expressions, phrases, and even names in eighteenth-century intellectual and/or court circles due to an anglophile inclination among some members of the cultural elite and nobility, as well as a concomitant resentment toward the great influence exercised upon German language, literature, and general culture by French language, thought, and custom. Unlike her other historical novels, *Das sanfte Joch der Vortrefflichkeit* employs a first-person rather than a third-person narrative voice, so it is Caroline who thinks of Wilhelm von Humboldt, an intimate of her circle, as "dem smarten Bill" (74). When she considers the fading of her physical passions and her inability as an older woman to have her heart struck by the glance of a man, she reflects, in English, "the time was over" (281). Feyl is certainly correct that such anglicisms gained a certain popularity in eighteenth-century Germany, particularly in the wake of Lessing's influential argument that German writers should replace France with England as a chief source for literary models. However, the use of English-language turns of phrase in a German historical novel published in the age of globalized English, which has produced a highly English-inflected German language (*Denglisch*), actually counteracts Feyl's efforts. Rather than evoking the particular ambience of eighteenth- and early nineteenth-century Germany, it jarringly brings her reader back into the twenty-first century. This is particularly the case when Caroline reflects on her and Schiller's bemusement at the style-conscious literary dandies of their environs as they strolled through "worldwide Weimar" (212). The most cosmopolitan globalized paradigm associated with the period of Weimar Classicism is Goethe's notion of *Weltliteratur* (world literature). Goethe believed that improvements in communication and transportation infrastructures in early nineteenth-century Europe — improvements he foresaw expanding across the world — as well as enhanced translation activity and the concomitant transnationalization of the book trade and literary reviews, were creating a fruitful interaction, an exchange of ideas among national literatures that he termed "world literature." As Reingard Nethersole has noted, this paradigm has been radically transformed in the age of global English and a fully "worldwide" capitalism. Thus, she discerns in our time a "hybrid new world literature in English at the nexus of center and periphery" that, "while articulating local experience in response to an internationalized culture of literacy, testifies to the widening gulf between the local and the global, to the particular realm of the vernacular, with its unique modes of making contingent historical experience intelligible, and to the general but vacuous vocabulary of commerce."[32] When Feyl has Caroline employ the term "worldwide Weimar," we are wrenched from the local, historical Weimar associated with Goethe and Schiller, and from the contingencies of the cityscape as historically experienced by Caroline and her circle, and plunged into the Anglophone "hybrid new world literature" — globally commercialized through the "worldwide" web of which contemporary Weimar is an infinitesimal element — described by Nethersole. Feyl's anglicisms thus undermine her otherwise successful effort to imbue her novel with a temporal and spatial ambience inspirational for German national consciousness through the reflections of a significant woman writer who, through the independence, strength, and resilience she displays in the novel, also promotes Feyl's feminist ideals.

A Sublated Eroticism: Sophie Charlotte and Leibniz

I will only briefly consider Feyl's last (as of this writing) historical novel, *Aussicht auf bleibende Helle*, for two reasons. First of all, it falls outside the pattern set by the previous novels: Its chief protagonist, Queen Sophie Charlotte, is not a writer, but seemingly plays the more historically traditional role of muse to a creative male intellect, the philosopher/mathematician Leibniz. Secondly, the novel's narrative time frame falls mostly outside the period that is the focus of this book, for her death (with which *Aussicht auf bleibende Helle* concludes) occurred in 1705. This novel does share one significant trait with *Das sanfte Joch der Vortrefflichkeit*. As she is writing Schiller's biography, Caroline considers the mingling of the spiritual/intellectual and the sensual in her relationship with the late author. What she had felt for him when he was alive comes to the surface once again: "die Lust, die ein geistiges Gewand trug, im ewigen Versteck geblieben war und nur sichtbar wurde in den Spiegelungen der Seele" (309; the desire that wore an intellectual/spiritual robe, remained in an eternal hiding place and was only visible in the reflections of the soul). Precisely this description, in all its nuances, captures the nature of the bond between Sophie Charlotte (married to Friedrich the Third since the age of sixteen) and Leibniz as constellated in Feyl's novel.

As with Caroline's relationship to Schiller, the erotic impulse connecting Sophie Charlotte to Leibniz is sublimated into intense intellectual exchanges that are highly productive for both of them. In her analysis of Volker Ebersbach's novel *Caroline* (1987), one of two significant GDR novels on the life of Caroline Böhmer-Schlegel-Schelling, Stephanie Bird claims that this key figure among the young German Romantics becomes in Ebersbach's work "in effect a passive muse with enough intelligence to participate or comment"[33] in her verbal intercourse with the young men of the circle, including her second husband, the literary historian August Wilhelm Schlegel, and her third spouse, the philosopher Friedrich Schelling. Sophie Charlotte is too much the strong, independent ruler, energetic pupil, and promoter of culture and learning in Prussia, to function as the "woman in the background" Bird sees in Ebersbach's Caroline Böhmer-Schlegel-Schelling.[34] Sophie Charlotte's "herausfordernde Wißbegier" (14; challenging thirst for knowledge) provides the élan to her conversations with the somewhat stiff and formal Leibniz. Though she is not a writer, she is cast in the same mold as Feyl's Luise Gottsched, Sophie La Roche, and Caroline von Wolzogen: a woman who does not allow herself to be defined by others, who exercises her influence through adroit social skills and diplomatic tact in a society where such female influence is legally constricted. Feyl's desire to provide her readers with a knowledge of their own history by painting a dense tableau informed by discrete local/historical coloring is achieved through a vibrant rendering of court life in that age. A key moment in the formation of German national identity occurred when Sophie Charlotte's husband Friedrich was elevated from Elector of Brandenburg to first King of Prussia, for Prussia as a kingdom became the driving force for the eventual unification of Germany. Feyl portrays Friedrich's coronation in all of its ornate pomp and circumstance (68–74).

A Different Kind of Feminism: Brigitte Struzyk's Caroline Böhmer-Schlegel-Schelling

Brigitte Struzyk's *Caroline unterm Freiheitsbaum*, on the life of Caroline Böhmer-Schlegel-Schelling, highlights by way of contrast Feyl's unique intertwining of feminism and national identity. Struyzk's novel has attracted more critical attention than Ebersbach's book on Böhmer-Schlegel-Schelling, much of it focused positively on Struzyk's somewhat postmodern avoidance of a cohesive and historically contextualized narrative in presenting Caroline's life.[35] Unlike Feyl, Struzyk provides her third-person narrator with a distinct voice; she enunciates a strong identification with the novel's eponymous protagonist.

Caroline unterm Freiheitsbaum and *Idylle mit Professor* constitute two of the four most significant GDR novels to focus on prominent, eighteenth-century women of letters. The other two, Sigrid Damm's *Caroline Goethe* and Johanna Hoffmann's *Charlotte von Stein*, are examined in the next chapter. The unique character of Feyl's contribution to the genre, both before and after the dissolution of the East German state, can be highlighted by contrasting her approach with that of Struzyk, since their works are almost completely antithetical with respect to style, narrative voice, and gender politics. While Feyl draws on period colloquialisms to heighten her novels' eighteenth- and early nineteenth-century ambience (with the glaring exception of those Anglicisms like "worldwide Weimar"), Struzyk concedes to such demands for historical atmosphere only though an ironic use of iambic meter (somewhat characteristic of the period) in her prose and an occasional resort (less frequent than that of Feyl) to the unique sartorial, architectural, and linguistic customs of the period.[36] Such evocations of the age in its material density — an evocation central to Feyl's project of enhancing contemporary German national consciousness — is countered in *Caroline unterm Freiheitsbaum* by a frequent employment of late twentieth-century slang, as when an English prince visiting Caroline's father, the prominent Orientalist Johann David Michaelis, comments regarding the recent loss of the American colonies: "Das ist uns scheißegal" (41; we don't give a shit about that). Where Feyl presents continuous, cohesive, reportage-like narratives focusing on the mature life of her heroines, Struzyk draws on random episodes in Caroline's life from childhood to old age and enacts them as discontinuous snippets presented by an ironic, highly intrusive narrator given to complex wordplay.

A reader with no background knowledge of the period would find Struzyk's historical, philosophical, and literary allusions nearly impossible to follow; her only concessions in this regard are a reprint of a brief biographical sketch of Caroline, written by Franz Muncker and published in 1890, that prefaces the novel, and poetic elucidations concerning the inspiration and source material for the book, as well as reflections concerning the narrated past, in what might be termed appendices, at its conclusion. Feyl does not force the reader to fill in such gaps. Though Struzyk suggests that the idealistic holism of the Jena Romantics can spur a productive engagement with the political present (187), thereby tacitly embracing the views enunciated by Christa Wolf and discussed in chapter 1, her Romantics are presented, albeit often sympathetically, as altogether idiosyncratic and earthy in their interactions with each other (see especially 112–16) — indeed, as inconsiderate slobs who force Caroline to engage in a major housecleaning (145–46) — rather than as profound thinkers. While Feyl presents the luminaries of Weimar with their petty foibles and jealousies in bringing the period to life, this is less a focus for her than for Struzyk. Indeed, Struzyk treats Caroline's lover, Georg Forster, a heroic figure in earlier GDR fictional treatments of this explorer, writer, and prominent member of the Mainz Jacobin circle,[37] as self-pitying and ineffectual. Although Struzyk's Friedrich Schelling is a strong and sympathetic figure (whereas Caroline's second husband, A. W. Schlegel, is reminiscent in Struzyk's novel of Feyl's Gottsched in his egotism and indulgence in extramarital liaisons), the Jena Romantics in *Caroline unterm Freiheitsbaum* are far less likely than Feyl's presentation of them to inspire a sense of German national consciousness through positive identification. Finally, whereas Feyl's feminist purport is obvious, gender politics are more understated in *Caroline unterm Freiheitsbaum*, reflecting Struzyk's aversion toward what she termed the "Emanzipationsgeplapper" (emancipation blabber) of the 1970s and 1980s,[38] although the sexual constraints experienced by Caroline and other women in the novel are thematized. Despite these substantive differences, Feyl and Struzyk both succeed in creating an empathetic identification with their leading female protagonists and in showing the relevance of the German past for the German present.

Conclusion

Broadly speaking, much Age-of-Goethe fiction published in the Federal Republic of Germany and the German Democratic Republic in the 1970s and early 1980s appropriated figures associated, not always accurately, with German Romanticism to engage with artistic and political concerns intimately connected to cultural life in those two countries, even when, as with Peter Weiss, these authors sometimes weave broader, pan-Western issues into their narratives. Renate Feyl's historical fiction, set in the eighteenth and early nineteenth centuries, reflects quite different contemporary priorities. Writing in a GDR that made the establishment of a positive German identity secondary to promoting the nation's USSR-dictated role in forging ever-stronger bonds of international socialist solidarity, and then in the post-Wall Berlin Republic that poses even greater challenges to establishing such a discrete identity due to cultural, commercial, and political globalization, Feyl wrote novels intended as a counterweight to these trends. Her thick descriptions of life among the literary elite in the period considered by many to be Germany's most glorious cultural epoch are designed to instill in her readers a recognition of the *Kulturnation*'s unique accomplishments and thus counteract homogenizing forces emanating from the Soviet and, now, Americanized global spheres.

At the same time, Feyl's novels are focused on the lives of pioneering women authors who had to establish their own identities and carve out a separate space for themselves within a domineering literary patriarchy during this putatively golden age of German culture. The protagonists of her Age-of-Goethe fiction are not, ultimately, casualties of this patriarchy like Wolf's Günderrode or Reschke's Henriette Vogel, but strong characters possessed of an iron will enabling them to be successful in the domain of belles lettres. By contrast, GDR author Brigitte Struzyk's novel on Caroline Böhmer-Schlegel-Schelling is a postmodern send-up mixing contemporary slang with postmodern narrative pastiche. Her book, contrary to Feyl's historical fiction, deliberately subverts the inculcation of German national identity and an uplifting feminist consciousness.

Notes

[1] Sue Thornham, "Introduction: Telling Stories; Feminism and Cultural Studies," in *Feminist Theory and Cultural Studies: Stories of Unsettled Relations*," ed. Sue Thornham (London: Arnold, 2000), 5–6.

[2] It should be noted that Feyl disparages the genre of the historical novel, at least as she believes it to be currently defined. In the course of my interview with her in August 2008, she sarcastically associated the historical novel with trivial fictions, whose covers are characterized by boldly printed gold letters and which might be written by "every administrative bureaucrat" (*jeder Verwaltungsangestellte*) who wishes to express his image of the Middle Ages. In contrast, she stated that she situates her novels in the eighteenth century because it was marked by a progressive attitude toward women, allowing her to make the events and people she depicts into a "metaphor for today." Despite Feyl's misgivings, and despite the concerns I expressed in the introduction regarding the limitations of the term "historical novel" (as delineated by previous scholars) for the works I am discussing in *Imagining the Age of Goethe*, Feyl's strong attention to period ambience and detail — a key factor in almost all definitions of the historical novel — allows this term to be used for her fictions anchored in the German eighteenth century.

[3] Renate Feyl, *Idylle mit Professor*, 6th ed. (Munich: Diana, 2007); *Die profanen Stunden des Glücks*, 7th ed. (Munich: Diana, 2007); *Das sanfte Joch der Vortrefflichkeit*, 9th ed. (Munich: Diana, 2007); *Aussicht auf bleibende Helle: Die Königin und der Philosoph* (Munich: Diana, 2008).

[4] Brigitte Struzyk, *Caroline unterm Freiheitsbaum: Ansichtssachen* (Darmstadt: Luchterhand, 1988).

[5] Renate Feyl, "Die Autorin im Gespräch," in *Aussicht auf bleibende Helle*, n.p.

6 Michael Holquist, introduction to *The Dialogic Imagination: Four Essays*, by M. M. Bakhtin, ed. Michael Holquist, trans. Caryl Emerson and Michael Holquist (Austin: U of Texas P, 1981), xix, xx.

7 Helen Bridge, *Women's Writing and Historiography in the GDR* (Oxford: Clarendon, 2002), 145.

8 Bridge, *Women's Writing and Historiography in the GDR*, 148.

9 J. H. Reid, *Writing without Taboos: The New East German Literature* (New York: Berg 1990), 189.

10 Following the practice of Helen Bridge (see note 7), I will refer to Feyl's female protagonists by their first names in order to distinguish them from their husbands, who are referred to by their last names.

11 Reid, *Writing without Taboos*, 189.

12 Martens, *The Promised Land?*, 198.

13 Kathleen L. Komar, "Klytemnestra in Germany: Re-visions of a Female Archetype by Christa Reinig and Christine Brückner," *Germanic Review* 69 (1994): 20.

14 Myra Jehlen, "Archimedes and the Paradox of Feminist Criticism," in *The "Signs" Reader: Women, Gender & Scholarship*, ed. Elizabeth Abel and Emily K. Abel (Chicago: U of Chicago P, 1983), 76. This passage is also cited by Komar in order to clarify Weigel's perspective. See "Klytemnestra in Germany," 26n5.

15 Arnd Bohm, "Authority and Authorship in Luise Adelgunde Gottsched's *Das Testament*," *Lessing Yearbook* 18 (1986): 129–40. A broader treatment of the development of her attitude toward female authorship and other gender-related issues with which she was engaged is provided by Susanne Kord, *Little Detours: The Letters and Plays of Luise Gottsched (1713–1762)* (Rochester, NY: Camden House, 2000).

16 See in this regard Bridge, *Women's Writing and Historiography in the GDR*, who regards Gottsched's literary patriotism in the novel as corollary to his embrace of poetry as an educational tool with a politically didactic role to play. In Bridge's view, "Gottsched takes on the role that the SED attributed to authors," and becomes an advocate of socialist realism *avant la lettre* (151). I agree with Bridge's view, but still believe Feyl intends Gottsched's embrace of a specifically German literature to be regarded positively.

17 Reid, *Writing without Taboos*, 189.

18 See Bridge, *Women's Writing*, 146–47.

19 Todd Kontje, *Women, the Novel, and the German Nation 1771–1871: Domestic Fiction in the Fatherland* (Cambridge: Cambridge UP, 1998), 11.

20 Martha Woodmansee, *The Author, Art, and the Market: Rereading the History of Aesthetics* (New York: Columbia UP, 1994), 104.

21 Veronica C. Richel, *Luise Gottsched: A Reconsideration* (Bern: Peter Lang, 1973), 7.

22 See note 15.

23 Woodmansee, *The Author, Art, and the Market*, 8 and 103–9. A more balanced view of Wieland's preface to *Sternheim* is provided by Claire Baldwin, *The*

Emergence of the Modern German Novel: Christoph Martin Wieland, Sophie von La Roche, and Maria Anna Sagar (Rochester, NY: Camden House, 2002), 105–12.

[24] Woodmansee, *The Author, Art, and the Market*, 103, and Feyl, *Die profanen Stunden des Glücks*, 299.

[25] Silvia Bovenschen, *Die imaginierte Weiblichkeit: Exemplarische Untersuchungen zu kulturgeschichtlichen und literarischen Präsentationsformen des Weiblichen* (Frankfurt am Main: Suhrkamp, 1980), 199. Both Woodmansee (*The Author, Art, and the Market*, 108) and Feyl (*Die profanen Stunden des Glücks*, 79–80) reference *Sternheim*'s influence on Goethe's first novel.

[26] C. M. Wieland, "Der Herausgeber an die Leser," in Sophie von La Roche, *Melusinens Sommerabende* (1806; repr. Eschborn: Dietmar Klotz, 1992), np.

[27] Kontje, *Women, the Novel, and the German Nation*, 11.

[28] The historical Schiller's attempt to bring about this triangle to serve his competing needs is particularly evident in a letter, clearly drawn upon by Feyl, addressed to Caroline while she was still married to Beulwitz and to the as-yet-unmarried Charlotte. The letter is dated 15 November 1789. See Friedrich Schiller, *Werke: Nationalausgabe*, ed. Eberhard Haufe, vol. 25 (Weimar: Hermann Böhlaus Nachfolger, 1979), 327–31.

[29] Jay Rosellini, "Zur Funktionsbestimmung des historischen Romans in der DDR-Literatur," in *DDR-Roman und Literaturgesellschaft*, 67–68.

[30] On this ambiguity on the part of German intellectuals on both sides of the wall, see Karoline von Oppen, "'Man muß jetzt laut schreien, um gehört zu werden': Stefan Heym, Walter Jens, Helga Königsdorf: An Intellectual Opposition?," in *Textual Responses to German Unification: Processing Historical and Social Change in Literature and Film*, ed. Carol Anne Costabile-Heming, Rachel J. Halverson, and Kristie A. Foell (Berlin: Walter de Gruyter, 2001), 109–29.

[31] See Lukács, "Erzählen oder Beschreiben?," in *Probleme des Realismus* (Berlin: Aufbau, 1955), 103–45.

[32] Reingard Nethersole, "Models of Globalization," *PMLA* 116 (2001): 640.

[33] Bird, *Recasting Historical Women*, 153.

[34] Bird, *Recasting Historical Women*, 153.

[35] See, for example, Bird, *Recasting Historical Women*, 87–113; Bridge, *Women's Writing*, 154–66; Maja Razbojnikova-Frateva, *Fiktionale Frauenbiographien in der Gegenwartsliteratur: Das Reden vom Geschlecht im Text hinter dem Text* (Berlin: trafo, 2003), 133–45. Razbojnikova-Frateva also provides a positive analysis of Feyl's *Idylle mit Professor* (90–107).

[36] See Bird, *Recasting Historical Women*, 98–99.

[37] These positive fictional treatments of Georg Forster by earlier GDR (male) writers are discussed in some detail and juxtaposed with Struzyk's treatment of this figure by Franziska Meyer, *Avantgarde im Hinterland: Caroline Schlegel-Schelling in der DDR-Literatur* (New York: Peter Lang, 1999).

[38] See Bird, *Recasting Historical Women*, 101–3, and Bridge, *Women's Writing*, 156–59.

4: Goethe Contra and Pro

THE PREVIOUS CHAPTERS OF THIS BOOK have hinted at a consistent antipathy toward Germany's most canonical writer, Johann Wolfgang Goethe, in German historical fiction from the late 1960s to the present. Chapter 1 examined Christa Wolf's *Kein Ort. Nirgends* in the context of the German Democratic Republic's embrace of Early Romanticism and its concomitant refutation of a postwar critical orthodoxy led by Georg Lukács, which valorized Goethe and the values of Weimar Classicism. In chapter 2, we saw that fictional treatments of Friedrich Hölderlin in both East and West Germany highlighted the cruel slights this poet received at the hands of Goethe. Goethe's subsequent refusal to aid Hölderlin's career was shown to have played a major role in driving him to madness. In Peter Weiss's play about the Swabian poet, Germany's "poet-prince" is portrayed even more negatively, as not only vengeful and unwilling to get past a petty grudge, but also as a toady to the nobility and the emerging bourgeois capitalist elite. In chapter 3, we noted how in Renate Feyl's novels on Sophie La Roche and Caroline von Wolzogen, Goethe was characterized as rather self-serving and egotistical, although Feyl mitigates this in her novels by casting him as a somewhat misunderstood victim, both of Sophie La Roche's failure to recognize his early genius and of Weimar society's vindictive attitude toward his common-law relationship with Christiane Vulpius. The following chapter will demonstrate that the treatment of Goethe as an iconic figure by Germany's fiction writers from the late 1960s to the present day has also been consistently negative when Goethe was a primary protagonist in novels and plays, regardless of whether the author was a citizen of the GDR, FRG, or the present day "Berlin Republic." However, I will conclude by showing how a number of recent works portray Goethe in a relatively positive manner.

This chapter will focus on works in which Goethe serves as the primary — or primary male — character. While Goethe has appeared in a large number of texts — particularly, but not exclusively, in German literature[1] — the present chapter will focus on a cross-section from the 1970s to the present day, consistent with this book's method of illustrating significant trends in recent German *Goethezeit* fiction through a close examination of selected works. Because the GDR was even more focused than the FRG on its cultural patrimony and how that patrimony should shape literary discourse in that country, Goethe fiction by East German authors is strongly represented in my investigation and will be analyzed at the outset of the chapter. I will begin by examining Peter Hacks's comedy *Ein Gespräch im Hause Stein über den abwesenden Herrn von Goethe*[2] (A conversation in the Stein house concerning the absent Goethe, 1974). This play is presented as a monologue by Goethe's erstwhile lover Charlotte von Stein but reveals the foibles and peccadilloes of both partners. The next work to be examined also focuses on the Stein-Goethe relationship. It was composed rather late in the GDR's existence: Johanna Hoffmann's novel *Charlotte von Stein: Goethe und ich werden niemals Freunde*[3] (Charlotte von Stein: Goethe and I will never be friends, 1988). Contrary to Hacks in his play, Hoffmann wrote her novel from a decidedly feminist perspective, and this is also the case with another work from the GDR elucidated in this chapter, Sigrid Damm's semi-fictional biography of Goethe's sister, *Cornelia Goethe* (1987).[4] I will then look at two works by the controversial author Martin Walser: the radio play *In Goethes Hand: Szenen aus dem 19. Jahrhundert*[5] (In Goethe's hand: Scenes from the nineteenth century, 1982), written when Walser was a resident of the FRG and concerning Goethe's relationship with his longtime amanuensis Johann Peter Eckermann, and the recent novel *Ein liebender Mann*[6] (A loving man, 2008), on the elderly Goethe's productive infatuation with a nineteen-year-old Ulrike von Levetzow. In another Eckermann novel, Jens Sparschuh's *Der große Coup: Aus den geheimen Tage- und Nachtbüchern des Johann Peter Eckermann*[7] (The great coup: From the secret day and night diaries of Johann Peter Eckermann, 1987), Goethe's secretary becomes the agent who steers Goethe's reception as the most immortal of Germany's writers by manipulating the tone and content of what was to be published as the *Gespräche mit Goethe* (Conversations with Goethe) in 1836, and Goethe comes across here as an intemperate dupe. In Henning Boëtius's novella *Tod in Weimar*[8] (Death in Weimar, 1999), Goethe is also duped, this time by a fictionalized Bettine Brentano, who arranges for her son's successful seduction of the poet shortly before the latter's death. The final work that strips the poet of his hagiographic status is Hanns-Josef Ortheil's novel *Faustinas Küsse*[9] (Faustina's kisses, 1998), an imaginative account of Goethe's life in Italy in the years from 1786 to 1787. The generally negative presentation of Goethe in recent German-language fiction does not constitute an exclusive trend, and this chapter concludes with three works in which the poet is presented in a mostly positive, even heroic light: Otto Böhmer's novel *Der junge Herr Goethe*[10] (The young Mr. Goethe, 1999); Rafik Schami's novel, also published in the Goethe Year 1999 and co-authored with Uwe-Michael Gutzschhahn; *Der geheime Bericht über den Dichter Goethe, der eine Prüfung auf einer arabischen Insel bestand*[11] (The secret report on the poet Goethe, who passed a test on an Arabian island); and Robert Löhr's novels *Das Erlkönig-Manöver*[12] (The earl-king maneuver, 2007) and *Das Hamlet-Komplott*[13] (The Hamlet conspiracy, 2010).

The Postwar Cult of Goethe

Before beginning to examine these plays and novels, it will be useful to examine briefly the historical foundations from which anti-Goethe fiction has emerged, and then to acknowledge that, particularly in the GDR, irreverent adaptations of Goethe's poetic oeuvre were considered a part of the rebellion against Goethe. As noted in the introduction, even before the war, exiled authors such as Thomas Mann persistently extolled Goethe as the most cogent face of cosmopolitanism, of transnational tolerance and exchange, as a counterweight to the xenophobia and crass nationalism of the Third Reich. After the fall of the Nazi empire, Goethe continued to serve as the ultimate point of reference in the attempt to rehabilitate Germany's image both at home and abroad, to reinfuse the nation — in both its Eastern and Western sectors — with the putatively humanist values of Weimar Classicism, of which Goethe was the most famous exemplar. He became, from 1945 until the late 1960s rebellions, Germany's ultimate historical authority figure, until both East and West German authors decided that he, having been embraced by their father's generation, was altogether too authoritarian.

The establishment of Goethe as a cultural beacon of light to whom his current fellow Germans must turn in the nation's darkest hour began immediately after the war. Scholars and politicians alike sought to recrown Goethe as the prince of the German *Kulturnation* — the cultural rather than political nation — hearkening back to the pre-unification, pre-militarist, indeed pre-Napoleonic past when Germans supposedly saw their country united not by politics, the army, or even ethnicity, but by its language and its culture. A new veneration of Goethe as Europe's ultimate cosmopolitan icon was seen as a way to rebuild the nation's spiritual links to the world at large. Fritz Strich expressed the hope in his *Goethe und die Weltliteratur* (Goethe and world literature, 1946) that the venerable concept of world literature itself, as coined by Goethe and discussed in the previous chapter, could make a major contribution to reestablishing a transnational intellectual milieu that would help overcome the virulent nationalism that had gripped the Western world from the 1930s until the end of Second World War. Even the historian Friedrich Meinecke, who had argued in *Weltbürgertum und Nationalstaat* that Germany's era as a *Kulturnation* marked an immature phase in the nation's history on its way to becoming a genuine, politically unified state, claimed after the war that Goethe and his heritage could lead to a revival of Germany's respected membership in the world at large. To be sure, German intellectuals and authors such as Friedrich Wolf, Theodor Plievier, and Theodor Adorno questioned whether a retreat to Goethean principles could really overcome the legacy of Nazi barbarism, and whether the Goethean ideals of *Kultur* and *Bildung* were really such a potent force

for a German renaissance — they had not only proven ineffective in pre-
venting the Holocaust and other Third Reich atrocities, but they were
even embraced by Nazis who murdered by day and reverently listened to
Beethoven at night. Nevertheless, the year 1949 marked both the two-
hundredth anniversary of Goethe's birth and the birth of Germany's two
political states, the GDR and the FRG. Functionaries from both brand-
new countries tripped over themselves in their eagerness to claim Goethe
as the exemplar of their particular nation. GDR intellectuals and play-
wrights such as Johannes Becher and Alexander Abusch went so far as to
argue that Goethe's thought was not only a precursor to Marxist dialectics, but that it also foreshadowed the Russian Revolution (this in spite of
Goethe's antipathy to the French Revolution). In the West, Goethe was
celebrated more for his supposedly timeless cultural ideals and contributions to science and morphology than for his putative ideology. The visit
of Thomas Mann, Goethe's self-styled successor, was the cultural highlight of the anniversary year 1949 in both countries.[14]

Karl Robert Mandelkow has noted that the hagiographic reception of Goethe in West Germany was largely restricted to educational
institutions and private readings; young FRG authors took little notice
of him. An early polemic against Goethe was issued by Walser in 1964
when he claimed that Goethe's plays could be characterized as a kind of
humanism without history, or even a humanism directed against history.
Goethe came to be seen increasingly in the West German intellectual
scene as, at best, a reactionary aesthete, and, at worst, as a forerunner of
Nazi barbarism and purveyor of its cultural décor.[15] In the East, as we
have seen, antipathy toward Goethe was largely generated in response
to GDR political and cultural orthodoxy. These trends will be further
explored in our discussion of the individual texts where Goethe functions as a protagonist or primary narrative object. First, however, it is
worth noting that Goethe was also instrumentalized against the GDR's
self-representation in highly satiric adaptations of his work. Reworkings
of classical German texts, including those of Goethe, constituted a central trend in twentieth-century German literature, as Gundula Sharman
has argued.[16] York-Gothart Mix has eloquently demonstrated that two
of these reworkings, Ulrich Plenzdorf's popular adaptation of *Werther*
entitled *Die neuen Leiden des jungen W.* (The New Sufferings of Young
W., 1973; first conceived as a play in 1968) and Volker Braun's various
Hinze und Kunze texts that began their evolution in the late 1960s,
represent the first successful attempts to subvert the GDR cultivation of
Goethe's "classical patrimony" as an immutable element of socialism's
national culture and its Lukács-inspired effort to use Goethe as a cudgel
against the allegedly decadent and formalist trends in modernism. By
productively reconfiguring Goethe's texts to make them more relevant
for a contemporary context, Plenzdorf and Braun problematized the

GDR's rigid, ossified postulation of a timeless classical heritage. Plenz-dorf's anti-hero Edgar Wibeau draws on Werther's letters to castigate the philistine narrowness of 1960s GDR society, and Braun parodies a passage from the second part of *Faust* to highlight the inability of the individual in the GDR to achieve genuine maturity (*Mündigkeit*) in a society regulated by dictates from an elite, authoritarian political caste. Plenzdorf and Braun engaged in polemics against their nation's fixation on classicism with its ritualistically invoked paeans to harmony as promulgated during the Age of Goethe — a harmony to be realized in the socialist future. Goethe's texts are thus mobilized against the Goethe-worshiping GDR state, and redeployed as subversive weapons in the struggle for aesthetic autonomy.[17] By the mid-1970s, a fictional-ized Goethe himself, a Goethe antithetical to the official GDR image of a cosmopolitan, tolerant, humanist paragon, became an agonistic instru-ment in this struggle.

Goethe was also the object of persiflage in 1950s West Germany. Arno Schmidt's desacralizing, chronologically playful treatment of the poet in his 1957 novella *Goethe und Einer Seiner Bewunderer*, a rela-tively obscure work, has already been mentioned in the introduction, but Goethe was also projected into a far more deleterious time-bending polit-ical conjunction in the most celebrated fictional narrative published in the FRG during this decade, Grass's *Die Blechtrommel* (The tin drum, 1959). Grass treats Goethe with parodistic disdain at several points in the novel, in a manner suggesting a certain affinity between the poet's supposed love of formal order and National Socialist attempts at attaining such har-mony through genocide.[18] This tendency culminates in the dream of the novel's central protagonist, Oskar Matzerath, who envisions himself on a merry-go-round along with thousands of children destined to be victims of the genocide. The two men propelling the carousel, by tossing in coins to make it turn, are Rasputin, who represents mass anarchy and mob rebellion, and Goethe, who consolidates "the forces of order."[19] Oskar's dream fantasy clearly suggests that Grass saw in National Socialism a fatal blend of rigid, homogenizing orderliness and chaotic popular violence. The metonymic instrumentalization of Goethe as a cipher for Nazi elimi-nationist regimentation foreshadows Goethe's irreverent treatment in the FRG later in the twentieth century and in the Berlin Republic from the 1990s to the present.

Goethe in Absentia: Peter Hacks

Hacks wrote adaptations of Goethe's plays: *Das Jahrmarktsfest zu Plun-dersweilen* (The market festival at Plundersweilen, 1976) and *Pandora, Drama nach J. W. von Goethe* (Pandora: Drama adapted from J. W. von Goethe, 1981). Philip Brady has characterized these adaptations as

"Hacks's defence of Goethe against what he sees as the depredations of modernizers,"[20] and thus clearly at odds with the reworkings of Plenzdorf and Braun. Nevertheless, though the only speaker in Hacks's *Ein Gespräch* is an unreliable narrator (she addresses her remarks to her husband, but he is a lifeless puppet) — Charlotte von Stein, who has just been abandoned by Goethe in October 1786 when, unbeknownst to her, he departed on his Italian journey — *Ein Gespräch* itself is hardly a defense of Goethe. Stein's barely suppressed rage at Goethe's sudden disappearance — only at the conclusion of the play does a letter arrive indicating Goethe's presence in Venice — leads, to be sure, to her creation of an image of the poet clearly intended by Hacks to strike the reader or spectator as highly distorted. Stein's class prejudices and her superficial view of poetry are on clear display. She claims Goethe was a coarse, vulgar, Storm-and-Stress ruffian when he arrived in Weimar, and she saw it as her task to give him the polish necessary for intercourse with polite, courtly Weimar society. Responding to Goethe's reputed eager desire to convert the human race to genuine humanity — an image of Goethe clearly cherished and unquestioned in orthodox GDR circles — Stein displays her reactionary side in revealing that she informed Goethe how progress would surely come but that she was happy to live where it would *not* come, and calling into question the very idea of humanity: "Humanität, was ist das Rechtes? Brauchte das Ding einen lateinischen Namen, wenn es sich fühlen ließe?" (424–25; Humanity, what is that really? Would this thing need a Latin name if it could be felt?). Her continued erotic attachment to Goethe is revealed at key moments when her stuttering and clumsiness belie her self-representation as resolute in resisting his advances (especially 404, 419, and 445).

Anna Kuhn has argued that in portraying Stein as deeply repressed, fearful of men, and ultimately deluded in her judgments of Goethe (whom, in Kuhn's view, Hacks intended to demythologize and render more human in this monodrama), Hacks upholds the GDR's underlying patriarchal attitudes toward women.[21] While Kuhn effectively sustains her argument, the play does not only humanize Goethe, but it also reveals his foibles, which were overlooked in the GDR hagiography of the poet. Or, more accurately, in humanizing Goethe, Hacks engages in an early display of his weaknesses and idiosyncrasies. In his afterword to the volume of Hacks's selected dramas cited here, the GDR intellectual Peter Fix indicates that the nineteen-year-old Hacks took note in a class paper of the horrified bourgeois response to Mann's *Lotte in Weimar* — expecting reverential treatment of the "poet-prince," the middle-class viewers accused Mann of defaming their idol and creating a disgusting, even dangerous work. In contrast, Fix claims the socialist state engages in the task of dismantling the sort of "Weihrauchkessel" (incense burner) the bourgeoisie were accustomed to find employed in the sanctification of

Goethe, and that "we" are undisturbed by the various representations when Goethe is the chief personage in a socialist drama (481). In his own notes to the play, Hacks asserts that he does not personally identify with Goethe, but that what he found compelling in the Stein-Goethe relationship was its "cold heat": The lovers were bound by neither inclination, common interests, common goals, nor customs. Contrary to Damm, who, as we will see, embraced the contemporary psychoanalytic view of Goethe as deeply neurotic and possessive, Hacks finds that he was happy even though he was generally in despair, while Stein was generally in despair but presumably lacked Goethe's capacity for happiness. Despite explicitly refuting Weiss's view that Goethe was a reactionary "defender of the status quo," and even finding plausible the thesis Stein proposed in her drama *Dido* that Goethe was part of a triumvirate of Jacobin conspirators, Hacks emphasizes that Goethe was fully prepared to drive the tenant farmers of the Steins' Kochberg estate into bankruptcy in order to raise sufficient tax funds. However, Hacks acknowledges the absence of a political component in *Ein Gespräch*, claiming a drama is not a work of history.[22] The essay makes clear that Hacks views Goethe as a genius but not as a socialist *avant la lettre*, as prior socialists intellectuals like Abusch and Becher claimed.

Hacks asserts that Stein's disagreement concerning the Kochberg taxes led to her break with Goethe,[23] but this issue does not come up in the play. As it develops, Stein drops layer after layer of a protective denial of her love for Goethe, and is crushed at the conclusion when his missive from Italy contains no profession of love, but only superficial pleasantries (454). While the stream of invective she utters concerning her former beloved throughout the course of *Ein Gespräch* is clearly revealed to be a cocoon belying her continued passion for him, Hacks does not intend her account of actual episodes that reveal his character to be regarded as mere invention. Thus, when she describes Goethe as acting like a petulant child, grinding his teeth, thrashing about on the floor, and pulling at his hair when she upbraids him concerning some matter by way of illustrating his "Anspruch auf uneingeschränkte Selbstsucht" (416–17; claim to unbound selfishness), there is no reason for the reader or spectator to doubt her veracity, especially since Goethe's titanic egotism has been historically established. His unexpected professions of happiness at the weather in Italy in the letter Stein reads at the close of the play are consistent with his neurotic sensitivity to and obsession with atmospheric conditions, as evident in her description of his chronic dissatisfaction with all seasonal meteorological variations in Weimar (425–26). In his comments on *Ein Gespräch*, Hacks emphasized his effort to avoid treating Goethe as a paradigmatic genius, but acknowledges that Goethe corresponds to the genus of genius in certain essential points.[24] Self-centeredness, egotism, vanity, and narcissism:

These are the attributes commonly associated with genius, and whatever her unreliability as narrator, Stein presents a convincing case that Goethe fully embodied these characteristics of the great man, the poet towering above mere mortals.

While Goethe's rather callous attitude toward the plight of Kochberg's lower class does not come to expression in this play, it does manifest itself in another drama by Hacks, the first dramolette in the tetralogy *Musen* (Muses, 1979). In this episode, Goethe is conversing with his secretary, Friedrich Wilhelm Riemer, concerning work on a number of projects, including the further composition of *Faust* after a thirteen-year hiatus. Their conversation is interrupted by Charlotte Hoyer, the aggressive maid of the Goethe household and eponymous focus of the piece. She has actually managed to intimidate Goethe's own industrious, down-to-earth housewife, Christiane Vulpius, who insists Goethe fire the servant. Despite Goethe's efforts to avoid Hoyer by hiding, the plan goes awry and Goethe gets into an argument with her concerning the household's menu for the day. The angry Goethe confirms her firing and gives her a certificate of discharge, attesting to her two years of service but also underscoring her stubborn recalcitrance. When he hands her this certificate, she tears it to shreds in front of him and leaves the room in uncharacteristic silence. The enraged Goethe then begins to draft a denunciation addressed to the Weimar police director, announcing to his secretary: "Und sehen Sie, Riemer, bevor ich keinen geeigneten Koch gefunden habe, werde ich den *Faust* nicht schreiben"[25] (And see, Riemer, before I have found a suitable cook, I will not write Faust). As Manfred Durzak has noted, the scene reveals Goethe's impotence in this collision with a reality he cannot adroitly manage, and his recognition that he will be unable to continue work on his masterpiece until he can find a cook is to be regarded as a confession of failure, confirming the image in *Ein Gespräch* of a genius thrown out of balance by mundane annoyances.[26] One can add that the scene with Charlotte Hoyer confirms the image of Goethe in Hacks's essay of a man of means who has little empathy for the tribulations of the lower class and cannot abide their disagreements with him. Thus, Hacks's Goethe is hardly portrayed as a forerunner and model citizen of the proletarian GDR state. Mandelkow has noted, based on Hacks's essay "Saure Feste" (Sour festivals, 1979), that this East German playwright constituted an exception to the GDR intellectuals' embrace of Romanticism and concomitant refutation of Goethe. In this essay, Hacks contrasted the Weimar-Classical embrace of a reality-based ideal of duty with the Romantics' supposed surrender to the temptation to replace "Wirklichkeit durch Utopien des Unwirklichen"[27] (reality through utopias of unreality). In his plays, by contrast, Hacks portrays a Goethe as distant from quotidian reality as any Romantic may have been.

The Goethe-Stein Relationship from Another Angle

Though Johanna Hoffmann's novel *Charlotte von Stein*, on the relationship between Stein and Goethe, was published very late in the GDR's existence (1988), and thus at a time when, as Mix states, the cultural politics of that country were hardly in a position to be actively enforced,[28] it adhered more closely to Marxist dictums than did Hacks's play, and Helen Bridge has noted that *Charlotte von Stein* pays a "conventionally Marxist attention to class relations." While Hoffmann intends the reader to empathize with Stein's limited opportunities as a woman, her tyrannical behavior toward her servants diminishes any positive image of her, and "the idea that Charlotte belongs to a social class whose role in history is almost at an end pervades the novel."[29] In *Ein Gespräch*, her class prejudices are more manifest in her attitude that Goethe was, at base, a bourgeois parvenu than in any disparaging remarks about her servants or tenant farmers. Indeed, Hacks's Stein senses that Goethe actually assumed that she could have been eternally *his* maid, even though she felt also elevated by his love (441). Rather, it is the class arrogance of Goethe that comes to the fore in *Musen*, though the portrayal of his cruelty toward Charlotte Hoyer is secondary, as Durzak indicates, to his representation as a lofty genius who is helpless, indeed impotent, when it comes to dealing with mundane matters. Of course, there is also a practical reason for this difference in the treatment of class issues by Hacks and Hoffmann. *Ein Gespräch* is a brief dramatic representation of one moment in this historically significant liaison, a snapshot of Stein's feelings toward the departed Goethe. Dimensions extraneous to the portrayal of her conflicted emotions at this moment would have lessened the play's comic/dramatic impact. *Charlotte von Stein*, on the other hand, is a novel that traces their affair from beginning to end, and is thus able to examine other facets of the two chief protagonists' personalities and attitudes.

Goethe, as well as Stein's husband Josias and the other figures who constellated around Goethe and Stein from the time of their first meeting to Goethe's departure for Italy (and briefly after his return) are also fleshed out and given active roles in Hoffmann's novel. Nevertheless, Stein is the text's chief point of reference. The subtitle of this work — *Goethe und ich werden niemals Freunde* — leads one to expect a first-person narration, but this is only the case for half the chapters. The opening episode is entitled "Die Nacht vom 8. zum 9. September 1788" (The Night from September 8 to September 9). Goethe has returned to Germany after having abandoned Weimar, and thus Kochberg and Stein, for his Italian journey, and this chapter is constituted by her lonely, first-person ruminations on her affair with the poet, chiefly marked by her regret that it came to pass. The second chapter, "November 1775," finds Stein dining with the Weimar court, and the chief object of discussion is the impending arrival of the "unbändiges Genie" (uncontrollable genius) in the duchy (13). All subsequent chapters observe this alternating pattern with respect to narrative voice and time: a first-person reflection, entitled "Die Nacht," is followed by a third-person account of key events marking the course of the Stein-Goethe liaison, with the heading of the month and year the event took place. The third-person chapters stretch from November 1775 to 5 September 1788, when Stein sees Goethe for the first time after his return from Italy (this is the only such episode with a specific date), and it is clear that the first-person chapters take place during the September evening marking Stein's awareness that the relationship is truly at an end. With the exception of the more broadly conceived ruminations of the first (and only dated) "night" segment, they delineate Stein's reflections on the events of the immediately preceding third-person segment. This unusual alternating pattern allows Hoffmann to present a fuller picture of Stein's psyche, from the inside and the outside, as it were. Her interactions with Goethe are thus externally described by an omniscient narrator who injects neither irony nor subjective nuances that might call her objective reliability into question, and by Stein's first-person voice, which seems designed to reflect the historical Charlotte von Stein's ambivalences and regrets.

The multidimensionality afforded by Hoffmann's use of a holistic representation of Stein's affair with Goethe, and her feelings as the affair evolves and concludes, cannot be confused with historical veracity. At the outset of his essay on *Ein Gespräch*, Hacks claimed: "Ich erzähle die wahre Geschichte, die Geschichte, wie sie stattgefunden hat"[30] (I narrate the true story, the story, as it took place), but his exploration has no more objective truth content than does Hoffmann's, because only Goethe's letters and diaries give a full account of the relationship; the historical Charlotte von Stein demanded her letters back from Goethe and destroyed them. Only Goethe's feelings are available for a comprehensive account (though they are themselves not fully reliable), but it is Stein's psyche that is most closely explored by Hacks and Hoffmann. Of course, some facts about the historical Charlotte von Stein's state of mind seem clearly established; For example, she apparently had no inkling that Goethe was departing Weimar for an extended period of time when he left for Italy.[31] Bridge accurately notes that "Hoffmann endows her Charlotte with a modern feminist consciousness which enables her to interpret her relationship with Goethe in terms of their society's gender roles."[32] Thus, Stein reflects that women could achieve as much as male court officials if they were educated to assume such responsibilities. They would also be equal to men intellectually if they were not trapped by the burdens of domesticity: "Gäbe man uns die Zeit, uns mit etwas anderem zu beschäftigen als mit Haus, Kindern, Küche, Musik, Mode und all den Dingen, die uns zwar dauernd beanspruchen, innerlich aber leer lassen, dann wären wir nicht weniger klug als die Männer" (40; If one were to give us the time to occupy ourselves with something else than house, children, kitchen, music, fashion, and the things that constantly claim our time but leave us empty inside, then we would not be less intelligent than men).

With respect to Goethe, Stein's growing love turns to hatred after his departure. She is as baffled, hurt, and surprised at his abrupt, unannounced disappearance as the historical Charlotte von Stein was, though she expresses an unmitigated hatred — "Wolf, ich hasse dich!" (Wolf, I hate you!) — that the reserved, subtle, eighteenth-century Frau von Stein would not have articulated. In the same passage, she feels an inner rage at a request Goethe sends from Italy that she make a copy of his travel sketches, asking whether Goethe now thinks of her as one of his servants (213), a sentiment we also saw expressed by Hacks's Charlotte von Stein. The best example of her treatment of the underclass occurs when she accuses her tenant farmer, with no evidence, of mismanaging Kochberg's harvest so that little profit was made, implying possible embezzlement on his part. Stein uses the distancing third-person form of address, and his entreaties about his family and the difficulty of finding new employment in the winter bring the cruel reply that his children are of no concern to her (24–25). This is the best example of what Bridge referred to as Hoffmann's conventional Marxist treatment of class relations, but Goethe, in a different context, also appears in a less-than-flattering light. Stein accuses him of hypocrisy for not allowing Weimar's Prince Konstantin to wed a woman of the lesser nobility, but Goethe pleads that the prince is second in line to inherit the ducal throne, making a marriage between the two young people, who are deeply in love with each other, an impossibility (126–27). On other hand, Goethe is unhappy at having to raise taxes on the masses in order to underwrite the court's festivities and at having to conscript soldiers for the ducal army (133–34). Nevertheless, his egotism and lack of tact in his dealings with Stein are clearly thematized in the novel. His tactless behavior toward Stein after returning from Italy is most cogently expressed not by her, from whom it would be expected, but by her cuckolded husband, Josias, who is given agency in Hoffmann's text after his stint as a lifeless stuffed puppet on Hacks's stage. Josias von Stein is annoyed about Goethe's abrupt departure from their home after a brief sojourn with other guests in Kochberg: "Mochte er doch sein Blumenmädchen kommen lassen, sooft er wollte. Mußte er sich deshalb seiner langjährigen und gealterten Freundin gegenüber so distanziert verhalten?" (228–29; He could have had his flower girl come as often as he wanted. Did that mean he had to behave so distantly toward his aged friend of many years standing?). Clearly the answer is no, for Hoffmann's Goethe is cast as a charismatic genius lacking in delicacy regarding the feelings of a former lover.

Interestingly, the modern feminist *avant la lettre* whom Bridge accurately discerns in Hoffmann's Charlotte von Stein rarely comes to the fore in her interactions with — and, in the "night" chapters, ruminations on — Goethe. The previously cited passage in which she asserts that women could fulfill the duties expected of court officials were they given the time and the freedom from domestic chores are prompted by her experiences in Duchess Anna Amalia's inner circle, and are unconnected to Goethe's later arrival. This episode represents the novel's most direct enunciation of feminist principles, though Stein is sometimes exasperated that Goethe, always demanding of her time and energy, fails to appreciate the obligations placed upon her as wife, mother, lady at court, and manager of the Kochberg estate. The historical Stein expressed the right of women to independence and self-determination subtly, through her own poetry and drama, often written as a critical riposte to Goethe's all-too-self-sacrificing heroines, such as Iphigenie.[33]

Sigrid Damm's *Cornelia Goethe* offers a much more unsparing look at Goethe from a feminist perspective. Hoffmann's Goethe describes his sister's marriage as a loveless union undertaken to escape the narrowness of her parents' household (43), and Stein speculates that Goethe feared his sister's children may have inherited her unfortunate disposition, which she feels might explain his greater attachment to her own son, Fritz (165–66). Stein's harshest criticism of her former lover is that he denied his terminally ill sister a last, comforting letter because he found her suffering oppressive, much as he was cold toward the Storm-and-Stress playwright Reinhold Lenz after he began to display signs of madness (231). *Cornelia Goethe* is harsher in its portrayal of Goethe through its examination of his complex relationship to his sister — much harsher, in fact, than Damm's treatment of Goethe's relationship to Lenz in her earlier biography on this latter tragic figure.[34]

Goethe as Evil Brother

As is the case with her book on Lenz, *Cornelia Goethe* is sometimes classified as a biography, but recent critics have cogently argued that this latter work cannot be so easily categorized. With its table of contents and relatively dry, objective style, the book on Lenz has not been treated by most literary scholars as belonging to any genre beyond that of literary biography, and the same is true of Damm's more recent examination of Goethe's relationship with his wife, Christiane Vulpius, a commercially and critically successful work entitled *Christiane und Goethe: Eine Recherche* (Christiane and Goethe: An investigation, 1998), as well as her biography of Schiller, *Das Leben des Friedrich Schiller: Eine Wanderung* (The life of Friedrich Schiller: An excursion, 2004). Her more recent *Goethes letzte Reise* (Goethe's last journey, 2007) is written in a somewhat speculative vein, posing questions for which she provides no definitive answers, as is the case with *Cornelia*

Goethe. Goethes letzte Reise treats Goethe's later years in a relatively benign fashion, and, like *Christiane und Goethe* but unlike *Cornelia Goethe,* is structured as a scholarly tome, with an extensive list of works cited. *Cornelia Goethe* can be characterized as a "hybrid biography," a term coined by Ina Schabert but pithily summarized by Dorrit Cohn as a "casting away" of "all historiographic inhibitions," applicable to works marked "by their unlimited irradiation of the minds of their historical subjects."[35] *Cornelia Goethe* does not treat the poet and his sister with quite such imaginative abandon, but it has justifiably been treated by critics as among the significant works of late GDR historical fiction. Hannes Krauss, for example, categorizes *Cornelia Goethe* as "eine Mischform aus wissenschaftlicher und fiktionaler Prosa ('faction')" (a mixed form out of scientific and fictional prose ["faction"]), which adheres to what he terms a genuinely Marxist objective to think through the subjective aspect of history.[36] Stephanie Bird includes *Cornelia Goethe* as an example of the German biographical fiction centered on female identity that is the focus of her 1998 study *Recasting Historical Women,* arguing that "what is special about Damm's approach is that the elements of supposition and fantasy are treated with the same rigorous academic tone as the facts and so can never become an escape from what is known."[37] Bridge terms Damm's book on Goethe's sister a "semi-fictional biography," and interprets it in a book chapter subtitled "Biographical Fictions about Women."

Although, like Hoffmann's *Charlotte von Stein, Cornelia Goethe* was written and published late in the GDR's history, it still belongs to those works written in that country that represent a refutation of Goethe and a concomitant embrace of Romanticism. Though Damm's book does not actually treat the Romantic movement, its mix of genres allows Krauss to analyze it as an example of what his essay terms the "Romantic reception of (not only) Romantic literature." In the late 1970s when the GDR's engagement with Romanticism had its fullest flowering, Damm edited a selection of Caroline Böhmer-Schlegel-Schelling's letters in which the sort of "subjektive Erkenntnisinteresse"[38] (subjective interest in recognition) is manifest that characterizes the previously examined novels of Christa Wolf and Brigitte Struzyk. This identification with Romanticism and refutation of Goethe also characterized more conventionally biographical works such as Günter de Bruyn's *Das Leben des Jean Paul Friedrich Richter* (The life of Jean Paul Friedrich Richter, 1975). Contrary to official GDR literary doctrine, the noted East German author de Bruyn treats the decidedly ironic, non-realist writer Jean Paul as a man of the people, and Goethe, as well as Schiller, as incapable of recognizing and accepting talent that does not conform to their literary orientation.[39]

We noted that Hoffmann's novel on the Stein-Goethe relationship makes a number of references to Goethe's sister and his relationship to her, and we will draw on these sparse but significant details to show how

Cornelia Goethe can be seen to flesh them out in a manner that casts the brother's behavior in the worst possible light. While Hoffmann's Goethe tells Stein that Cornelia married to escape her constricted life in the parental home, Damm shows how Goethe is partly to blame for this. The novel's early passages show the siblings enjoying an excellent education through the attention of their father, Johann Caspar, who, living on his inheritance, largely devotes himself to the thorough acculturation of his children. Goethe and his sister develop a very close bond. However, when Goethe, as a young man, leaves their Frankfurt home to pursue further studies in Leipzig, Wetzlar, and Strasbourg, he fails to fulfill his promise to have Cornelia join him. In his letters, he expresses jealousy of her leisure time, admonishing her to write longer missives because he, with much more to do, sends her such detailed reports (55). She comes to realize that all her early education is for naught since, as a woman, she must either marry or languish at home. This causes her bouts of depression, for which her brother shows little sympathy. Her engagement and marriage to Goethe's friend Johann Georg Schlosser is actually marked by early happiness, although it provokes the jealous brother's rage (131). She lapses into another depression when the couple move to Emmendingen, where her husband is a court official, because she feels completely isolated there. Goethe's neglect of Cornelia's daughters after her death — both children passed away at a young age, like their mother who died shortly after giving birth to the second daughter — is connected by Damm both to a latent sense of guilt on the poet's part, and to his belief in his later years that the individual's personal responsibility extended even to matters of health and longevity. That Cornelia and her daughter Lulu could not, in Goethe's view, exist in holistic, harmonious unity with the world becomes associated for him with "Lebensunfähigkeit," an inability to live (249–50). Damm seems deliberately to make Goethe's perspective a forerunner to the Nazi view that certain individuals (as well as races) were unfit to live, *lebensuntauglich*. Damm also infers that Goethe's cruel neglect of his sister because she married, and thus failed to meet his selfish expectations, had much to do with her depression and early death; in one of the book's most clearly imaginative turns, Cornelia's deathbed delirium causes her to perceive her brother's voice, nearby and full of the tenderness she vainly craved (257). Stein surmises in Hoffmann's novel that Goethe failed even to maintain a comforting epistolary connection with his sister during her last illness because he felt oppressed by her suffering and dying, but Damm treats this neglect as an additional extension of his egotism; because Cornelia did not assume the role in his universe the brother had assigned her, he simply let her fall entirely out of this universe. He is even silent for nearly two weeks after hearing of her death, finally writing his mother that he has always been fortunate and that Cornelia's death is all the more painful because it surprised him in happy days. As Damm puts it: "Sein Wohlbefinden und Cornelias Tod in einem Atemzug" (246; His well-being and Cornelia's death in a single breath). This is one of Damm's most subtle but effective means of expressing her belief that Goethe was an unmitigated narcissist whose self-centeredness strongly contributed to his sister's early demise.

Bird has argued that, "Damm's personal identification with Cornelia Goethe is intense, and it manifests itself in the desire to portray her positively as a strong-minded, independent character, worthy of our sympathy and respect."[40] This was certainly Feyl's intention with regard to the female protagonists of her historical novels, and she succeeded admirably. Damm, on the other hand, while showing that Cornelia exhibited signs of strength and self-determination — for example, she expresses admiration for the courage Cornelia displays in her epistolary diary, and even avers that her brother "provoked" this literary bravery (81–82) — is so focused on Goethe's destructive narcissism in his treatment of his sister that Cornelia's independence of spirit fades into relative insignificance in the overall portrayal of her victimization. While Goethe is away and Cornelia forced to live under her father's heavy-handed tutelage, he still tries to control her through his letters. As with Charlotte von Stein's missives to Goethe, those of his sister are lost to posterity (Goethe burned them). Damm therefore claims that only the "Anstrengung unserer Phantasie" (exertion of our fantasy) allows the addressee in Goethe's letters to emerge as a personage in her own right, but ultimately fails to engage her own fantasy at this narratively self-conscious moment in the hybrid biography, choosing instead to focus on Goethe's narcissism and patriarchal authoritarianism as he tries to control his sister from afar (54–55). As Bridge notes: "Cornelia's life is presented as a series of passive responses to other people's demands, and Damm denies the idea that Cornelia could have had any autonomy over, or responsibility for, her 'fate,' by suggesting that it followed an inevitable pattern."[41] While Cornelia's father and husband are shown to bear a significant share of responsibility for denying her any genuine agency, it is Goethe whom Damm casts as the chief villain in this regard. *Cornelia Goethe* is somewhat mistitled, for the book is as much about her brother as it is about the eponymous protagonist. Of all the anti-Goethe images to emerge in the GDR, Damm's is the most negative: He is cast as deeply neurotic, possessive, somewhat incestuous — a self-centered, vindictive, controlling, destructive monster.

Goethe as Aging Lothario in Two Works of Martin Walser

As mentioned at the outset of this chapter, Karl Robert Mandelkow singles out an essay of Martin Walser as an early harbinger that West Germany, at least outside official classroom discourse, was emerging from its immediate postwar embrace of Goethe as the embodiment of its best intellectual traditions, from a Goethe cult that made the "poet-prince" the figurehead in its attempt to infuse the country with the spirit of a new humanism. In his 1964 essay "Imitation oder Realismus" (Imitation or realism), Walser argued that Goethe's humanism lacked a historical dimension. Walser also seemed to pave the way for the depiction of Goethe as a villainous figure in the wave of Hölderlin fiction discussed in chapter 2 when he argued in 1970 that one cannot praise Hölderlin without scorning the mature (or Weimar) Goethe.[42] Walser's play *In Goethes Hand* also makes Goethe into the egotistical manipulator of a powerless man, but this time the victim is the amanuensis of his later years, Johann Peter Eckermann.[43] As Gerald Fetz notes in his essay on this drama, Walser's "antiheroes are generally struggling, somewhat neurotic individuals with lower middle-class sensibilities, occasionally situated in the shadows of the limelight of others, incapable of generating much light themselves,"[44] and this is the case with Walser's Eckermann. Drawn to Goethe in the hope the now-elderly (and clearly senile) poet can advance his own literary career, Eckermann instead becomes a poorly paid factotum to his master, editing his collected works and otherwise helping to manage Goethe's affairs at the cost of his own ambitions, financial stability, and marriage plans. Eckermann's long-postponed wedding to his fiancée Hannchen becomes the play's most grotesque thread, as he glosses over her repeated protestations that Goethe is exploiting him. Eckermann points to hopeful but clearly illusory signals from his master that his prosperity and success lie just around the corner. Thus, the first two acts are sardonically entitled "Glaube" (faith) and "Hoffnung" (hope), underscoring the illusions harbored by the factotum. The name of the third act, "Liebe" (love), is ironic because it finds Eckermann already widowed in 1848 after Hannchen has died in childbirth, their married life having only lasted two-and-a-half years; in fact, "Liebe" refers to Eckermann's conflicted love for Goethe. Reflecting the circumstances of the historical Eckermann, Walser's protagonist, ill and impoverished, lives in a virtual menagerie (including birds of prey, martens, moles, etc.) with his teenage son Karl.

Similar to his characterization in *Cornelia Goethe*, Goethe in Walser's play is deeply neurotic, unable to abide eyeglasses, beards, or dogs. Just as he tried to control his sister in Damm's fictionalized biography, he manipulates Eckermann, though mainly through flattery and the vague promises communicated at intervals by Eckermann to Hannchen. Goethe's control even extends beyond the grave; in a dream long after Goethe's death, Eckermann is unable to hear his late wife's entreaties as he is consumed with expressing his hatred of the "Excellency," but then he falls back into apologetic adulation, equating a hatred of Goethe with a hatred of the sun, light, life, even God (153).

In addition to his manipulativeness and neurosis, Walser's Goethe possesses another attribute alluded to by Damm: a revulsion at death and ugliness. In the play's longest monologue, Eckermann recites for his employer a speech he intends to give to a group of artists gathered in Weimar to paint the great man. Eckermann insists that Goethe be represented as beautiful, that indeed his physical beauty is the product of his work (77), making an argument similar to Damm's Goethe, who maintained that infirmity and early death are an individual's personal responsibility. As Heike Doane notes in summarizing Eckermann's monologue, the protégé finds that "Goethe's art has come to triumph over life's miseries, even over death itself," through its instantiation of "beauty and harmony." However, citing another Walser essay, "Goethes Anziehungskraft" (Goethe's power of attraction, 1983), Doane notes that Walser found Goethe's obsession with harmony, happiness, and beauty masked a deep fear of mortality.[45] This may explain why, as *Cornelia Goethe* indicates, he focused on his own health and happiness in writing to his mother about his sister's death. Walser's Eckermann continues this view of Goethe as a writer whose guiding motif was not to suffer (84). At the conclusion to the rehearsal of his speech — which he cannot actually deliver in front of the assembled artists due to the interruptions of Goethe's drunken son, the profligate August — Eckermann revels in his own poverty and unrequited love for the great man (86), a further sign of Goethe's mastery over Eckermann's soul.

One important distinction between Walser's Goethe and the Goethe configured by Hacks, Hoffmann, and Damm is his advanced age. Whereas Goethe was still young and vigorous when he ended his affair with Charlotte von Stein, and was only twenty-seven when his sister died, he first met Eckermann in 1823, only nine years before his own death. In Walser's play, Goethe's senility is evident in his memory lapses; having recited a poem to two young ladies, Getrud and Gustchen, he repeats it moments later (34, 36). Indeed, this elderly Goethe is not only a manipulator, but is himself manipulated by the teenaged Gustchen, who seduces him on a coach ride as a means to achieve her goal of becoming an actress at the Weimar theater. He is also manipulated by his daughter-in-law Ottilie, who is indeed Goethe's equal in exercising her control of Goethe's factotum. Like Goethe, she manages to steer Eckermann into acting against his own best interests, and the play's conclusion witnesses her, who expresses contempt for Christine Vulpius and for her own alcoholic late husband, goading Eckermann into kissing her hand (169–70). She does this in order to perceive herself as ennobled once again despite her current poverty. Eckermann is thus a victim of all three adult Goethes in the course of the play, enhancing Walser's characteristic portrayal of lower-class suffering in the shadows of more elite figures. As Doane notes, *In Goethes Hand* illustrates a postulate thematized throughout Walser's oeuvre: "dependence destroys."[46]

Walser's view concerning the emptiness of Goethe's humanism postulate finds expression again when Gustchen defends Getrud after she has fallen asleep during a conversation where Goethe's pettiness and attention to insignificant detail are on full display — Gustchen explains that this apparent expression of boredom actually resulted from the young lady's fainting from excitement. Goethe exclaims that Gustchen's benevolent gesture reveals the heartfelt goodness of Germany's women: "Schon Bildung tilgt diese Fähigkeit. Wer weiß, was Humanismus ist, hat keinen" (44; Acculturation already eliminates this capacity. Whoever knows what humanism is does not have any). This line is reminiscent of the observation of Hacks's Charlotte von Stein that "Humanität" itself would not need a Latin signifier if it could be felt. Clearly, Walser is challenging once again postwar Germany's infatuation with, indeed desperate embrace of, Goethean "humanism" by showing it to be a fatuous, empty ideal.

Walser's negative portrayal of Goethe continues in the last act, which takes place in the revolutionary year 1848, some sixteen years after Goethe's death. Walser creates a fictional meeting between Eckermann and the 1848 revolution's most eloquent poetic advocate, Ferdinand Freiligrath. Eckermann has pinned his final desperate plan to escape penury on successfully completing the third volume of his *Gespräche mit Goethe*, and Karl Marx has engaged Freiligrath to interview him for the *Neue Rheinische Zeitung*, which Marx edits. Citing the views of the Young Germany–adherent Ludwig Börne, Freiligrath claims that Goethe belongs not in the classroom, but in the literary salon, and also asserts that Goethe was a toady to such reactionaries as the King of Bavaria. This is the image of Goethe presented by Weiss in *Hölderlin*, and both Weiss and Walser thereby anticipate the more elaborate scholarly critique of Goethe's reactionary political tendencies as privy counselor in Weimar by contemporary academics such as W. Daniel Wilson.[47] By 1848, the Age of Goethe was at an end (135–37), and in death he became a tool of reactionary forces, according to the fictional Freiligrath: "Der Goethe-Kult, den der reaktionäre Teil des Bürgertums betreibt, ist Politik, Eckermann. Klassiknarkose!" (133; the Goethe cult propagated by the reactionary element of the bourgeoisie is politics, Eckermann. Classicist narcosis!). Günter Niggl has accused Walser of creating a completely distorted view of Freiligrath's image of Goethe because, as Niggl shows, Freiligrath was a strong devotee of the sage of Weimar.[48] Walser himself was somewhat distressed by the judgment of critics and academic Germanists when they assumed, based on his 1982 radio play, that his attitude toward Goethe was entirely negative. He softened the vehemence of the drama's anti-Goethe thrust when he adapted it for the stage in 1984, and his personal pronouncements on Goethe around that time suggest a greater ambivalence than the radio play would indicate.[49] Nevertheless, the message *In Goethes Hand* offered to listeners through the medium of a distorted

Freiligrath in the Goethe Year 1982, the 150th anniversary of the poet's death, was similar to Walser's groundbreaking youthful perspective: The cult of Goethe is reactionary and destructive, whether it manifests itself in the 1840s, the 1940s, the 1960s, or the 1980s.

In Goethes Hand alludes to the elderly Goethe's affair in Bohemia with the young Ulrike von Levetzow. Indeed, early in this work, Goethe's absurd pettiness is illustrated when he goes into a tirade about her age; he is furious at the gossip circulating in Weimar and given voice by his son August that she is nineteen years old; Goethe insists to August that she is already twenty (40–41). This affair of the aged Goethe with the much younger Ulrike von Levetzow is the central theme of Walser's recent novel, *Ein liebender Mann*. The first two-thirds of the novel take place in Marienbad and Karlsbad, and constitute an imaginative account of the relatively little-known details concerning Goethe's affair with Levetzow in the two Bohemian spa towns. In the last section of *Ein liebender Mann*,[50] Goethe is back in Weimar and his letters to Levetzow, who, as he gradually realizes, will never enter into a genuine relationship with him, are interspersed with third-person descriptions of Goethe's increasing despair at his seemingly permanent separation from his beloved. The most famous work of Goethe's inspired by the affair, the *Marienbader Elegie* (Marienbad elegy, 1823), is discussed as it evolves when Goethe leaves Karlsbad for Weimar, tracing a circuitous path allowing for mineral-gathering expeditions with friends, and the entire poem is reprinted in the novel (198–204). In an interesting inversion of Goethe's insistence in the radio play that Levetzow is not a teenager, it is she who attempts to play down her lover's age in the novel; when he decisively states he is seventy-four, she passionately claims he is, for her, seventy-three, "eine wunderbare Zahl" (107; a wonderful numeral). The Goethe of Walser's novel bears little resemblance to the Goethe of Walser's radio play; even the vanity and neurotic aversion to common objects such as eyeglasses are treated in a more nuanced manner in the later work, as Walser delves into Goethe's imagined subconscious. For this purpose, he even briefly employs the stream of consciousness technique (241–45).

As the title of Walser's novel indicates, Goethe's obsession with Ulrike transforms him from the tyrant of the earlier drama into "a loving man," making him a much more agreeable, even sympathetic, figure. Nevertheless, he is also made to seem, in numerous passages, quite ridiculous. He is most reminiscent of the Walser protagonist Helmut Halm, who, like the fictionalized Goethe, appears in two of Walser's works. Halm is relatively young in the novella *Ein fliehendes Pferd* (Runaway horse, 1978). In the novel *Brandung* (Breakers, 1985), he has an awkward infatuation with a much younger female student while he is a guest professor at a California university. Just as Halm is constrained in his pursuit of this student, Fran Webb, by another woman, Carol Elrod, a departmental secretary who exercises substantial control over him, so Walser's Goethe is constrained by two domineering women, in Bohemia by Levetzow's shrewd manipulative mother Amalie, and in Weimar by his daughter-in-law Ottilie, who is as vindictive and controlling in *Ein liebender Mann* as she was in the radio play. Walser's second Goethe is also consumed by jealousy of a much younger rival, de Ror, a mysterious purveyor of jewelry to Europe's patrician ladies, who attempts to seduce Levetzow in Marienbad and then, while Goethe is in Weimar, visits her at her boarding school in Strasbourg. Goethe is only aware of this impending visit because he has received a letter in Weimar from Levetzow alluding to the ominous development concerning the mysterious de Ror, who in Marienbad had confided his first name to the object of his passion as though it were a great secret she must hold in confidence. Goethe's obsession and sense of helplessness regarding this — for him — fearsome new event typifies the persona with which Walser invests him throughout the course of the novel. This persona is completely antithetical to the domineering, manipulative Goethe who is displayed in the radio play. Although he assumed the role of shrewd master to the slave Eckermann in the early work, *Ein liebender Mann* shows the poet to be a slave to his unrealizable infatuation, incapable of acting, only capable of writing and obsessing. This weakness is manifest in the run-on sentence, a common syntactic technique in the novel for illustrating Goethe's feverish, circular musings, through which his speculations concerning Ulrike's second meeting with de Ror are conveyed. This sentence communicates Goethe's typically entangled mix of hope and despair:

> Der stürmische Schmuckmann will verkaufen, die Mutter ist schon ganz wild auf die Steine aus Übersee, Ulrike wird ihn diesmal fragen, ob sie ihrem Freund Goethe den Vornamen sagen dürfe, sie kommt doch gar nicht mit in sein Hotelzimmer, Steine interessieren sie einfach nicht, gut, beleidigen will sie den Stürmischen auch nicht, aber eine Kundin wird sie nie, dafür hat die Mutter gesorgt, de Ror hat die Nacht im Sommer vielleicht vergessen, der ist sicher immer so stürmisch, kann er ja, falls sie mit denen hingeht, um neun muss sie zurück sein im Internat, die Mutter will eine Sondererlaubnis, will sie nicht, warum auch, obwohl, wenn sie mitginge, interessant wäre, ob er, wenn man ein zweites Mal mit ihm die Mitternachtsgrenze passierte, wieder den selben Vornamen preisgäbe. (228)

> [The tempestuous jewelry man wants to sell, the mother is already completely wild about the stones from overseas, Ulrike will ask him this time if she can say his first name to her friend Goethe, she will certainly not accompany him into his hotel room, she is simply not interested in stones, good, she also does not want to insult the tempestuous one, but she will never become a customer, the mother

took care of that, maybe de Ror forgot the night in the summer, he is certainly always so tempestuous, he can indeed, in case she goes with them, at nine she has to be back in the boarding school, the mother wants a special permission, does not want it, why should she, although, if she went along, it would be interesting, if he, if one were to cross the midnight limit with him a second time, would reveal the same first name.]

In *Brandung*, Halm exhibits a similar neurotic obsession about a much younger potential romantic rival.[51] To a certain extent, *Ein liebender Mann* transforms Goethe into the Eckermann figure of Walser's radio play, as he allows his life to be governed by a futile dream.

Aside from the *Marienbader Elegie*, the key Goethean text alluded to in *Ein liebender Mann* is the so-called *Altersroman* (old age novel), *Wilhelm Meisters Wanderjahre oder Die Entsagenden* (Wilhelm Meister's travels or the renunciants, 1829). Several references are made to Goethe's reworking of this novel, and Walser's Goethe mentions, on a number of occasions, a novella inserted into the *Wanderjahre*, "Der Mann von fünfzig Jahren" (The man of fifty years). Though the plot of this novella is never discussed, its citation is ironic, given that its eponymous protagonist, a retired major, is the object of his prospective young daughter-in-law's romantic interest while his son Flavio falls in love with a somewhat older widow. Ultimately, the major marries the widow and Flavio marries his original intended. This is ironic because Levetzow's widowed mother, Amalie, betrays a certain erotic interest in Goethe in Walser's novel, but Goethe's own obsession with her daughter never wavers. Goethe scholars have naturally taken the motif of renunciation (*Entsagung*) seriously in analyzing the *Wanderjahre*, given its centrality in that novel,[52] and Goethe has been traditionally presented in biographies as heroic in his own renunciation of erotic fulfillment late in his life. As Arthur Henkel has noted: "Goethe als der große Entsagende, das ist eine geradezu gängige Identifizierung. Und für den alten Dichter, den Weisen, vor allem ist der Zug der gelösten Entsagung, der heiteren Lebensdistanz derjenige, welcher kaum einer Darstellung der 'Epoche seiner Vollendung' fehlt"[53] (Goethe as the great renunciant, that is a really common identification. And for the old poet, the wise one, particularly the quality of the relaxed renunciation, of the cheerful life's distance, is that which is hardly ever missing in an account of the "epoch of his completion"). The image of the elderly Goethe as a heroic, benign renunciant is a central element in the various Goethe cults in their otherwise disparate historical manifestations. The Goethe of Walser's novel, alluding to his status as an iconic figure in Weimar who is expected to maintain a certain reputation in this "Feindesland" (enemy territory), where he must keep his passion a secret, is angry that he must play the role of renunciant as never before, that he must not exude (*ausstrahlen*) anything but renunciating (265). At the conclusion to *Ein Liebender Mann*, he regrets his waste of energy "in einem Affentheater der Entsagungs-Schau" (277; in an ape theater of renunciation display). Indeed, the closing line has Goethe awakening with an erection, having dreamt of Levetzow (285). Walser's recent Goethe is a more sympathetic figure than his earlier dramatic protagonist, because his response to frustrated passion exposes his vulnerable humanity. However, by making Goethe so appealingly down-to-earth, even with respect to his use of a modern-day idiom, *Ein liebender Mann* represents another attack on the poet's Olympian venerability and cult status, albeit from an entirely different angle than is to be found in the portrayal of Goethe as a manipulative tyrant in Walser's earlier fictional treatment of the poet.

Sparschuh's Take on the Goethe-Eckermann Relationship

The Goethe figure in Jens Sparschuh's *Der große Coup* bears a strong resemblance to the poet-prince of Walser's *In Goethes Hand* in his relationship to Eckermann. Both display a manipulative self-centeredness in their dealings with their acolyte. The two texts also treat Eckermann's fiancée as a voice of reason who tries to persuade her betrothed that he is being duped and exploited. However, unlike Walser's Eckermann, the amanuensis of *Der große Coup* is implied to have effectively managed the contours of his master's immortality.[54] Theodore Ziolkowski has noted that Eckermann's "secret" diaries in the novel reveal his suppressed desires and wishes, as well has his observations concerning Goethe's pettiness, superficiality, and exploitative behavior. Ziolkowski contrasts the directly expressed hatred revealed in the fictional diaries in Sparschuh's novel with the tendency toward a more underscored self-deception, as well as a continued feeling of pure love toward Goethe, in another work where Eckermann plays the role of narrator, Hans Peter Renfranz's tale *Eckermann feiert Goethes 100. Geburtstag* (Eckermann celebrates Goethe's hundredth birthday, 1990).[55] The key point here is that Sparschuh's Eckermann, unlike the utterly duped figure in Walser's play and in Renfranz's story, possesses genuine agency and uses it to instrumentalize his former employer.

To be sure, Sparschuh's Eckermann is as emotionally and professionally manipulated by Goethe as the character created by Walser and Renfranz. The Goethe of *Der große Coup* constantly tells the fortyish Eckermann that he is still a young man whose time will come and whose talents will be realized, while, to the despair of Eckermann's fiancée Hannchen, Goethe never intervenes with the ducal court in Weimar to create a remunerative and stable position for his secretary. When Eckermann requests to examine a letter from Schiller, Goethe deliberately misreads the request as a wish to organize his entire correspondence, claims he will consider the wish, and on the following day reminds Eckermann of his promise to engage in this enormous task! (67). Eckermann's obedience, agreement, and acquiescence to Goethe are so complete that, late in the novel, this circumstance causes the ailing poet to fly into a rage (200–201). Nevertheless, the diary entries constituting most of the novel (which are interspersed with the historical fiancée's actual correspondence, printed in italics) reveal what we are to assume is the real Goethe — an insecure, cynical, deeply pessimistic, often petty tyrant. By implication, the conversations the historical Eckermann was to publish from 1836 until 1848 under the title *Gespräche mit Goethe* are to be regarded as a virtual fiction, the product of Eckermann's effort to create a harmonious, perfect, indeed hagiographic image of the poet, as Eckermann himself admits when he contrasts the "Konversationen" (conversations) with the "Geheimtagebücher" (secret diaries) that constitute Sparschuh's novel (155–56). The clever conceit of *Der große Coup* is that the *Gespräche mit Goethe*, and not the novel composed by Sparschuh, are the real work of fiction. Thus, the *Gespräche* are to be regarded as Eckermann's instrumentalization of Goethe into the near-divine paragon of Weimar Classicism later worshipped by generations of Germans, including those alluded to at the outset of chapter 4 who tried to employ this hagiographic image in order to rehabilitate Germany's ruined reputation in the immediate aftermath of World War II, and, in the present day, by Schami.

The "coup" alluded to in the title signifies the plan, conceived by Goethe and assisted by Eckermann, to find suitable last words to be attributed to the poet on his deathbed. Much of the narrative is occupied by the research and discussions of the two men devoted to finding the phrase that will have both the greatest impact on posterity and most effectively immortalize the poet to whom it is attributed. At one point, Goethe suggests the phrase "Mehr nicht" (187; no more), which would accord well with this fictionalized poet's dispirited, profane, pessimistic worldview. Of course, the last words popularly attributed to the historical Goethe are "mehr Licht" (more light), which fits the image of Goethe as the eternal striver for knowledge and clarity, and Sparschuh implies that Eckermann is responsible for this legendary quote. Sparschuh's Eckermann describes himself toward the close of the novel as Goethe's sacrificial victim, but he finds this relationship allows him the greatest possible insight into Goethe. This supreme insight is Eckermann's reward for being "das lebendige Opfer der Menschheit an den Minotauros G." (197; the living sacrificial victim of humanity to the minotaur G.). Sparschuh implies that in sacrificing himself to Goethe on behalf of humanity, Eckermann has created the Goethe known to subsequent generations; the "victim" instrumentalizes the "minotaur" so that the world can have a poet-prince of inestimable value for posterity's various needs.

Goethe as Dying Lecher

The year 1999 marked the 250th anniversary of Goethe's birth, and *Der geheime Bericht* was one of several works of prose fiction published that year in which Goethe was the center of focus. Boëtius's novella *Tod in Weimar* (Death in Weimar) was inspired by the circumstance that Siegmund von Arnim, the son of Bettine and Achim von Arnim, was the last visitor outside his intimate Weimar circle to have been received by Goethe before his death. Siegmund spent six days in Weimar, from the tenth to the fifteenth of March 1832, departing exactly one week before Goethe expired. Boëtius imagines Bettine sent her attractive son to seduce the putatively bisexual poet and thereby arrange for her procurement of the letters she had sent him so that she could begin composing *Goethes Briefwechsel mit einem Kind*; indeed, she commenced with this book shortly after his death.[56] As the title of the novella hints, the relationship between Goethe and Siegmund is patterned to a large degree after the much more famous homosexual relationship — the unconsummated infatuation of an older man for an adolescent boy — between the aging intellectual Gustav Aschenbach and the Polish youth Tadzio in Thomas Mann's *Der Tod in Venedig* (Death in Venice, 1912).[57] Goethe's brilliant insights, as depicted by Boëtius, born of a loneliness brought on by the relative isolation of his advanced age, make him reminiscent of the Goethe in Mann's *Lotte in Weimar*. However, his loathing of Bettine von Arnim, her husband, other Romantics, Eckermann as a toady who seems all ears, as well as of his own vividly described physical decay and decrepitude make this Goethe, in contrast to Mann's Goethe, singularly unattractive. This ugliness is enhanced through accompanying lithographs by Johannes Grützke.

Goethe's Italian Sojourn from a Fictional Italian Perspective

Hans-Josef Ortheil's novel *Faustinas Küsse* offers an imaginative account of Goethe's long residence in Italy at the end of the 1780s. Goethe is an "absent" figure in Hacks's monodrama and in much of Hoffmann's novel; despite their different approaches to how Charlotte von Stein copes with this absence, both authors powerfully evoke the distress it causes her. Not only does the she obsessively dwell on Goethe's sudden flight to Italy in both works, but also on how to understand his identity in the light of his seemingly impetuous disappearance. Ortheil's novel shifts the focus and locus from Goethe's absence from Weimar (and Kochberg) to his physical presence in Rome. However, far from answering any questions about Goethe's identity that Hacks and Hoffmann raised via the Stein figure — and left for their audience or readers to ponder — *Faustinas Küsse* engages in such radically postmodern play with the very issue of identity that the figure associated with the name Goethe is as absent in Rome in 1786 and 1787 as he was in Weimar. To put the matter somewhat differently, Ortheil's novel challenges the reliability of *any* Goethe image — positive or negative — shaped by readings of his works, his biographies, his critical reception, and by other Goethe fiction. Ortheil deconstructs the relation between the signifier "Goethe" and a fixed, unified persona by investing all of his main characters in the novel, including the poet, with multiple, unstable, and shifting identities.

The chief protagonist of *Faustinas Küsse* is the entirely fictional Giovanni Beri, an impoverished young native of Rome who latches onto the traveler Goethe when he first arrives, drawn by his powerful charisma and an awareness that attaching himself to this figure will somehow allow him to realize his fortune. Indeed, Giovanni comes to spy on Goethe for the Holy See, and invents stories about the privy counselor's putative attempts to conspire against Rome and the Austrian emperor at the behest of his employer, the Duke of Weimar, and his Prussian allies. Giovanni does this in order to enhance his value as a spy for the Vatican, but he himself comes to form an image of Goethe based almost exclusively on his reading of *Werther*; having heard rumors about Goethe's liaison with a married woman in Weimar, and observing Goethe's celibate life in the exclusive company of men such as the painter Johann Heinrich Wilhelm Tischbein and the writer Karl Philipp Moritz (who are, of course, genuine historical figures whom Goethe knew in Italy), Giovanni assumes Goethe has a Werther complex and is unable to get over his obsession with the unnamed woman in Weimar. Goethe himself adopts a fabricated identity in Rome; he becomes — as he did in real life — the German painter Filippo Miller, a name Giovanni continues to associate with Goethe even when he learns his real name and background. Giovanni also passes himself off as a painter to Goethe once the latter returns from a stay in Naples and the Italian instigates direct contact. He attempts to cure Goethe of his "Werther complex" by initiating an amorous liaison between the poet and his childhood friend Rosina, whom he claims to Goethe is his sister. Reading *Werther*, and railing against its eponymous protagonist, helps Giovanni to overcome a bout of depression while Goethe is in Naples, and dressing in Werther's costume — casting himself psychically as an anti-Werther — helps him win the affections of Faustina, the title character. Giovanni's plans backfire when Filippo/Goethe remains indifferent to Rosina, and unaware of Giovanni's relationship to Faustina, starts his own affair with her after Giovanni introduces them in a tavern. Alone and depressed after Goethe departs for Weimar, Giovanni adopts the identity of the German painter Filippo Miller at the novel's conclusion (350).

Ortheil's entanglement of identities extends to his manipulation of his own source material. As Anthonya Visser has noted, the name Faustina derives from the eighteenth of Goethe's *Römische Elegien* (Roman elegies, 1795; composed 1788–90). In this verse, the poet describes Faustine (Goethe's spelling in the poem) as having made him happy by sharing his bed. The lyrical "I" of the elegy describes Faustine as completely fulfilling his erotic wishes, and as being fully faithful to her faithful lover. Ortheil's Faustina, on the contrary, has two lovers, a circumstance of which Goethe — unlike Giovanni — is unaware. While the narrating ego in Goethe's poem cycle is stable, self-assured, and allows for no possibility of having his veracity called into question, Ortheil's Faustina is, like Giovanni and Goethe, duplicitous, and possesses multiple identities.[58] For Goethe, she is the faithful, fulfilling lover, while she presents herself to Giovanni as a gold digger in her relationship to the poet, interested only in obtaining money from a man she describes as a boring lover (293).

Ortheil's postmodern destabilization of identity and author-ity is evident not only in his playful tweaking of a poetic intertext. The most obviously significant source for the book's personalities and events are Goethe's diaries of his Italian sojourn, collectively published as the *Italienische Reise* (Italian journey, 1816). Ortheil undermines the status of these diaries as a historical document, as pure nonfiction, not only by having historical figures such as Tischbein, Moritz, and, of course, Goethe, interact with purely imaginary figures like Giovanni and Rosina, but also by putting a creative spin on quite specific incidents chronicled by the diaries. For example, in an entry dated 8 December 1786, Goethe relates that Moritz broke his arm when his horse slid and fell on the slippery Roman pavement, an incident that represents a profound misfortune for the small German circle.[59] Ortheil reconfigures this by having Giovanni, who is annoyed at Moritz's monopolization of Goethe's time, give Moritz's horse a furtive but powerful blow to its flank as they ride past him. This makes the horse rear up and gallop out of control, spilling its rider and causing the broken arm (63). In discussing this episode in the *Italienische Reise*, Richard Block claims that Moritz's "handicap allows Goethe to take control of the hand of writing,"[60] a pun conveying the idea that Goethe assumed more autonomy as an author after the episode. For Giovanni's purposes, the plan backfires because Goethe becomes *less* autonomous as a tourist, spending even more time with Moritz as the latter recuperates. The novel infers that only Goethe's affair with Faustina ultimately succeeds in bringing about Giovanni's fondest wish for his friend's career, namely, that he shift his focus from a dilettantish dabbling in painting and sketching to a resumption of his true vocation, imaginative writing. However, in a further deconstruction of the authority of Goethe's authorship, Ortheil has Giovanni resolve to write the definitive account of Goethe's sojourn in Rome. As the second incarnation of Filippo Miller, "ein Maler aus Deutschland" (350; a painter from Germany), the new Goethe seems to be the figure authorized to write this account, rather than the man who is returning to Weimar.

As Katya Skow has indicated, Ortheil also made use of the incidents Goethe describes in the *Italienische Reise* to make him seem childish, eccentric, and even blasphemous in the devoutly Catholic Giovanni's eyes, particularly early in the novel.[61] Of course, given Giovanni's clearly unreliable perspective, one cannot say that this presentation belongs to the sort of anti-Goethe polemic evident in the other works discussed in this chapter. Rather, through his postmodern multiplication and conflation of identities, Ortheil subverts the Goethe cult by deconstructing the very image of the poet as a discrete, cohesive genius, worthy of veneration across the ages because his authority and authorship — vested in a stable persona produced by his life and work, or by his life as one coherent artwork — transcends time. Traditionally, the veneration and instrumentalization of Goethe have depended on the secure existence of a single historical figure, even if different aspects of this figure have been drawn upon for different needs. If, as Ortheil's novel suggests, even the historical Goethe is a product of the imaginary (whether on the part of a fictional Italian who "experienced" him first-hand, or in our own day), then the cult of Goethe, which has been the object of a consistent attack from his death up to modern writers like Hacks and Walser, simply becomes an impossibility.

Goethe as a Positive Protagonist in Recent Fiction

A sympathetic, albeit ironic, view of the poet from the Goethe Year 1999 is evident in Otto Böhmer's novel *Der junge Herr Goethe* (Young Mr. Goethe). As the title indicates, the focus is the poet's youth rather than his last days. Like Boëtius's Goethe, we see him struggle with intertwined bouts of vanity and self-loathing. He frets over the image he will leave to posterity, suffering prophetic nightmares about a modern-day professor who disparages his life and work in his lectures to bored twentieth-century students. Nevertheless, among all contemporary fictional Goethe portraits, Böhmer's poet, along with that of Rafik Schami and Robert Löhr, is the most positive. In stark contrast to the decadent debaucher of *Tod in Weimar*, this "young Mr. Goethe" consistently radiates with vitality, physical attractiveness, and love of life. This is evident even in the novel's last sentence: "Schließlich hat er noch viel vor, im Leben — von dem er *mehr* will und *immer mehr* (334; After all, he still intends to do a great deal in life — from which he wants *more* and *ever more*; italics in the original). However, Rafik Schami's novel *Der geheime Bericht* is unique in its enactment of Goethe and his oeuvre in the service of a specific social and cultural agenda. The discussion of Schami's Goethe will be followed by a look at Robert Löhr's two recent novels, *Das Erlkönig-Manöver* (The earl-king maneuver, 2007) and *Das Hamlet-Komplott* (The Hamlet conspiracy, 2010), in which Goethe is the leader of a heroic group of well-known scholars and poets as they battle Napoleon.

Schami's Goethe: A Role Model for Contemporary Multicultural Germany

Given Schami's priorities, he had to recuperate Goethe from his Oriental-ist reputation, as established by Edward Said in the first edition of *Orientalism* (1978). Said's position was that the "German Orient" was merely "scholarly" or "classical" — never "actual" as it was for French and English scholars and/or imaginative writers — because "there was nothing in Germany to correspond to the Anglo-French presence in India, the Levant, North Africa."[62] In making this assertion, Said singles out two authors and their respective works as exemplars of "scholarly" Orientalism: Friedrich Schlegel with his *Über die Sprache und Weisheit der Inder* (On the language and wisdom of the Indians, 1808) and Goethe's *West-östlicher Divan* (The west-eastern divan, 1819). While these works draw on writing that originated from the empires of France and Great Britain, Said finds it significant that they came into being as a result of Schlegel's forays into Parisian libraries and of a Rhine journey undertaken by Goethe, respectively.[63] Indeed, the *West-östlicher Divan* serves as Said's foremost poetic example of what he sees as Germany's penchant for engaging in a purely imaginative, even dialogic, Orientalism, one which is divorced from an Anglo-French linkage of scholarly investigations (and even poetic writing) to the extension of imperial authority in the Orient. Said would emphatically deny that Goethe belonged to "the *guild* of Orientalists" marked by "a specific history of complicity with imperial power."[64] In his brief analysis of the *Divan* in *Orientalism*, Said emphasizes Goethe's association of timelessness, boundlessness, and an originary purity with the Orient — a romantic projection that reflects the German author's fantasy rather than the realities of the Eastern world. In his later writing, Said has expressed an unreservedly positive view of Goethe as a comprehensive, dialogically oriented thinker. For example, in his preface to the twenty-fifth edition of *Orientalism*, he links Goethe's world-literature paradigm to broad-minded scholarly cosmopolitanism *tout court*, finding that "philology as applied to *Weltliteratur* involved a profound humanistic spirit deployed with generosity, and, if I may use the word, hospitality. Thus the interpreter's mind actively makes a place in it for a foreign Other." In his preface, Said also speaks approvingly of Goethe's "interest in Islam generally, and Hafiz in particular" — something Said believes was "a consuming passion" that resulted in the *Divan*'s composition.[65]

Precisely this view of Goethe as a seeker of respectful, mutual understanding between self and Other, particularly as exemplified by the *Divan*, is advanced by Schami in *Der geheime Bericht*. The positive image of Goethe conveyed by this novel puts Schami into conflict with other contemporary writers and scholars regarding Goethe's Orientalism. Zafer Şenocak, who has accused Schami of serving up Orientalist clichés to his

German readers by presenting himself as a purveyor of "authentic" Arab fairy tales,[66] also finds Goethe guilty of buttressing European racism in his poetry cycle by employing damaging stereotypes: Arabs are bellicose but unquestioningly accept the dictates of their rulers, reject change, and obsessively thirst for revenge when they feel slighted.[67] Todd Kontje expresses criticism of *Der geheime Bericht* in asserting that it presents "an image of Goethe as a child-loving, politically correct advocate of multicultural understanding."[68] While Kontje's description of Schami's novel is not inaccurate, Schami does attempt to move Goethe beyond the Orientalist epithet, and *Der geheime Bericht* exemplifies Schami's own ongoing attempt to promote an East-West dialogue.

The core of Schami's novel is constituted by the "Bericht," a report on discussions concerning Goethe's life and works as a model for humanist education by a scholarly commission on the imaginary island of Hulm. The "Bericht des wohlgeborenen Prinzen Tuma" (Report on Prince Tuma of noble birth) is divided into nine "nights" (the "first night," the "second night," etc.); on each of the nights constituting the nine chapters, the German-born character Tuma, who has become a prince on the island, and the commission discuss one of Goethe's works or body of works. The texts discussed on the respective evenings are: *Die Leiden des jungen Werthers*; *Wilhelm Meisters Lehrjahre* (Wilhelm Meister's apprenticeship, 1795–96); *Reineke Fuchs* (1794); a selection of the most popular poems; *Faust* (1808 and 1832), with Mephistopheles as the focus; *Die Wahlverwandtschaften* (Elective affinities, 1809); *Die Farbenlehre* (Theory of colors, 1810); and *Der West-östliche Divan*. On the final evening, when the decision on the merits of including Goethe in Hulm's curricula is to be made, episodes and relevant facts connected to Goethe's life are elaborated upon, interspersed with citations from Eckermann's *Gespräche mit Goethe* and a concluding recitation of the poem "An den Mond" (To the moon, approx. 1777). All the chapters are structured in a similar manner. Tuma begins to discuss the merits of the work in question, members of the commission make comments when they find interesting parallels between passages and thoughts in Goethe and the Middle Eastern texts, philosophies, and figures with which they are familiar, or when a work recited or summarized by Tuma strikes a personal chord. Naturally, the commission responds with enthusiasm to each of the texts elaborated upon by Tuma, for otherwise he would not have been granted nine whole evenings for a discussion of Goethe's oeuvre. At the conclusion of the ninth night, Tuma is assigned the task of overseeing the translation of Goethe's poems in the House of Wisdom (157), where the books approved by the commission are to be placed and where the youth of Hulm will learn about European culture.

Since the nine chapters are almost identical in structure, my analysis will focus on the discussion of the *Divan* on the penultimate night, because this work is the focal point of the current critical discourse on Goethe's Orientalism. The *Divan* chapter represents the culmination not only of Tuma's effort to win Goethe's acceptance into the pantheon of European authors assigned for the edification of Hulm's youth, but also of Schami's own endeavor to instrumentalize Goethe as a precursor — and thus authorizing voice — for his own role as an intercultural ambassador, as a mediator between East and West, Orient and Occident.[69] After Tuma opens his presentation of the *Divan* by reciting two of its poems, the first response from Sultan Hakim, the island's ruler, is incredulity that Goethe had never visited the Orient. Tuma then remarks on the Romantic Orientalist context that informs the historical period of the cycle's composition, noting how early European Romantics made the Orient the extravagant locus and goal of their own prelapsarian fantasies (132). The audience responds to Tuma's presentation with unadulterated pleasure at what they perceive to be Goethe's grasp of ancient Oriental wisdom, his positive reply to Arab enthusiasm for poetry, the respect — not at all universal among the Europeans with whom the commission is familiar — he displays towards the East. Tuma discusses Goethe's profound engagement with the Persian poet Hafiz, the diversity of subjects taken up by the cycle, as well as its historical background. He intersperses his elucidations with a recitation of other poems from the cycle.

On several levels, Tuma's presentation of the *Divan* and the dialogue of his audience in response tend to counteract the charge leveled by Said and others that this work is an exemplary instance of scholarly and imaginative Orientalism. We recall Said's claim that the *Divan* embodied a profound Western yearning to return to a pure, prelapsarian paradise filled with limitless potential and temporal plenitude.[70] In responding to the sultan's query as to whether he is certain that Goethe had never visited the Orient, Tuma points out the region had indeed become "zum neuen Paradies, zum schwärmerischen Ziel" (a new paradise, a raved-about destination) at the beginning of European Romanticism (132), thereby suggesting that Romanticism per se, and *not the* individual poet Goethe, is to be associated with the extravagant topos of the Orient-as-paradise that Said finds in the *Divan*. Said's more serious charge is that the *Divan* provided Karl Marx with his most authoritative support for viewing Asia as a torpid, decadent, unindividuated morass in need of regeneration from Europe — however cruel some of this regeneration's manifestations might be. Said claims Marx's defense of English colonialism in "crumbling," "ancient" Asia was inspired by the *Divan*, which provided "the sources of Marx's conceptions about the Orient."[71] Creating individuated Arab exclamations of pleasure at Goethe's perceived insights into, and respect for, Oriental Islam, Schami implicitly refutes the charge that Goethe could be held responsible for the Orientalist views of Marx and others that Asia itself lacked any internal dynamism or individuation, and thereby upholds Germany's most famous writer as a champion of multicultural dialogue. Said cites Marx's citation of Goethe's verse on the cruelty of Timur to underscore his belief that the *Divan* inspired Marx's views on the Orient's seemingly undifferentiated "human material," finding that the founder of the Communist movement transformed Goethe's poetic equation of Timur's devouring of innumerable souls with the aesthetic pleasure one finds, despite any personal bitterness, in "the spectacle of the crumbling of the ancient world"[72] into a justification of England's brutal colonial policies in India. Tuma, on the other hand, claims Goethe accurately described the Mongolian prince as a merciless conqueror, but that the German author gave him "einen Anstrich von Humanität und sogar von Humor gegenüber Beleidigungen eines Untergebenen" (139; a layer of humanity and even of humor in the face of the insults of a subordinate).

In *Der geheime Bericht*, British greed for oil triggers the profound dystopian conclusion narrated in the novel's brief final chapter, "Wie die Geschichte zu Ende ging" (How the story came to an end). This denouement begins quite cheerfully, with the posthumous triumph of the cosmopolitan writer whose work and personage Schami dedicates himself to promoting in this fiction: "Goethe hatte Herz und Geist der Kommission erobert. Sie war von seinem Werk so beeindruckt, dass sie einstimmig beschloss, das Haus der Weisheit mit der Übersetzung seiner Werke zu beauftragen. Als erster deutscher Dichter wurde Goethe an allen Schulen und Universitäten des Landes im Unterricht eingeführt" (159; Goethe had conquered the heart and the spirit of the commission. It was so impressed by his work that it unanimously decided to authorize the House of Wisdom to translate his works. Goethe was the first German poet introduced into all the schools and universities of the country). Among German authors, the only other nineteenth-century luminary who receives such an unreservedly enthusiastic reception is Heinrich Heine, who also combined the gifts of literary imagination, a poetically expressed love of the Islamic world, and the ability to mediate literature between cultures (159). Indeed, at the end of the nineteenth century, the House of Wisdom comes to embody Goethe's ideal of *Weltliteratur*, attracting scholars and translators from all of Arabia, who translate not just European but Asian literature as well (160). However, once the British discover that Hulm is rich in oil, the island's fate is sealed. Claiming as a pretext that civil war has broken out in Hulm, the British Navy bombards and quickly conquers the island. Oil firms pump Hulm so dry of petroleum that the entire island sinks into the gulf. In the novel's last sentence, Schami reveals "Hulm bedeutet auf Arabisch Traum" (164; Hulm means dream in Arabic). Clearly, Schami recognizes that genuine intercultural and international respect, appreciation, and equality are, in the nineteenth century as well as in the current age, only dreams not close to realization. An appendix on the life of Goethe attributed to Prince Tuma, along with a second appendix with cursory descriptions of the works discussed on the nine "nights" as well as tips on consumer-available theater, television, and musical productions of Goethe's work, follow the novel's denouement. The informal/informational but didactic tone of these appendices underscore the fact that the two authors composed the book with a young (high-school age) target audience in mind. The unadorned prose style evident in the "Dokument zum Leben des deutschen Dichters Johann Wolfgang von Goethe" (Document on the life of the German poet Johann Wolfgang von Goethe) — a style quite uncharacteristic of Schami — as well as Gutzschhahn's background as a Germanist and editor of children's and young adult literature for the Hanser Verlag (*Der geheime Bericht* is categorized on trade websites as *Jugendliteratur*, literature for young people) lead one to surmise that the two appendices are the latter's primary compositional contribution to *Der geheime Bericht*.

A brief overview of the critical remarks Şenocak directed towards Goethe and Schami for allegedly buttressing Orientalist stereotypes shows that Schami instrumentalizes Goethe for a subtler reason than merely positioning him as the most exemplary German figure in the greatest age of his nation's literature, as a source of pride and inspiration for young German readers when they experience the "land of poets and thinkers" simplistically juxtaposed with greedy, imperialist Great Britain. Şenocak's most sustained critique of Goethe and his *Divan* is contained in the essay "Das Buch mit den sieben Siegeln. Über die vergessene Sprache der osmanischen Dichtung" (The book with the seven seals: On the forgotten language of Ottoman poetry), originally published in 1992. Şenocak accuses Goethe of promoting stereotypes such as Oriental passivity and obeisance, Arab lust for vengeance and war, Middle Eastern despotism and changelessness. Goethe's fear of going beyond formal and sensual boundaries (*Entgrenzung*) does not allow him to recognize the essential feature of divan poetry: "nämlich der Typus des *rend*, des weisen Spielers, des Genießers, der mystische und erotische Töne zu einem den Geist bezaubernden Klang vereint"[73] (namely the type of the *rend*, of the wise player, of the epicure, who unites mystical and erotic tones into a sound that enchants the spirit). A genuine "West-East Divan," based on liminal experience and genuine contact and without authorizing the reader as "traveling salesman," as Goethe modeled himself in the "Noten und Abhandlungen" (Notes and treatises), the scholarly apparatus to the *Divan*, remains to be written, in Şenocak's view.[74] In the article "Wann ist der Fremde zu Hause? Betrachtungen zur Kunst und Kultur von Minderheiten in Deutschland" (When is the foreigner at home? Observations on the art and culture of minorities in Germany), originally published in French in 1992, Şenocak complains that minority literature not reflective of Western clichés has few buyers in Germany. The most successful — albeit, for Şenocak, perfidious — strategy is to reinvigorate the oral Arab fairy-tale tradition: "Sie wird vor allem von arabischen Autoren wie von dem Syrer Rafik Schami, der seine Märchen nicht vorliest, sondern sie auf zahlreichen Veranstaltungen 'authentisch' mündlich vorträgt, mit Erfolg praktiziert"[75] (Above all, it is most success-fully practiced by Arab authors like the Syrian Rafik Schami, who does not read his fairy tales aloud, but rather orally declaims them in an "authentic" manner at numerous performances).

It is unlikely that Schami would entirely disagree with Şenocak's characterization either of the *Divan* or of his own writing. While Tuma has nothing but praise for the *Divan* in *Der geheime Bericht*, he empha-sizes the discrete character of its diverse themes, a "Verschiedenartigkeit" (133; diversity) not conducive to the all-encompassing synthesis Şenocak associates with true divan poetry. The secondhand character of Goethe's acquaintance with the Middle East is persistently underscored in the nov-el's *Divan* chapter as well. However, his service as a mediator between East and West, and as creator of new poetic avenues, is also acknowledged in the *Divan* chapter of *Der geheime Bericht*. The West-East hybrid pro-tagonist Thomas/Tuma constantly banters with his audience while mak-ing it clear that introducing Goethe's works into Hulm's curricula would greatly enhance the fictive island's educational program. Throughout his writing, Schami underscores the genuine liberatory potential of storytell-ing as an oral medium informed by dialogue and not just an unbridge-able divide between active speakers and passive listeners. In *Der geheime Bericht*, Schami instrumentalizes Goethe into the catalyst of such oral dia-logue. In so doing, he hopes not only to overcome Orientalist clichés about Middle Eastern passivity, but also to inspire the transcendence of what William Paulson has termed the consumption-oriented and "pas-sive" nature of Western "print-culture reading" itself.[76] The scholarly dis-cussions of Goethe's life and works that constitute the core of *Der geheime Bericht* show that this transcendence might be accomplished by reviving a constituent feature of the Age of Goethe: the literary salon.

Goethe as Hero in the Campaign against Napoleon in Two Novels by Robert Löhr

Goethe was an admirer of Napoleon, seeing in him an exemplar of the demonically possessed genius, which is to say, a man imbued by a natu-ral force propelling him to achievements beyond the reach of almost all other mortals, destined to attain titanic heights but also doomed to a tragic end. In two novels by Robert Löhr, *Das Erlkönig-Manöver* and *Das Hamlet-Komplott*, Goethe is transformed into the leader of bands of well-known authors from the period who engage in audacious ploys designed to topple the emperor from power. In *Das Erlkönig-Manöver*, Goethe and fellow adventurers Friedrich Schiller, Heinrich von Kleist, Alexander von Humboldt, Bettine Brentano, and Brentano's future husband Achim von Arnim travel to French-occupied Mainz to rescue the putative heir to the Bourbon throne, Louis XVII, in order to bring him to Weimar, from where he can inspire a campaign to topple the emperor and restore the Bourbon dynasty. However, this Louis XVII, after his liberation, is revealed to be an impostor, a circumstance leading to unexpected plot twists and infighting among the band of poetic and scholarly luminaries. In *Das Hamlet-Komplott*, set in 1807 (two years after the previous novel's time frame), a new group of authors, still including Goethe and Kleist but now accompanied by the Romantic figures Ludwig Tieck and August Wilhelm Schlegel, as well as Schlegel's real-life paramour Madame de Staël (who famously celebrated Germany as the land of poets and thinkers in her *De l'Allemagne*, published in 1813), travel as an acting troupe whose real mission is to bring the imperial crown, excavated by Kleist from an island in Lake Constance, to Prussia after smuggling it through French-occupied German territory. In both novels, Löhr blends autobiographical facts culled from the authors' lives, literary snippets from canonic works of the age, and actual historical episodes into fast-paced adventure stories tinged by humor and pathos.

More than any other author discussed in *Imagining the Age of Goethe*, Löhr's style is marked by historical and literary pastiche. According to Ingeborg Hoesterey, "postmodern pastiche is about cultural memory and the merging of horizons past and present." In Hoesterey's reading of the contemporary enactment of the pastiche genre, postmodernists borrow copiously from the Occident's cultural archive of architectural, cinematic, artistic, and literary motifs and quotations and insert them into their work.[77] The result is a mélange of different quotations and sources lifted from earlier authors, as is evident in Löhr's historical fiction. With the possible exception of Christoph Hein, discussed in the following chapter, few other German writers engaged in Age-of-Goethe fiction employ this form of pastiche, nor do they adopt the extended imitation of an earlier author's style (another variation of the pastiche genre). Whereas Wolf's Kleist emerges as a sexually ambiguous figure largely through an occluded narrative voice in *Kein Ort. Nirgends*, and Feyl borrows from the *Bildungsroman* tradition in evolving her characters through broad chronological stretches of their lives, Löhr tends to draw on assumptions rooted in popular cultural memory concerning his Age-of-Goethe figures, as a way of lending otherwise wild events and episodes a certain historical plausibility. Kleist's sexual ambiguity and Humboldt's presumed homosexuality allow Löhr to cast them into a passionate erotic relationship. The historical Brentano's apparent impetuousness, impulsiveness, and presumed dalliance with Goethe make credible her constant, nearly simultaneous careening between Arnim and Goethe as lovers. Kleist's hot temper and Schiller's idealism are juxtaposed with Goethe's caution as the group passes from one nearly fatal adventure to another, but Goethe's heroic historical stature is transformed into a martial valor not generally attributed to Germany's most canonic writer. All the authors display courage verging on bravado as they enter Mainz, use subterfuge and violence to wrest Louis XVII from Napoleon's forces, and make their way back to Weimar pursued by the villainous Bavarian Captain Santing and French and allied troops, but Goethe is clearly their leader, possessing the authority to make the daring rescue through Duke Carl August. The duke, along with allied foreign supporters of the Bourbons who are staying at his castle, makes his privy counselor responsible for carrying out the rescue.

A good example of Löhr's employment of literary and historical pastiche can be found in his treatment of Schiller's death. The historical Schiller died of tuberculosis in 1805, a slow demise portrayed with relative historical accuracy by Feyl in *Das sanfte Joch der Vortrefflichkeit*. Löhr makes Schiller's fatal pulmonary disease the consequence of a long immersion in the Rhine River as the literary group flees Mainz with Louis XVII, and then a long outdoor sojourn on the Kyffhäuser Mountain as they hide from Santing and his troops. After he and Goethe return to Weimar, and Carl August and his allies are forced to admit that the Louis XVII delivered to the ducal castle is a fraud, Schiller resolves to write a historical drama that deals with a much earlier episode of royal duplicity, but that clearly alludes to this deception. As Schiller is dying, Santing, who now works for the Bourbonists, steals the manuscript of the play because, if read correctly, it might cast aspersions on the false Louis XVII who is to be restored to the Bourbon throne. Goethe discovers this theft and, despite his own illness, bravely dashes after Santing. Kleist, as so often in the novel, rescues Goethe from death after capture by Santing and the Bourbonists in their castle, and then also saves the manuscript from being burned when he snatches it from a fire. Schiller's play turns out to be *Demetrius* — the fragmentary status of which was, in fact, caused by Schiller's untimely death, but which did revolve around a historical figure who assumed the title of Russian Czar in the early seventeenth century by falsely claiming to be the son of Ivan the Terrible. Thus, both Schiller's death and his dramatic fragment are turned into pastiches of fact and fiction in the service of Löhr's narrative.

Ironically, Löhr's Goethe had himself burned pages of Kleist's play *Der zerbrochene Krug* (The broken jug, 1803) in order to light a fire to warm the ailing Schiller on the Kyffhäuser. Indeed, Kleist had pursued Goethe to Mainz in a desperate attempt to get him to read the manuscript. Goethe's burning of the play's first pages nearly causes the enraged Kleist to shoot him. The novel's conclusion, however, shows them joyously riding back toward Weimar together after the rescue of Goethe and a portion of the *Demetrius* manuscript. The novel's final

words are "Heinrich, Heinrich!" (362), called out by Goethe as they
gallop together toward the Werra Valley (362) right after Goethe
decides, contrary to his initial impression, that he thinks highly enough
of the play to stage it. The historical Goethe did in fact stage the play at
the Weimar Theater in 1808, but its popular and critical failure, which
Kleist blamed on Goethe's poor direction, led to the estrangement of
the two authors. Löhr's revision of these circumstances is a literary-historical pastiche in the service of appealing to the contemporary popular imagination in Germany. Both writers continue to be held in high
esteem, so their bond at the novel's conclusion fancifully and idealisti-
cally corrects a historical reality that perhaps disturbs those who revere
these two authors and the Age of Goethe as a totality.

Literary pastiche in the form of intertextual citation is a frequent stylistic element in the novel, often in ironic service to the plot. For example, Bettine Brentano pulls the petals off a flower in Goethe's presence
as she murmurs: "Er liebt mich — liebt mich nicht" (225–26; he loves
me — loves me not), echoing the lines of Gretchen in *Faust I* (1808).
As Goethe collects flowers for a bouquet that inspires her recitation from
Faust, he requests Schiller's assistance by asking him: "Seien Sie so hilfreich und gut, mir bei der Suche nach einigen schönen Blüten zur Hand zu
gehen" (223; Be so helpful and good as to assist me in the search for some
pretty blossoms), drawing thereby on the frequently cited opening couplet
of Goethe's 1783 poem "Das Göttliche"[78] (On the divine). Commenting
on the haste with which French troops are galloping toward them, Schiller questions whether it might be the earl king and his daughter engaged
in wild gallop (205), the novel's only allusion to its title, derived from the
famous poem "Der Erlkönig" (The earl king, 1782). Goethe delivers two
crushing punches with his fists to Santing's servant toward the novel's conclusion, calling his first fist blow "Faust eins" (literally, "fist number one"
but a clear allusion to part one of his most famous play), and the second,
with the left hand, "Faust zwei" (344; fist number two).

Löhr also inserts narrative episodes from Goethe's works into the
novel. For example, as the group of writers is being ferried over the Rhine
by a fisherman to the French-occupied bank, Schiller accidentally drops a
coin into the river as he attempts to pay him. The fisherman is horrified,
claiming this event will bring both the group and himself disaster (64–
65). The incident is clearly adopted from Goethe's *Das Märchen* (Fairy
tale, 1795), in which will-o-the wisps outrage their boat pilot when they
attempt to pay him with gold coins; he declares that if a coin dropped
into the water a catastrophe would ensue. In both works, the respective ferrymen assert that the river cannot tolerate such coins.[79] In *Das
Erlkönig-Manöver*, Schiller's companions blame his careless accident for
a number of their misfortunes at various times in the novel. Such intertextual allusions and citations also enact cultural memory for the reader

at least minimally conversant with Age-of-Goethe writing, a form of pastiche designed both to amuse and to enhance the novel's literary-historical ambience.

The historical Goethe's admiration for Napoleon comes to expression in *Das Hamlet-Komplott*, where the fictional Goethe refers to the emperor as a god (84). While such direct adulation is not enunciated in *Das Erlkönig-Manöver*, the two novels are marked by other similarities. Not only does *Das Hamlet-Komplott* employ the same varieties of literary pastiche evident in Löhr's earlier novel, but its narrative is driven by an almost identical plot conceit: A group of prominent intellectuals, tacitly led by Goethe, seeks to smuggle a valuable cargo from French-occupied Germany to a safe haven in a German domain still largely free of Napoleonic rule. To be sure, the circumstance that this cargo is an inanimate object rather than a human being alters the dynamics of the adventures experienced by the group, as well as their interpersonal interactions, but the novel is to a great extent, like its predecessor, constituted by alternations between chase scenes as the group tries to smuggle its cargo from French-occupied Germany to Prussia, and flamboyant physical and verbal exchanges, interspersed by literary and historical allusions, among the traveling luminaries. The novel's Kleist continues to rescue the novel's Goethe from precarious situations, but his hatred of Napoleon, France, and their German allies is even more intense in *Das Hamlet-Komplott* than it was in *Das Erlkönig-Manöver*, resulting in a series of foolhardy deeds culminating in an attempt to assassinate the emperor during a staging by Goethe of a Voltaire play at the Weimar Theater. Goethe continues to be the charismatic guiding star of his fellow author-adventurers, despite moments of weakness (such as an opium-induced fantasy that he is being haunted by Schiller's ghost) as well as arguments with other troupe members.

The new German characters, Tieck and August Wilhelm Schlegel, were leading Romantics, so the divide between this movement and that of Weimar Classicism, briefly alluded to in *Das Erlkönig-Manöver* when Arnim challenges Goethe by favoring Romantic "heart" over the "pure head" of Classicism (247), is more frequently thematized in *Das Hamlet-Komplott*. For example, Kleist proclaims Goethe to be the king of Classicism and Tieck to be the king of Romanticism (189), and when Tieck witnesses Goethe and Schlegel engaging in chatty, pleasant conversation, he says that such a scene makes it appear that the dispute between Weimar (the center of German Classicism) and nearby Jena (the seat of early Romanticism) never took place, ascribing Goethe's new openness and empathy to Schiller's death (241). Tieck is portrayed as somewhat childlike and helpless, lacking the talent of his fellow Germans but compensating for this lack through sheer force of will, while Schlegel's primary character traits are the intellectual/critical acumen associated with

his historical model, an abject romantic attachment to Staël (who nee-
dles him mercilessly), and a tendency to contribute to his group's martial
engagements by bashing in the skulls of its tormentors. Staël's character is
marked by quick wit, courage, and sexual aggression toward Kleist (whose
homosexuality is more understated in the later novel) and Goethe.

Löhr's tendency to intersperse his narrative with literary and historical pastiche is as pronounced in *Das Hamlet-Komplott* as it was in *Das
Erlkönig-Manöver*. As the coach sets off from Staël's estate in Coppet to
rescue Kleist from imprisonment in Fourt de Joux, where the historical
Kleist was actually confined due to his suspicious behavior in France, they
are pursued by a black poodle who bears an obvious resemblance to the
dog who follows Faust and turns out to be Mephistopheles in Goethe's
play. However, the name of the poodle in Löhr's novel is Stromian (42–
43), recalling the dog in Tieck's most canonic story, *Der blonde Eckbert*
(Fair-haired Eckbert, 1797). In Tieck's story, the dog was left to die by
the female protagonist, Bertha, when she runs away from home; Bertha
has repressed the dog's name, and its mention triggers the novella's cata-
strophic chain of surreal events. In Löhr's novel, Stromian is cared for by
Eleonore, a young Italian actress who becomes part of the troupe, and
with whom Tieck falls in love. At various times in *Das Hamlet-Komplott*,
Staël announces to the characters that she is taking note of their words
and deeds for the book she is composing, a clear allusion to the historical
Staël's *De l'Allemagne*. After a night in which the group has consumed
a copious amount of wine and opium, Schlegel asks Tieck whether he
has a "Kater," German slang for a hangover. Tieck responds: "Ja, und
zwar einen gestiefelten" (184; Yes, and in fact, one in boots), an ironic
reference to the historical Tieck's most canonic comedy, *Der gestiefelte
Kater* (Puss in boots, 1797). Goethe, tired of the stressful misadventures
he has had to endure as a member of the traveling troupe, announces
he is leaving the group by saying "Meine Wanderjahre sind vorüber"
(264; My years of traveling are at an end), drawing on the title of the
actual Goethe's novel *Wilhelm Meisters Wanderjahre oder Die Entsagenden*. However, events force Goethe to stay with the group, and when
Eleonore is buried after having died from inhaling smoke from a fire in
the castle where the travelers spent the night after a disastrous *Hamlet*
performance, Goethe recites a quatrain adopted from an elegy composed
by the actual Goethe on the occasion of the death of the court carpenter and stage decorator Johann Martin Mieding, entitled "Auf Miedings
Tod" (On Mieding's death, 1782); however, it is altered slightly to reflect
that Eleonore was relatively still a child, and not a grown man.[80] As with
Das Erlkönig-Manöver, Löhr engages in these diverse enactments of pastiche in order to enhance his novel's literary-historical ambience, evoke
cultural memory, and entertain those readers who have some familiarity
with works composed during the Age of Goethe.

Nevertheless, *Das Hamlet-Komplott* is structurally distinct not only from Löhr's earlier novel, but from other works examined so far in *Imagining the Age of Goethe*, through its consistent grounding in one specific intertext. Despite its quite diverse literary and historical allusions, *Das Hamlet-Komplott*'s primary narrative foil is Goethe's novel *Wilhelm Meisters Lehrjahre*. Unlike Plenzdorf's *Die neuen Leiden des jungen W.*, which is an ironic send-up of Goethe's *Werther*, the adaptation of motifs and episodes from *Wilhelm Meisters Lehrjahre* in *Das Hamlet-Komplott* simply constitutes Löhr's broadest enactment of literary pastiche. In other words, this intertextuality can be regarded as supporting Löhr's effort to evoke cultural memory (in this case, through re-instilling an awareness among his readers of one of German literature's most canonic works) while driving his narrative plot forward. I will mention only a few of the most obvious strands common to the novels. In both cases, the main casts of characters evolve into theatrical troupes who perform *Hamlet*. Both works contain broad theoretical discussions of Shakespeare's play and how it is to be performed. In both novels, a disastrous fire breaks out after a staging of *Hamlet*. Like Mignon in Goethe's novel, Eleonore in *Das Hamlet-Komplott* is an Italian girl originally attached to a loutish group of entertainers, and who dies of heartbreak at a perceived loss of love. Mignon loses hope after she sees Wilhelm kiss another woman. Eleonore is a victim not only of the fire (she inhales too much smoke trying to save the imperial crown from the flames), but also of a loss of hope when she is rejected by Tieck after confessing that she is, in fact, a spy for Joseph Fouché, Napoleon's Minister of Police.

To be sure, the theatrical portion of Goethe's novel constitutes only one part of its early narrative content, while in Löhr's much shorter novel, the fire occurs near its conclusion. The "Wilhelm" of *Das Hamlet Komplott* is August Wilhelm Schlegel, who turns out to be the shrewdest among the group despite his misguided, indeed masochistic, relationship to Staël, for the Catholic Romantic is able to transport the crown to Vienna after the troupe breaks up, thwarting the Protestant Kleist's effort to ferry it to eastern Prussia. While *Das Hamlet-Komplott* is not a *Bildungsroman* like *Wilhelm Meisters Lehrjahre*, its conclusion shows that Kleist and Goethe have absorbed valuable lessons as a result of their experiences. Kleist learns to renounce his murderous passions, and Goethe overcomes his morbid aversion to anything associated with death, as he proves by cheerfully stepping over a corpse (359). As in *Das Erlkönig-Manöver*, this conclusion shows the two men having reconciled and engaging in friendly colloquy. Löhr once again rewrites literary history in a manner appealing to those who treasure the Age of Goethe and its personalities, but who may be disturbed by one of its bitterest, most unfortunate rivalries.

Conclusion

Not surprisingly, the literary figure most prominently thematized in Age-of-Goethe fiction from the 1970s to the present day is the man for whom the period is named. This circumstance can only be partially explained by Goethe's towering presence in German literature from the 1770s to his death in 1832. Rather, the frequency with which late twentieth- and early twenty-first-century German authors actualized him in their work must also be seen as a backlash against the revival of the Goethe cult in the years immediately following the Second World War. The attempt to reinvent Germany as the *Kulturnation* it was perceived to be — perhaps incorrectly — during the *Goethezeit* by invoking the great genius's authority in festivals, critical laudatios, and somewhat kitschy fiction was seen by writers in the 1970s and the early 1980s as a conservative, even reactionary, effort to return to values they perceived as outdated, and, at best, irrelevant in the present day: inwardness, *Bildung*, spiritual metaphysics, and elitism, among others. Given Goethe's instrumentalization in the GDR as a progressive hero who could further the socialist revolution, the negative reaction to Goethe was as common in the GDR as it was in the FRG.

The backlash against Goethe in West German literature is evident in fiction on Hölderlin, where Goethe was cast as a reactionary antipode to the revolutionary Jacobin Swabian. In works more centrally focused on the sage of Weimar, his reputedly slavish adherence to monarchic, antidemocrat rule was coupled with a tendency to portray him as duplicitous, sexually deviant, and as both a tyrant toward and duped instrument of his secretary Eckermann. East German feminists treated him as a completely egotistical lover and brother. In the Berlin Republic, such fictional vituperation has frequently given way to playful pastiche, as authors blended historically established episodes from his life with fantastic tableaus created in connection with his sojourns in Bohemia and Italy, his activities during the Napoleonic Wars, and events surrounding the last days of his life. To be sure, some of these recent works have treated Goethe sympathetically as a dynamic young man, the inspirer of multicultural understanding as well as holistic learning on a fictitious Arabian island, and as a hero in the period when Napoleon's troops occupied much of Germany. Nevertheless, the general irreverence in twenty-first-century treatments of Goethe tends to throw more dirt on the coffin of the Goethe cult already buried by the literary portraits of this figure in East and West Germany in the 1970s and 1980s.

Notes

[1] A broad comparative overview of such literature from the beginning of the twentieth century to the present day is provided by Theodore Ziolkowski, "Das Treffen in Buchenwald oder Der vergegenwärtigte Goethe," *Modern Language Studies* 31 (2001): 131–50.

[2] Peter Hacks, *Ein Gespräch im Hause Stein über den abwesenden Herrn von Goethe*, in *Ausgewählte Dramen 2* (Berlin: Aufbau, 1976), 389–454.

[3] Johanna Hoffmann, *Charlotte von Stein: Goethe und ich werden niemals Freunde*, 3rd ed. (Berlin: Verlag der Nation, 1991).

[4] Sigrid Damm, *Cornelia Goethe*, 3rd ed. (Frankfurt am Main: Insel, 1989).

[5] Martin Walser, *In Goethes Hand: Szenen aus dem 19. Jahrhundert* (Frankfurt am Main: Suhrkamp, 1982).

[6] Walser, *Ein liebender Mann* (Reinbek bei Hamburg: Rowohlt, 2008).

[7] Jens Sparschuh, *Der große Coup: Aus den geheimen Tage- und Nachtbüchern des Johann Peter Eckermann*, 2nd ed. (Cologne: Kiepenheuer & Witsch, 1996).

[8] Henning Boëtius, *Tod in Weimar*, 2nd ed. (Gifkendorf: Merlin, 1999).

[9] Hanns-Josef Ortheil, *Faustinas Küsse* (Munich: Luchterhand, 1998).

[10] Otto A. Böhmer, *Der junge Herr Goethe* (Munich: Albrecht Knaus, 1999).

[11] Rafik Schami and Uwe-Michael Gutzschhahn. *Der geheime Bericht über den Dichter Goethe, der eine Prüfung auf einer arabischen Insel bestand* (Munich: Hanser, 1999).

[12] Robert Löhr, *Das Erlkönig-Manöver*, 4th ed. (Munich: Piper, 2010).

[13] Löhr, *Das Hamlet-Komplott* (Munich: Piper, 2010).

[14] An excellent summary of the ideological appropriation of Goethe in the immediate postwar years in Germany, culminating in 1949, is provided by Stephen Brockmann, *German Literary Culture at the Zero Hour* (Rochester, NY: Camden House, 2004), 115–41. For a detailed overview of the intellectual currents that manifested themselves during the postwar Goethe renaissance and the Goethe year 1949, see Mandelkow, *Goethe in Deutschland*, 2:135–64.

[15] Mandelkow, *Goethe in Deutschland*, 2:218–24.

[16] Gundula Sharman, *Twentieth-Century Reworkings of German Literature: An Analysis of Six Fictional Reinterpretations from Goethe to Thomas Mann* (Rochester, NY: Camden House, 2002).

[17] York-Gothart Mix, "Mit Goethe und Diderot gegen die Pächter des klassischen Erbes: U. Plenzdorfs *Die neuen Leiden des jungen W.*, V. Brauns Texte zu *Hinze und Kunze* und die Kontrolle der literarischen Kommunikation in der DDR," *Jahrbuch der deutschen Schillergesellschaft* 42 (1998): 401–20.

[18] For an elaboration of this treatment of Goethe in the novel, see Peter O. Arnds, *Representation, Subversion, and Eugenics in Günter Grass's* The Tin Drum (Rochester, NY: Camden House, 2004), 135–45.

[19] Grass, *Die Blechtrommel*, 6th ed. (Frankfurt am Main: Fischer, 1962), 342.

[20] Philip Brady, "On Not Being Intimidated: Socialist Overhauling of a Classic," in *Goethe Revisited: A Collection of Essays*, ed. Elizabeth M. Wilkinson (London: John Calder, 1984), 48.

[21] Anna K. Kuhn, "Peter Hacks' *Ein Gespräch im Hause Stein über den abwesenden Herrn von Goethe*: A Feminist Reinterpretation of the *Geniebegriff*?" *Germanic Review* 60 (1985): 91–97.

[22] Hacks, "Es ließe sich fragen . . . Zu *Ein Gespräch im Hause Stein über den abwesenden Herrn von Goethe*," in *Die Maßgaben der Kunst: Gesammelte Aufsätze* (Dusseldorf: Claassen, 1977), 388–94.

[23] Hacks, "Es ließe sich fragen," 392.

[24] Hacks, "Es ließe sich fragen," 389–90.

[25] Hacks, *Musen: Vier Auftritte*, in *Ausgewählte Dramen 3* (Berlin: Aufbau, 1981), 317.

[26] Manfred Durzak, "Ein Gespräch im Hause Hacks über den anwesenden Herrn von Goethe: Goethe-Einflüsse und Goethe-Adaptionen in Stücken von Peter Hacks," in Bauer Pickar and Cramer, *The Age of Goethe Today*, 143.

[27] Mandelkow, *Goethe in Deutschland*, 2:233.

[28] Mix, "Mit Goethe und Diderot," 418.

[29] Bridge, "Biographical Fiction by GDR Women Writers: Reassessing the Cultural Heritage," in Durrani and Preece, *Travellers in Time and Space*, 161.

[30] Hacks, "Es ließe sich fragen," 388. Hacks notes in the same passage that in creating this "true story," he does not claim to use the tools of philology, tools he finds inadequate for the reality of the episode. He is not out to "prove" anything, but to relate a truthful account from the perspective of art.

[31] See Helmut Koopmann, *Goethe und Frau von Stein: Geschichte einer Liebe* (Munich: C. H. Beck, 2002), 202–3. Koopmann claims that Charlotte inadvertently or willfully overlooked clear signs of the crisis in their relationship prior to Goethe's departure for Italy.

[32] Bridge, "Biographical Fiction by GDR Women Writers," 160.

[33] See Markus Wallenborn, *Frauen. Dichten. Goethe.: Die produktive Goethe-Rezeption bei Charlotte von Stein, Marianne von Willemer und Bettina von Arnim* (Tübingen: Max Niemeyer, 2006), 15–172, esp. 152 and 171.

[34] Damm, *Vögel, die verkünden Land: Das Leben des Jakob Michael Reinhold Lenz* (Berlin: Aufbau, 1985), esp. 247–56.

[35] Dorrit Cohn, *The Distinction of Fiction* (Baltimore, MD: Johns Hopkins UP, 1999), 28. Cohn is referring here to a trend, especially popular in the 1920s, to create rather imaginative biographies that used literary techniques such as free indirect style. This genre was termed the "New Biography."

[36] Hannes Krauss, "Die Kunst zu erben — zur romantischen Rezeption (nicht nur) romantischer Literatur: Über Sigrid Damm, Christa Moog und Brigitta Struzyk," in *Neue Ansichten: The Reception of Romanticism in the Literature of the GDR*, ed. Howard Gaskill, Karin McPherson and Andrew Barker (Amsterdam: Rodopi, 1990), 43–44. The term "faction" became fashionable in the 1980s to describe the hybrid of fact and fiction characteristic of works such as *Cornelia Goethe*. See, for example, Richard Johnstone, "The Rise of Faction," *Quadrant* (April 1985): 76–78.

[37] Bird, *Recasting Historical Women*, 115.

[38] Krauss, "Die Kunst zu erben," 43.

[39] Günter de Bruyn, *Das Leben des Jean Paul Friedrich Richter*, 5th ed. (Halle-Leipzig: Mitteldeutscher Verlag, 1975), 162.

[40] Bird, *Recasting Historical Women*, 116.

[41] Bridge, *Women's Writing*, 140–41.

[42] Mandelkow, *Goethe in Deutschland*, 2:219, 227.

[43] The employment of Eckermann as a fictional character has a long history, and is particularly common in recent German literature. See Ziolkowski, "Das Treffen in Buchenwald," 140–45.

[44] Gerald A. Fetz, "Cultural History on Stage: *In Goethes Hand*," in *Martin Walser: International Perspectives*, ed. Jürgen E. Schlunk and Armand E. Singer (New York: Peter Lang, 1987), 146.

[45] Heike A. Doane, "Love vs. Life: Martin Walser describes Johann Peter Eckermann's Development," in Bauer Pickar and Cramer, *The Age of Goethe Today*, 159–60.

[46] Doane, "Love vs. Life," 164.

[47] Wilson's most well-known critique of Goethe's reactionary political tendencies in Weimar was his best-selling study *Das Goethe-Tabu: Protest und Menschenrechte im klassischen Weimar* (Munich: dtv, 1999).

[48] Günter Niggl, *Zeitbilder: Studien und Vorträge zur deutschen Literatur des 19. und 20. Jahrhunderts* (Wurzburg: Königshausen & Neumann 2005), 164–66.

[49] See Kruse, "Walsers Eckermann-Stück: Goethe-Schelte oder Liebeserklärung?," *Monatshefte* 79 (1987): 439–48.

[50] There is also a sort of afterword, a "Letzte Nachricht" (last news) relating an anecdote concerning Ulrike's deathbed act of having Goethe's letters to her burned, placed in a silver capsule, and buried with her (287).

[51] Walser, *Brandung* (Frankfurt am Main: Suhrkamp, 1985), 167–68.

[52] See, for example, Melitta Gerhard, "Ursache und Bedeutung von Goethes 'Entsagung,'" *Jahrbuch des freien deutschen Hochstifts* (1981): 110–15, and Mauro Ponzi, "Zur Entstehung des Goetheschen Motivs der 'Entsagung,'" *Zeitschrift für Germanistik* 7 (1986): 150–59.

[53] Arthur Henkel, *Entsagung: Eine Studie zu Goethes Altersroman* (Tübingen: Max Niemeyer, 1954), 1. Henkel borrows the phrase "Epoche seiner Vollendung" from Otto Harnack's book on Goethe with this title.

[54] See also Elizabeth Margaret Dick, "Rewriting the Past: Goethe and Contemporary Literature," Ph.D. diss., Washington University, 2004, 116–17. Dick notes that Walser's intention was to "offer a new picture of Goethe" in his play, while "Sparschuh focuses more of his attention on Eckermann."

[55] Ziolkowski, "Das Treffen in Buchenwald," 144–45. Another creative work centering on Eckermann and Goethe cited by Ziolkowski (145), in which the amanuensis is devoted to his master but capable of irony and even rebellion, is a radio play described by its authors as actually renouncing all fiction, but rather arranging in a dramatic manner episodes from Eckermann's *Gespräche mit Goethe*. See F. W. Bernstein, Bernd Eilert, and Eckhard Henscheid, "Eckermann und

sein Goethe: Ein Schau-/Hörspiel getreu nach der Quelle," in *Unser Goethe: Ein Lesebuch*, ed. Eckhard Henscheid and F. W. Bernstein (Zurich: Diogenes, 1982), 975–1110, esp. 977 and 978.

[56] Boëtius discusses these circumstances in the afterword to the novella, 99–103.

[57] For a discussion of Boëtius's conscious adaptation of Mann's novella, see Dick, "Rewriting the Past," 201–2.

[58] Anthonya Visser, "Hanns-Josef Ortheils *Faustinas Küsse* — ein postmoderner Künstlerroman?," in Ester and van Gemert, *Künstler-Bilder*, 187–205, esp. 191–96.

[59] Johann Wolfgang Goethe, *Gedenkausgabe der Werke, Briefe und Gespräche*, ed. Ernst Beutler (Zurich: Artemis, 1950), 11:161.

[60] Richard Block, *The Spell of Italy: Vacation, Magic, and the Attraction of Goethe* (Detroit, MI: Wayne State UP, 2006), 106.

[61] Katya Skow, "Goethe Lite: The Fictionalization of German Literati," *Popular Culture Review* 17 (2006): 25–26.

[62] Edward W. Said, *Orientalism* (New York: Vintage Books, 1979), 19.

[63] Said, *Orientalism*, 19.

[64] Said, *Orientalism*, 341. Italics in the original.

[65] Said, "2003 Preface to the Twenty-Fifth Anniversary Edition 5 November 2003," *Princeton Alumni Weekly* (November 5, 2002), http://www.princeton.edu/~paw/web_exclusives/plus/plus_110503orient.html.

[66] Zafer Şenocak, "Wann ist der Fremde zu Hause? Betrachtungen zur Kunst und Kultur von Minderheiten in Deutschland," in *Atlas des tropischen Deutschland: Essays*, 2nd ed. (Berlin: Babel, 1993), 70–71.

[67] Şenocak, "Das Buch mit den sieben Siegeln: Über die vergessene Sprache der osmanischen Dichtung," in *War Hitler Araber? IrreFührungen an den Rand Europas: Essays* (Berlin: Babel, 1994), 39.

[68] Kontje, *German Orientalisms* (Ann Arbor: U of Michigan P, 2004), 119.

[69] For a reading of Schami that elucidates his effort to bridge the cultural division between East and West in his novels by problematizing the very idea that contemporary Arab and European lands are still characterized by essentialist Occidental and Oriental cultures — a reading that argues that Schami infuses the paradigm of Orientalism with a positive nomadic alternative to the ideal of a fixed, rooted, chthonic nationalism — see Arnds, "Orientalizing Germany in Rafik Schami's *Die Sehnsucht der Schwalbe* and *Sieben Doppelgänger*," *Seminar* 41 (2005): 275–88.

[70] Said, *Orientalism*, 167–68.

[71] Said, *Orientalism*, 153–54.

[72] Said, *Orientalism*, 154.

[73] Şenocak, "Das Buch mit den sieben Siegeln," 41.

[74] Şenocak, "Das Buch mit den sieben Siegeln," 47.

[75] Şenocak, "Wann ist der Fremde zu Hause?" 70–71.

76 William Paulson, *Literary Culture in a World Transformed: A Future for the Humanities* (Ithaca: Cornell UP, 2001), 162.

77 Ingeborg Hoesterey, *Pastiche: Cultural Memory in Art, Film, Literature* (Bloomington: Indiana UP, 2001), xi. Hoesterey discusses a number of "Goethe Pastiches" (85–90), but among them only one German-language work, the story by Thomas Bernhard on Goethe's death briefly analyzed in the introduction to the present book.

78 The famous opening couplet of the poem reads as follows: "Edel sei der Mensch/ Hilfreich und gut!" (Let people be noble, helpful and good!). Goethe, "Das Göttliche," in *Gedenkausgabe* 1: 324.

79 See Goethe, *Das Märchen*, in *Gedenkausgabe* 9: 369, and Löhr, *Das Erlkönig-Manöver*, 65.

80 See Goethe, "Auf Miedings Tod," in *Gedenkausgabe* 2: 95, and Löhr, *Das Hamlet-Komplott*, 319.

5: Savaging and Salvaging the German Enlightenment

THE EUROPEAN ENLIGHTENMENT placed great faith in human reason and scientific progress. Its adherents believed that rational thought and progressive education could help curb humanity's dark impulses, create greater social harmony, and promote equality and peace among nations. Already during the German Storm-and-Stress and Romantic periods, this focus on reason at the expense of faith and emotion provoked resistance. However, it was the employment, particularly in more recent times, of scientific progress for human exploitation, the use of technology for ever-more-destructive wars, and the massive despoiling of nature in the pursuit of its resources that helped inspire German authors from the 1970s to the present to call the Enlightenment's ideals and priorities into question through fictional caricatures of its leading adherents. The following chapter examines in detail three novels that pursue such caricature: Daniel Kehlmann's *Die Vermessung der Welt* (Measuring the world, 2005),[1] Klaas Huizing's *Das Ding an sich* (The thing-in-itself, 1998),[2] and Gert Hofmann's *Die kleine Stechardin*[3] (The little flower girl, 1994).

We will begin, however, by briefly examining Heiner Müller's play *Leben Gundlings Friedrich von Preußen Lessings Schlaf Traum Schrei: Ein Greuelmärchen*[4] (Gundling's life Friedrich of Prussia Lessing's sleep dream scream: A horror story, 1976). With respect to postmodern Enlightenment critiques that caricature well-known intellectuals from the Age of Goethe, Müller's play is the pioneering work in German-language imaginative literature, and provides a logical starting point. Following this, an examination of the philosopher Hans Blumenberg's *Der Prozeß der theoretischen Neugierde* (The process of theoretical curiosity, 1973) will offer a crucial context for our analysis. Blumenberg's book examines a key Enlightenment motif — theoretical curiosity — by means of an examination of three paradigmatic figures: Georg Christoph Lichtenberg, Immanuel Kant, and Alexander von Humboldt. Through a fortuitous coincidence, all three of these figures, as well as the trope of a scientific curiosity that is divorced from theological concerns and human emotions, figure prominently in the novels under discussion here.

Finally, the analysis of texts negatively portraying the Enlightenment will conclude with Jens Sparschuh's novel *Lavaters Maske*[5] (Lavater's mask, 1999). This text is set primarily in the present day, but includes flashbacks to the life of the eponymous protagonist, the famous physiognomist Johann Kaspar Lavater. His study of faces inspires in a contemporary researcher the quest for all-encompassing surveillance through facial analysis, a panoptic surveillance first envisioned in the Enlightenment period.

As with the novelistic presentations of Goethe, Age-of-Goethe fiction from the 1970s to the present has not been entirely negative regarding the Enlightenment, and this chapter also includes a discussion of two works emphasizing the positive side — its cosmopolitanism, search for scientific truths, and tendency toward tolerance. Thus, I will precede my examination of *Die Vermessung der Welt* by looking at Christoph Hein's epistolary tale "Die russischen Briefe des Jägers Johann Seifert"[6] (The Russian letters of the hunter Johann Seifert), part of the collection *Einladung zum Lever Bourgeois* (Invitation to the Lever bourgeois, 1980). Hein's treatment of Humboldt through the deliberately distorted lens of his assistant Seifert provides a useful pendant to Kehlmann's creative look at the explorer because Hein's unusual technique allows his Humboldt to emerge, in contrast to that of Kehlmann, as a somewhat heroic exemplar of a *valorized* Enlightenment. At the conclusion of this chapter, I will contrast Hofmann's Lichtenberg with the Lichtenberg protagonist in Boëtius's *Der Gnom: Ein Lichtenberg-Roman*[7] (The gnome: A Lichtenberg novel, 1989), which presents a less caricatured portrait of the scientist/aphorist and his thought than does Hofmann's book.

Christian Stahl opens his review of Kehlmann's *Die Vermessung der Welt* — which focuses on the explorer/geographer/scientist Humboldt and the mathematician/astronomer Carl Friedrich Gauß — by claiming that the author resorts to a well-known, reliable formula: One selects a figure prominent in German intellectual history (*Geistesgeschichte*) and creates literary capital from the intellectual's eccentricity (*Verschrobenheit*). As examples of this tried-and-true approach to composing a historical novel, Stahl cites three recent works from the same vein tapped by Kehlmann: Bernhard Setzwein's novel on Nietzsche *Nicht kalt genug* (Not cold enough, 2000); Hofmann's *Die kleine Stechardin*, whose central character is the late eighteenth-century scientist and aphorist Lichtenberg; and Huizing's fictional treatment of the relationship between Kant and his friend, the philosopher Johann Georg Hamann, *Das Ding an sich*. Stahl closes his brief review of Kehlmann's book by congratulating the author for his entertaining and intelligent novel, and for being nominated for the inaugural German Book Prize.[8]

Though Kehlmann's novel did not win, it did claim several other prestigious awards, such as the Candide Prize, the Heimito-von-Doderer Prize, and the Kleist Prize. It was also an enormous commercial success, staying atop the German magazine *Spiegel*'s bestseller list for thirty-five weeks.[9] It is by far the most acclaimed work among the novels cited by Stahl as profitably mining the eccentricities of well-known German intellectuals from the past. While Setzwein's novel on Nietzsche falls outside the time period of this study, the other novels constitute the primary object of analysis for the current chapter. This is not because these works create exemplary caricatures of key figures from the Age of Goethe. There is much in the way of successful caricature in the texts discussed in the previous chapter on Goethe himself: Hacks, Ortheil, and Walser are particularly adept at mining his eccentricities to imbue their works with humor. Instead, I will examine *Die Vermessung der Welt*, *Das Ding an sich*, and *Die kleine Stechardin* primarily in order to show how such caricature serves a purpose prominent in contemporary German letters, and one not treated in previous chapters: the critique of the German Enlightenment.

Heiner Müller's Pioneering Creative Intervention into the German Enlightenment

The pastiche of scenes constituting Müller's play features, among the primary speaking roles, not only Lessing, but Friedrich II of Prussia and Johann Paul Freiherr von Gundling, who succeeded Leibniz as the president of the Prussian Academy of Sciences during the reign of Friedrich's father, Friedrich Wilhelm I. All three characters succumb to the brutality of Prussian militarism, most clearly exemplified by Friedrich Wilhelm. Gundling is symbolically castrated by Friedrich Wilhelm's soldiers and is seen to proffer his position for the furtherance of authoritarian state control. Forced to witness the execution of his friend, Lieutenant Katte, Friedrich II adopts his father's ruthless style of rule. The once-rebellious Lessing is portrayed as on the verge of death, wishing only for sleep. He is in the process of forgetting everything, including the words of his text, and he believes he will soon hear only his own voice asking about the forgotten words (35). While Lessing's characters Nathan der Weise (Nathan the wise) and Emilia Galotti have often been proclaimed to be Enlightenment heroes, they are, in Müller's play, "presented as the victims *and the* accomplices of the orthodox external paternalistic authority," as Arlene Teraoka notes.[10] This is also the case with Schiller and Kleist in *Leben Gundlings*; largely through gesture and pantomime, they reveal a betrayal of Enlightenment ideals and acquiescence to the Prussian dictatorship. Schiller recites his idealistic poem "Der Spaziergang" (The walk, 1795) while King Friedrich forces a peasant family to recognize their turnips as oranges. Schiller's recitation, interrupted by fits of coughing, annoys Friedrich, who has a turnip sack placed over the poet's head (29–31). Kleist acts out the role of his Michael Kohlhaas, but decapitates his horse doll, reversing his hero's anti-authoritarian defiance of insisting his horses be returned to him in their original healthy state. Wearing the horse's head, the Kleist character executes a Kleist doll (33). Stage workers costumed as theatergoers pour sand onto the stage while "waiters" fill the stage with busts of "poets and thinkers." They place a bust of Lessing onto the poet himself, who vainly tries to free himself from this covering (36–37). Clearly, he becomes a victim of his own canonization, molded into an immortal representative of a Prussian culture in which Enlightenment and oppression fit together like hand and glove, or, in Lessing's case, bust and torso. In Müller's play, Lessing, Schiller, and Kleist — all champions of a liberatory Enlightenment in their youth — help perpetuate, but are sacrificed to, the Prussian instrumentalization of this movement for its own authoritarian ends. Müller's characterization of his drama as a "Greuelmärchen" (literally, a horror fairy tale) anticipates the approaches of Huizing and Hofmann, who adopt the Romantic fairy-tale genre to varying degrees in their historical novels. Despite the brevity of its treatment of Schiller, Lessing, and Kleist, *Leben Gundlings* also anticipates a tendency, particularly evident in Kehlmann's novel, to show how significant figures of the German Enlightenment reveal the imbrications in the movement of ratio-based scientific authority with authoritarianism in a rigidly hierarchical society.

Hans Blumenberg on Lichtenberg, Kant, and Humboldt

In his historical/philosophical treatise, Blumenberg treats Lichtenberg, Kant, and Humboldt as key figures in the development of the paradigm of scientific curiosity from the time of its subordination to theological concerns in the pre-Enlightenment to its full realization as a discrete domain in the psychoanalytic/anthropological age characterizing the turn to the twentieth century. Blumenberg regards Lichtenberg as a particularly significant transitional figure whose reflective curiosity marks a threshold from the need to justify the claims of knowledge to a period when the success of scientific insight was paramount and could be ruthlessly, single-mindedly pursued. Thus, Lichtenberg shuttles between the spheres of "Experiment und Tagebuch" (experiment and diary), an oscillation deftly captured in Hofmann's novel. According to Blumenberg, Lichtenberg learned from Kant, or believed he learned from Kant, that humans come to recognize and develop *themselves* in nature, that nature does not simply exist for humans to cognitively perceive. Lichtenberg goes on to realize, independently from Kant (though also in his footsteps), that the scientific description of reality can abruptly transform into a distancing from it; this is a lesson Hamann comes to learn more profoundly than Kant in Huizing's novel, and even more profoundly than Lichtenberg in *Die kleine Stechardin*. Blumenberg reveals the authoritarian political strain in Kant's later treatment of the self-imposed problem of the lack of maturity and the regulative rather than random principle of knowledge when the Enlightenment is regarded as the self-preservation of reason. Kant's famous argument in the essay "Was ist Aufklärung?" (What is enlightenment?, 1784) presumed that such immaturity was based on one's inability to engage personal understanding without external guidance, an inability stemming from a lack of courage and decisiveness. In 1786, he came to believe that state guidance — what Blumenberg terms "politische Nothilfe" (political emergency aid) — is necessary to preserve order, implying that freedom of thought independent of the laws of reason destroys itself. The authoritarian streak of the late Kant is reflected in the personality with which Huizing imbues him. Kant, in Blumenberg's view, comes to face an irresolvable dilemma: Reason, driven by theoretical curiosity and thirst for knowledge, tries to comprehend the conditional from its own conditions and thereby arrive at the unconditional; however, reason cannot grasp something that, according to Kant, does not exist under the conditions of comprehensibility. This ungraspable, unknowable essence to which Blumenberg refers is the thing-in-itself, and the irresolvable aporia in Kantian philosophy that Blumenberg sees is precisely the dilemma faced by Hamann, Kant, and Kant's servant Lampe — the three main characters in Huizing's novel — in confronting the physically manifest thing-in-itself alluded to by the book's title. For Blumenberg, Humboldt exemplifies the type of curiosity evident in the first half of the nineteenth century, which prizes scientific objectivity and accuracy. Humboldt therefore comes to deplore twin tendencies increasingly evident by the middle of that century: popular curiosity fanned by increasing media interest in scientific exploration, and enhanced state intervention into such pursuits. These are also among the chief irritants faced by the fictional Humboldt of both Hein and Kehlmann. In a passage cited by Blumenberg, Humboldt deplores the steering of science into the support of political agendas, and claims he is anything but a friend of such tutelage.[11] Particularly in Hein's story, but in Kehlmann's novel as well, Humboldt is forced to chafe precisely under such state, and state-mediated, tutelage.

Christoph Hein's Positive View of Humboldt and the Enlightenment

Einladung zum Lever Bourgeois encompasses an eclectic range of stories written and published when Hein was a citizen of the GDR. Most have a contemporary East German setting, including one, "Der neuere (glücklichere) Kohlhaas: Bericht über einen *Rechtshandel* aus den Jahren 1972/73"[12] (The New [More Successful] Kohlhaas: Report on a *Legal Dispute* from the Years 1972/73), that adapts Kleist's tale to a modern setting in narrating a chair factory bookkeeper's relentless battle against the state to obtain forty marks he felt were unjustly withheld from his annual incentive bonus; Hubert K.'s triumph and the obvious dispro- portion between the miniscule gravity of his grievance and the effort he expends to redress it turn Kleist's tragedy into a comedy. Two of the tales are historical fictions featuring prominent intellectuals. The collection's title story, "Einladung zum Lever Bourgeois," shows the playwright Jean Racine as an aging, ill man tormented by his failure to have reported a horrible crime by French soldiers that he witnessed, feeling the absolutist state would have papered over an offense perpetrated by its troops against foreign (in this case, Dutch) victims. The other historical fiction is "Die russischen Briefe des Jägers Johann Seifert." Johann Seifert was Hum- boldt's valet and servant from 1827 until Humboldt's death in 1859. Indeed, Humboldt made Seifert his sole inheritor. Seifert was married when he began his service for Humboldt, and his wife helped supervise Humboldt's household.[13] Seifert accompanied Humboldt on the latter's Russian expedition and Hein's tale consists of fictional letters written by the servant to his wife in Berlin, where the three of them lived together. Uniquely among all the authors covered in this book, Hein employs a completely colloquial eighteenth-century German diction in composing Seifert's letters. Hein captures the period style so accurately that Günther Drommer, editor of the collection's East German edition, believed Seifert actually wrote the letters, and only discovered later that nothing written by the servant remains to posterity.[14]

Hein's Seifert is naïve, chauvinistic, zealously religious, and pro- foundly bigoted, as well as being a man with a limited education. From the very first letter, he seems in constant despair, plagued by insects, sur- rounded by people and customs he does not comprehend, gullible, and utterly homesick, a homesickness enhanced by his wife's apparent failure to respond to his letters, thus arousing his suspicions. Given this circum- stance, Hein clearly intends for the reader to sympathize with the forlorn servant, but also to assume his views are dubious at best, particularly when he reports on his disputes with Humboldt. Seifert describes his master as an unpatriotic cosmopolitan, and reveals a clear dislike for Russia and Rus- sians. Because an internationalist perspective and deference to the Rus- sian-led Soviet Union were expected of GDR citizens, this circumstance alone would enhance Humboldt's image and underscore Seifert's unreli- ability among those East German citizens — perhaps even then a minor- ity — whose attitudes adhered to those of their nation's leaders. Seifert alludes to Humboldt's reputation at the Sanssouci Palace as among the "reddest" of the Jacobins (122), though he reveals that Humboldt pre- fers to remain silent on the extreme social injustices he observes in Russia when he believes protests on his part might impede his scientific pursuits. Nevertheless, Humboldt comes across as a man of the Enlightenment in the most positive sense of that term, tolerant, cultivated, cosmopolitan, and a defender of the Other. Seifert reports on how, in the course of upbraiding him for his anti-Semitism, Humboldt argues that the hatred of Jews reflects the philosophy of mediocrity. The unsuccessful and the dilettante seek their salvation in denouncing the Other and the foreign. Rejected suitors call all women whores. Jews and homosexuals, in this Humboldt's view, are a favorite target of those who blame the Other for their own failures and shortcomings: "Und mit ganz besonderer Vorliebe stürze sich der Chorus dieser Kuemmerlinge auf die Männerliebe (sic!) und die Juden, um sich für sein banales, unglueckseliges Leben zu rächen" (And with special fondness this chorus of wretches pounces on manlove [sic!] and the Jews, in order to take revenge for their banal, unfortunate life). Seifert finds Humboldt's perspective here eccentric and seems not to comprehend it (139–40).

Humboldt's antinationalist cosmopolitanism becomes evident in his response to Seifert's question concerning how long they will have to travel through Siberia before their grasp of their mother tongue becomes little more than a distant memory: "Er lachte, schüttelte den Kopf und antwortete, er sei, habe er nur eine LandesGrentze ueberschritten, unfähig, weiterhin ein Deutscher zu sein, und man würde im gesammten TransUral keinen national gesinnteren Sibirjaken finden als ihn. Er sei, wenn er sich auch nicht dazu verstehe, auf sein Vaterland zu verzichten, keinesfalls ein Vaterländer" (He laughed, shook his head and answered, he was incapable of remaining a German once a national border was crossed, and one would find in the entire Trans Urals a no more nationally oriented Siberiack than he was. While he would not agree to renounce his fatherland, he was absolutely not a fatherlander). He goes on to note that one can forget one's own language comfortably at home; a trip is not suitable for such purposes (110–11). Through the veil of Seifert's eighteenth-century conversational German, Humboldt emerges as both possessed of sardonic humor and as a true citizen of the world. However, it is particularly this former quality that is completely lacking in the figure as represented by Kehlmann, and precisely this deficiency makes Humboldt in *Die Vermessung der Welt* seem relentlessly Prussian, diminishing the dynamic, trans-Atlantic globalism that contemporary scholarship has discovered in his work and in his person. This explains the negative reception of Kehlmann's novel by academics such as Ottmar Ette, discussed below, though I will argue that Humboldt's cosmopolitanism is nevertheless evident in the portrayal of the explorer in *Die Vermessung der Welt*.

Humboldt has been assumed by many commentators, both then and now, to have been a homosexual. Hein's Seifert alludes to these rumors at times in the narrative, though he categorically denies them (for example, 137 and 145–46). At any rate, Humboldt is not victimized by such rumors in the tale, but rather by the sort of political interventions into his scientific expeditions and experiments that Blumenberg regarded as a hallmark of Humboldt's later years and that he finds complaints about in Humboldt's writing. However, Hein's Humboldt is quite adroit at minimizing the impact of this state interference, and not solely by turning a blind eye to the oppression he witnesses. As Marianne Krumrey observes in analyzing the story, Humboldt makes use of the narrow-mindedness and infantilism of the Czarist bureaucrats and military officials in order to appease them, holding their mistrust in check even though the courtiers and petty state officials, motivated by jealousy, resentment, and a hatred of intellectual, creative endeavor, continuously make his life difficult.[15] Through the filter of Seifert's letters, Humboldt's contempt for such figures becomes clear; they are poisonous toads (*Kröten*) who give vent to their own spleen by hiding their malicious intent behind a veneer of sanctimonious moral and political pretence (180–81). Like all GDR authors who dared veer from socialist realist orthodoxy, Hein had to deal with such state servants as well, and his identification with Humboldt in this regard is obvious.[16] However, Humboldt is not merely the target of Russian jealousy in the story. The mineralogist Gustav Rose, who accompanied Humboldt on his Russian expedition, complains to Seifert that courtiers such as Humboldt, Goethe, and Schelling are anxious to sit "in the shadows of power," in contrast to "modest gardeners" such as himself, who must content themselves with useful but more modest accomplishments (136). Nonetheless, in spite of his political expediency, Hein's Humboldt emerges in Seifert's letters as a thoroughly sympathetic Enlightenment figure, a misunderstood victim of those who resent his genius.

A Stay-at-Home Skeptic and a Globe-Trotting Kantian: Daniel Kehlmann's Gauß and Humboldt

Kehlmann's *Die Vermessung der Welt* contains a chapter that includes an account of Humboldt's journey to Russia. Indeed, it is the novel's penultimate episode, in which both Humboldt and Gauß make their final appearance; the denouement narrates the voyage of Gauß's son Eugene to America, the result of a forced exile after he is arrested at a rally featuring an agitator in the mold of German nationalist Turnvater Jahn. Kehlmann's treatment of the Russian expedition, like Hein's story, features the mineralogist Rose and the zoologist Christian Ehrenberg (who also accompanied the actual Humboldt on the trip), though Seifert himself is never mentioned. As is typical in *Die Vermessung der Welt*, and unlike Hein's story, the narration of the Russian expedition is suffused with a comic nuance at once subtle and ribald, as when a Kalmuck Buddhist lama pats his substantial abdomen as a sign of his inner strength, then touches Humboldt's more meager chest and proclaims: "Aber da sei nichts. Wer das nicht verstehe, werde rastlos, laufe durch die Welt wie der Sturm, erschüttere alles und wirke nicht" (But there is nothing there. Whoever does not understand that becomes restless, runs through the world like the storm, upsetting everything and effecting nothing). The perplexed Humboldt replies that he does not believe in nothing, but in the fullness and richness of nature, and assumes there is a translation problem when the lama claims in turn that nature is unredeemed and breathes despair (285–86). This brief exchange reveals the antithetical perspectives of Hein and Kehlmann with respect to Humboldt as an Enlightenment figure. Through the confused lens of Seifert's letters, Humboldt emerges as a shrewd, albeit calculating, champion of Enlightenment scientific progress, rationality, and tolerance, while it is Kehlmann's Humboldt who is obviously confused, displaying the limits of Enlightenment rationality in comprehending a culture radically at variance with that of contemporary Western Europe.

While Hein's epistolary tale derives entirely from Humboldt's Russian expedition, *Die Vermessung der Welt* can be described as an unusual, double *Bildungsroman* (a genre that traditionally follows the growth of one individual from childhood to maturity via acculturation and life experience), for its initial chapters alternately narrate the separate childhoods, educations, and personal and career development of Humboldt and Gauß. The two men do not meet until some two-thirds of the way through the novel, when Humboldt succeeds in persuading Gauß to travel from his home in Göttingen for a court reception in Berlin, where Humboldt resides after 1827. At other times, Gauß follows these adventures as they are related by newspaper accounts. Kehlmann employs a somewhat dialectical approach in narrating the lives of the two scientists until well into the novel, alternating chapters devoted exclusively to one or the other of the two scientists in their early lives, showing them to be virtually antithetical in their personal makeup, experiences, and proclivities. The polarities in their personas continue to be evident even after they meet. To be sure, both suffer somewhat brutal childhoods: Gauß through his alcoholic father and a grammar school teacher who treats him (until he discovers his genius) with the same cruelty he employs with the other lower class children, and Humboldt through his older brother Wilhelm, portrayed as a sadist who tries to lure him to his death on two occasions. Gauß follows his mathematical calling somewhat reluctantly, disappointed that he cannot become a Latin scholar. He develops into a passionate, earthy man who comes close to suicide when his first proposal of marriage is spurned and, expecting the same result the second time around, he is on the verge of poisoning himself with a substance Humboldt investigated on his South American explorations when her consent arrives by mail. He detests travel, his work as a surveyor, and his pedagogical duties as a Göttingen professor, where he must teach mathematics to students who cannot grasp even simple principles. Humboldt, by contrast, is entirely devoted to "measuring the world" in South America and the Caribbean. Kehlmann portrays him as so single-minded in his pursuit of scientific truth that he is virtually devoid of personal needs, and seemingly asexual. Neither a young girl nor a young boy sent on different occasions to his dwellings during the journey are capable of seducing him, though he is somewhat excited by the latter, and late in the book admits to his homosexual inclinations. While he deplores human and natural exploitation and slavery in the abstract, even affronting American Secretary of State James Madison by speaking of the "Alpdruck der Sklaverei" (nightmare of slavery) before Madison hints at President Jefferson's slave holdings (212–13), he seems oblivious to individual suffering. To the astonishment of his assistant and traveling companion, Aimé Bonpland, who is periodically upbraided by Humboldt for seeking to fulfill the appetite he shares with Gauß, he does not realize that a screaming adolescent girl they come across was the victim of rape, believing she must be lost and suffering from the heat (104–5).

Kehlmann casts Humboldt as an almost blind adherent of the Enlightenment, with his zealous belief in reason and his conviction that geographical domains only become real once they have been measured and their coordinates determined (for example, 135–36). Gauß, by contrast, believes such measurements rob the natural world of its corporeal facticity and comes to perceive that his surveying activity does not merely measure tracts of land, but invents them (268). Though Humboldt's measuring mania takes him around the world, from Spain to the Americas and later to Russia, while Gauß stays at home in pursuing his mathematical, astronomic, and surveying activities, Kehlmann clearly intends us to regard Gauß as the true forerunner of scientific modernism. As Mark Anderson has observed in an essay on Kehlmann, Humboldt's belief in the universality of time and space is shown to be in error, and he works with outmoded media not adapted to the terrain he explores; Gauß, on the other hand, with his postulate on "curved space," is shown to establish the foundation for the contemporary scientific perception of the world.[17] Thus, when Humboldt claims understanding (*der Verstand*) forms natural laws, Gauß replies that this is old Kantian nonsense: "Der Verstand forme gar nichts und verstehe wenig. Der Raum biege und die Zeit dehne sich" (220; Understanding forms nothing and understands little. Space curves and time expands). It is clear that Kehlmann's sympathies lie with Gauß's anti-Kantian, anti-Enlightenment perspective.

In Acapulco, Humboldt tells a journalist, while lying on his back and looking through a telescope (he is clearly more comfortable with the popular press than the Humboldt of Blumenberg or Hein), that a precise atlas of New Spain will promote the settlement of the colony and the domination of nature (196). The image of a supine Humboldt, not ceasing to survey the heavens even as he talks to a reporter, adds a tone of levity to his advocacy of the Enlightenment's telos of dominion over nature and indigenous people. The contemporary reader is expected to recognize this utterance as portending the global ecological catastrophe humanity faces in the twenty-first century. As Heinz-Peter Preußer has argued, the phenomenal popularity of *Die Vermessung der Welt* stems from Kehlmann's ability to turn an ambience of future decline from tragedy to comedy, creating a classical critique of civilization by selling it as a means to pleasure (*Genussmittel*).[18] Kehlmann's Humboldt is the Enlightenment personified, progressive with respect to issues such as slavery and individual liberty but tone-deaf with respect to social and cultural nuance, as when he buys South American slaves, gives them their freedom, and is surprised when they simply do not know what to do next (70–71). Humboldt's desire to make nature productive by measuring and dominating it, setting the stage for future environmental catastrophe, is a major element in Kehlmann's humor-laced, anti-Enlightenment polemic.

Clearly, the image of Humboldt as a caricatured Enlightenment visionary, enhanced through dialectical contrast with the skeptical Gauß figure in Kehlmann's novel, does not necessarily do justice to the historical Humboldt. Chenxi Tang has argued persuasively that Humboldt was profoundly impacted by Romantic convictions concerning the landscape of mood, and convinced that an immersion in landscape painting and poetry furthered the study of nature, even though his ultimate aim was objective truth and a "universally valid scientific gaze" that could be extended to any geographic region.[19] Thus, a comic high point in *Die Vermessung der Welt*, Humboldt's translation of Goethe's celebrated poem that begins with the line "Über allen Gipfeln" (over all the treetops) into a literalizing Spanish[20] certainly would never have been conceived by the landscape-poetry loving historical Humboldt. Of course, as a creative writer, Kehlmann had to be free to take liberty with the true nature of historical personages such as Humboldt and Gauß, as with broader historical facts themselves. This is true of all authors who imaginatively engage with the past. Kehlmann eloquently defended the liberties he takes in *Die Vermessung der Welt* in his essay "Wo ist Carlos Montúfar?"[21] (Where is Carlos Montúfar?), an appropriate title since this traveling companion of Humboldt's in South America is nowhere mentioned in the novel. The key point here is that Kehlmann draws on his poetic license with respect to Humboldt with the goal of creating a pointed but humorous Enlightenment caricature.

In a recent study *Alexander von Humboldt und die Globalisierung* (Alexander von Humboldt and globalization, 2009), Ottmar Ette takes Kehlmann to task for distorting Humboldt by making him appear as a humorless adherent of the Enlightenment. Like Tang, Ette emphasizes that the explorer was deeply attuned to the literary sensibilities of his time, a circumstance Kehlmann's novel ignores. Ette argues that, in creating his

Humboldt, Kehlmann drew on clichéd representations of the explorer, such as Friedrich Schiller's 1797 letter to Christian Gottfried Körner claiming that Humboldt's thinking was marked by pure unadorned reason shameless in its surveying of nature. Ette indicates that Kehlmann preferred to draw on anecdotal remarks about Humboldt, such as Schiller's, rather than examining Humboldt's actual oeuvre. Ette regrets that the cosmopolitan, emancipatory character of Humboldt's perspective is masked by *Die Vermessung der Welt*, and claims that it is time to discover this strain in Humboldt's world view by renewed attention to the works themselves.[22] One might argue that passages such as the explorer's dialogue with Madison actually allow his progressive, cosmopolitan thought to emerge. While Ette is fundamentally correct in his analysis of Kehlmann's sources and about the one-sided caricature the novelist draws, it is also important to remember that Humboldt is only the secondary target of his satire; through his humorous treatment of this figure and his contrast with Gauß, the Enlightenment itself becomes the primary object of the novel's ridicule.

The issue of the historical Humboldt's relationship to the Enlightenment is a rather vexed one. In his comprehensive overview of Humboldt reception from 1848 to the present day, Nicolaas Rupke has shown that the explorer and scientist has been appropriated by various political and social groups according to their own ideological needs. For example, the National Socialists ignored the strong impact of the Berlin Enlightenment, including those of its Jewish adherents such as Moses Mendelssohn, on the shaping of Humboldt's thought. The Nazis twisted Humboldt into the adherent of an irrationalist strain of German idealism they wished to cultivate in its modern form. The intellectuals of the GDR, by contrast, saw him as a champion of the progressive humanist thinking they associated with the French Revolution and the European Enlightenment.[23] Not surprisingly, this latter Humboldt dominates in Hein's configuration, with some exceptions. For example, he argues strongly against the rationalist technique of stuffing young students with knowledge, which he feels dulls their sensibility. Here, Humboldt boasts that, up to the age of eighteen, he himself was a virtually unschooled child whom teachers saw as quite unpromising; his own early education was "naturhaft" (163; grounded in nature). Humboldt thus appears to be an advocate of Rousseau's pedagogy — a pedagogy, of course, which had a profound influence on the development of European Romantic thought. Seifert also cites Humboldt's advocacy for the progressive Young Germany movement in the 1830s, a movement that the servant associates with "Jidden-Bengel" (170; Jewish scoundrels). On the other hand, as in Kehlmann's novel, Hein's Humboldt advocates human domination of nature (150), revealing a negative Enlightenment tendency. Michael Dettelbach has noted that "like the historiography of natural science itself, historical assessments of Alexander von Humboldt have ever been pulled between the two poles of empiricism and idealism, Enlightenment and Romanticism,"[24] and that Humboldt's scientific work not only encompasses the priorities of both movements but highlights certain affinities between them. His argument is quite convincing, and it is safe to say that Hein's portrait of Humboldt is more nuanced in this regard than Kehlmann's.

A Bad-Luck Charm Defies Kant and Hamann

Kehlmann's Humboldt is an avowed Kantian; early in his travels with Bonpland, he catches the Frenchman in flagrante with a woman and, in upbraiding him for this deed, he asks him if he has never read Kant (48). Shortly after completing his magnum opus, the *Disquisitiones Arithemeticae*, as a young man, Gauß journeys to Königsberg to visit the famous philosopher and to deliver a copy of the book to him. He explains in detail the book's complex hypothesis, and Kant's immediate response is to ask his servant Lampe to purchase some sausages and stars (*Wurst und Sterne*). Realizing the hunched figure before him is an utterly senile old man, Gauß takes polite leave when he hears the song of male voices. Lampe says this is the prisoners' choir, which always disturbs his master (95–97). In creating this episode, Kehlmann may have drawn on Huizing's *Das Ding an sich*, where Kant's annoyance at the Königsberg prisoners' choir also comes up. Though Huizing's Kant is not the senile dwarf found in Kehlmann's novel, this definer of the Enlightenment also cuts a rather ridiculous figure as one of Huizing's three chief protagonists (along with Lampe and Hamann). The "thing-in-itself" is a clay shard proffered to Hamann by a Russian courier in London. The Russian not only does not demand compensation for this mysterious artifact, but pays Hamann to take it off his hands because it has brought him and his nation bad luck. He claims the impression found on the shard is the handprint of the Biblical Adam, who thereby sealed a pact with the devil. This Hamann is clearly naïve; he had been taken advantage of several times on his way from Riga to London, and then again in London itself. Given his credulity and the debt he has incurred through this unfortunate trait, it is unsurprising that he agrees to the bargain with the Russian. A humorously ponderous prologue to the novel had established that the shard had been found in Kant's tomb by early forensic anthropologists who had wanted to study the philosopher's skull to see if it could reveal the secret of his genius. The fictitious narrator had come across the report of their findings and, obsessed with discovering the truth behind the shard, he traces its progress from the time Hamann obtained it in London. The circumstance that the "thing-in-itself" is a physical object already parodies Kant's abstract signifier for the earth's phenomena, the noumenal essence of which cannot be grasped by humanity.

It soon becomes apparent to Hamann that the shard is indeed a sort of bad-luck charm that seems responsible for his lack of personal and professional success. In Königsberg, Hamann turns to Kant in the hope the genius can rid him of the object, and the philosopher employs his servant, Lampe, to destroy the obviously durable shard by means of modern science, thereby also hoping to cure his brilliant friend of his apparent superstition. Indeed, Kant accuses Hamann of having become a religious fanatic and, in admonishing him, sings the praises of reason, virtue, and a belief in the progress of humanity (55). Thus, Huizing's Kant constitutes the perfect Enlightenment role model for Kehlmann's Humboldt, who unwaveringly acts according to these dictates and tacitly admonishes men like Bonpland to do the same. Lampe, however, who seems a model of Prussian military rectitude, reflecting his career as a soldier prior to his employment with Kant, fails in his missions to destroy the clay shard. Instead, Lampe himself is injured in these attempts and they later bring misfortune to some of the individuals who attempt the most advanced contemporary scientific techniques to rid Hamann of the object. These techniques include electrocution through channeled lightening, steam cooking, artificially induced freezing, and an animal magnetism ceremony conducted by its celebrated inventor, Franz Mesmer. Hamann himself takes part in the journey to Braunschweig and the mesmerization procedure. All these undertakings fail to annihilate the ancient relic. Finally, an aesthetic approach in the form of a glass harmonica adagio composed and performed by Hamann, with hummed accompaniment by all three of the novel's chief protagonists, splits the shard into two pieces. However, when Kant later discovers the object as a once-again-seamlessly-reunified entity, he arranges on his deathbed, surreptitiously through his maid, to have it placed in his coffin prior to his burial. Between the chapters narrating the adventures of Hamann, Lampe, and the thing-in-itself, Huizing inserts letters, primarily correspondence between Hamann and the physiognomist Johann Casper Lavater, in which Hamann reveals the arc of an increasing estrangement from Kantian philosophy and toward the mystically tinged anti-Enlightenment sensual linguistics the actual Hamann indeed developed. Lavater's responses gradually reveal the mysterious history of the shard.

Gauß and Hamann do not have a great deal in common historically, and they cut quite disparate figures in the respective novels by Kehlmann and Huizing. Kehlmann's Gauß is a committed scientist who is able to establish a relatively stable life in Göttingen professionally, financially, and personally despite the unhappiness that the stresses and changes in all these domains cause him. Hamann, by contrast, is a rather unstable, itinerant philosopher who, goaded by his correspondence with Lavater, increasingly immerses himself in a seeming religious obscurantism unthinkable for the Göttingen scientist, who tends toward both skepticism and scientific prophecy. Nevertheless, the fictional Gauß and Hamann play similar roles as everyman-like foils to their seemingly soulless, emotionally stunted counterparts, Humboldt and Kant respectively. This character contrast in both novels enhances their anti-Enlightenment tenor because Humboldt and Kant come across as exaggerated specimens of unfeeling Enlightenment rationalism. This is particularly the case with respect to sexuality. Gauß, Hamann, and the novels' respective chief "servant" or assistant figures, Bonpland and Lampe, emerge as relatively sensual, passionate men, and the portrayals of their relationships with women, while tinged by humor, are clearly designed to evoke empathetic identification on the part of the reader. Humboldt's homosexuality is revealed rather late in Kehlmann's novel (264), though there are earlier hints. For the most part, he seems impervious to sensuality, or even annoyed by it when he finds Bonpland giving in to temptation. Kant, whom Humboldt cites in one of his admonitions to the Frenchman, is portrayed in *Das Ding an sich* as completely asexual. Indeed, the prologue, which parodies the scientific veneer of nineteenth-century phrenology, draws on one of the studies of Kant's skull to describe it as exhibiting both a dominant tendency toward "Vernünftigkeit," an exaggerated propriety and rationalism, and a correspondingly extreme lack of development with respect to libido (14–15). Huizing's Kant fully lives up to this phrenological report. In this respect, Kehlmann and Huizing employ similar character dialectics in the service of skewering the Enlightenment.

On a different plane, the imbuing of Kant's thing-in-itself concept with a physical form constitutes another example of Huizing's use of the sensual to deconstruct the Enlightenment. The Adamic shard driving the plot of *Das Ding an sich* almost literally embodies the impossibility of scientific reason's attempt to arrive at the unconditional through its own conditions, the aporia Blumenberg locates at the core of Kant's somatology. In yet another variation on the novel's employment of the corporeal in undercutting the Enlightenment, the shard as an irreducible and indestructible physical essence is seen to inspire the turn toward a sensual linguistics by the former Enlightenment-adherent Hamann. Thus, Huizing uses a fictional device to motivate an intellectual transformation that the historical Hamann actually experienced. Indeed, with the exception of the fabulous shard, Huizing's delineation of Hamann's religious conversion in London closely follows the historical record, with a couple of notable exceptions. In both cases, Hamann was in London at the behest of Christoph Berens, also a friend of Kant, who later tried to win Hamann back to Enlightenment rationalism. The historical Hamann did engage in a mission involving a Russian diplomatic official, though the nature of that mission, even whether it was mainly a political or commercial undertaking, remains unknown. As in *Das Ding an sich*, the historical Hamann enjoyed playing the lute, spent considerable time in London socializing with a professional lute player, but broke off this relationship when his patron's homosexual activities became evident. In substantial debt and in poor health, Hamann isolated himself and intensely studied the Bible, resulting in his conversion to a form of Christianity somewhat tinged by Pietism. In *Das Ding an sich*, this newfound religiosity leads Hamann immediately to doubts concerning human progress and "proud" reason (48).

Huizing's decision to have Hamann's initial response to his epiphany manifest itself as a refutation of Enlightenment reason and its embrace of teleological human progress underscores the anti-Enlightenment polemic inherent in his book. In their analyses of the London conversion, Hamann scholars James O'Flaherty and John Betz emphasize the intensely personal nature of his experience and the productive spur to the lyrical and philosophical writing it brought into being, but do not suggest its immediate result was a refutation of Enlightenment thought.[25] Huizing also employs poetic license in implying that Lavater had a significant role in the development of Hamann's theological perspectives. At the conclusion to his book, Huizing notes that "Die Briefe sind Centonen aus Briefen und häufig freie Erfindungen" (237; the letters are centos from letters and frequently free inventions). An example of such an approach can be seen in briefly comparing the novel's third "fliegender Brief" (flying scroll, a biblical allusion) — in which Hamann, among other things, attempts to ascertain the constitution of reason on the basis of Kantian doctrine — with its source, Hamann's letter to Lavater dated 18 January 1778. Some passages are virtually identical, as when Hamann notes a correspondence between Lavater's expressed need for courage in the face of an overwhelming burden created by the many tasks he faces, and his own loss of courage under the burden of his idleness and boredom.[26] However, while Kant is nowhere mentioned in the original letter, Huizing uses the third "fliegender Brief" as the occasion to have Hamann praise Kant's attempt in the *Kritik der reinen Vernunft* (Critique of pure reason, 1781) to establish the sensual basis of all knowledge while claiming, in rhetorical questions contra Kant, that even reason is dependent on language, and that such reason is perhaps still too "proud" (121–22). Of course, in evoking this key difference in the philosophies of the two men, Huizing adheres to intellectual history. Hamann did diverge from his friend in seeing the human capacity for reason as linked to the sensual imagery of rational language, and in seeing Kantian metaphysics as denuding language of its connection to the concrete, factical world.[27]

While the narrative in *Das Ding an sich* of Hamann's London sojourn largely adheres to history, and the letters, as Huizing himself notes, are a mélange of quotations, paraphrases from various sources, and pure invention, the body of the text, in which the shard and the attempts to destroy it are the centerpiece of the novel, is obviously the product of the author's imagination. In setting the stage for the shard adventures, Huizing maneuvers fact and fiction in a manner designed to heighten the effectiveness of the novel's anti-Enlightenment perspective. The historical Berens and Kant made two attempts after Hamann's return to Königsberg to undo his conversion and win him back to Enlightenment ideals. These meetings inspired Hamann to write his most famous treatise, the *Sokratische Denkwürdigkeiten* (Socratic memorabilia, 1759). Its subtitle concludes with the dedicatory missive "An Niemand und an Zween" (To Nobody and to [the] Twain),[28] and this "twain" consists of Berens and Kant. As Betz remarks, Hamann's "message to them, wrapped behind many veils and symbolic allusions was simple: He was not to be reconverted to the ideals of the Enlightenment."[29] Huizing makes this work and its immediate successors the product of the walk during which Kant accuses his new friend of having become a religious fanatic and praises virtue, reason, and human progress (55).

Huizing does not allude to the "simple message" in the *Sokratische Denkwürdigkeiten* summarized by Betz. To have done so would have undermined the efficacy of the shard adventures in making such a reconversion impossible, for it is the shard that brings about the defeat of science and the Enlightenment, and the concomitant victory of art and emotion. This becomes evident with particular vividness in the chapter "Das Rohe und das Gekochte" (The raw and the cooked), an allusion to the book of the same title by structural anthropologist Claude Lévi-Strauss. The steam machine not only fails to damage the shard, but scalds Lampe's arm and is itself nearly destroyed in the process. It is made to sing. The result shocks the French team who attempt the pulverization, and causes one of them, Jacques, to break into poetry. The shard's supernatural power confounds Enlightenment science and produces an aesthetic moment evocative of powerful feelings (114–16). Ultimately, the shard inspires Hamann's own lyrical profusion, transforms him into the "vociferous" critic of Kant, and the "Seher der radikalen Aufklärung" (214–16; seer of the radical Enlightenment). Kant, spurred by Hamann's negative review of his *Kritik der reinen Vernunft*, reverts to his typical coldness by allowing his relationship with this friend to taper off despite the emotional bond the two shared in the wake of Hamann's successful musical undertaking, which temporarily split the shard in half (209–11, 219). Near the novel's conclusion, Kant orders his maid to weave the shard, hidden in a little packet, into his burial shroud, and then dies, "preußisch, müde und lebenssatt" (229; Prussian, tired, and fed up with life). The contrast between the weary, resigned, expiring Kant and the revitalized Hamann evokes a victory of art over science, sensuality over abstraction, the "radical" Enlightenment over the "rational" Enlightenment. Huizing uses his fabulous Adamic shard to shatter Kantian reason and metaphysical idealism.

A Fairy-Tale Rendering of Lichtenberg

Das Ding an sich closes with an ironic epilogue suggesting that perhaps someday science might develop a method for the shard's ultimate destruction, for which the scholarly narrator already has an idea (234). The Enlightenment dream of domination over nature and mystery that the narrator's remark reveals is shown to transcend history. The opening line of the narrative, immediately following the prologue about the shard's discovery in the course of the scientists' phrenological research into Kant's skull, begins with the words "Es war einmal ein Handlungsreisender" (Once upon a time there was a business traveler), followed by a description of this man's current circumstances. This traveler is revealed to be Hamann (19). These three opening words, "Es war einmal," served as the opening to many fairy tales that were collected (most famously by the Brothers Grimm) or were composed during Germany's Romantic age, and are conventionally translated into English as "once upon a time." With their sensuality, vivid imagery, natural language, and enchanted supernaturalism, fairy tales appealed to the Romantics partly because they constituted a genre that was anathema to German Enlightenment predilections with respect to both form and content. Thus, Huizing's casting of his novel as a fairy tale is consistent with this intent. Hofmann's *Die kleine Stechardin* not only commences with a variation on the "es war einmal" prelude, but is completely suffused with a fairy-tale ambience and with Romantic irony. Both qualities are evident on the first page. The opening line: "Einmal, vor vielen, vielen Jahren, stieg der Professor Lichtenberg in seinen Rederock und wollte mal vors Haus" (7; Once many, many years ago Professor Lichtenberg climbed into his lecturing coat and wanted to go out in front of his house) slightly reworks the more standard fairy-tale prelude employed by Huizing, but both variants evoke the fairy-tale atmosphere of timelessness, a counterpoint to the Enlightenment telos of a routine, measured, and ordered temporality. In contrast to the complex hypotactic syntax evident in Huizing's "es war einmal" introduction of his Hamann figure,[30] designed perhaps to parody the run-on fulminations evident in the writing style of Enlightenment philosophers typified by Kant (but also by the narrator, a scholarly successor who originally intended to write a dissertation on the Enlightenment philosopher's theory of radical evil), Hofmann's opening line previews the child-like, credulous simplicity characteristic of *Die kleine Stechardin* as a whole, a tone similar to the modern sanitized versions of the Grimms' fairy tales that have been reconstituted for the very young. This is enhanced by another technique present throughout the novel and already employed on the first page: the interruption of the narrative by a rhetorical/pedagogical question of the sort found in children's books but related in this case to the Romantic parabasis discussed in chapter 2 in

connection with Härtling's *Hölderlin*. The narrator notes the diminutive Lichtenberg's enormous hump, claiming people not only wanted
to see it, but also to feel it: "Warum? / Es brachte Glück!" (7; Why? It
brought luck!). Like parabasis, such interruptions deliberately break the
narrative flow and call attention to the narrator himself, an enactment
of the kind of irony adopted in the early Romantic period to subvert the
Enlightenment ideal of poetic verisimilitude favored by Gottsched and
his followers.

As is evident in the title, *Die kleine Stechardin* focuses on Lichtenberg's relationship with Maria Dorothea Stechard, the young teenage girl
whom he originally employed as a servant and who became his lover. The
novel is first and foremost a love story, though it is a great exaggeration
to claim, as does Klaus Harpprecht, that nothing else counts as significant
in this work; science, literature, the epoch's din (*Getöse*), and the Enlightenment itself appear to him completely unimportant in comparison with
the novel's overarching theme of love, though he acknowledges that the
historical Lichtenberg was a man of the Enlightenment, an "Aufklärer."[31]
It would be more precise to say that Hofmann's unusual fairy-tale style,
with its almost grotesque and surreal underscoring of Lichtenberg's tiny
size and correspondingly enormous hunchback, as well as his superstitious
reception by the townspeople (all evident in the previously cited opening
page), both subvert the writer's stature as a serious Enlightenment figure
and mitigate the natural tendency of contemporary readers to see in the
relationship between a man in his mid-thirties and an adolescent of thir-
teen (her age when Lichtenberg first met her as a flower girl) an instance
of child abuse. In other words, Hofmann's ability to make this love story
plausible, even touching, to modern sensibilities, is closely related to the
subversion of the Enlightenment in and through its representative and
chief protagonist in the novel, the scientist and aphorist Lichtenberg.

Lichtenberg's hump also constitutes an example of the Bakhtinian
grotesque. In his book on Rabelais, *Tvorchestvo Fransua Rable* (Rabelais and his world, 1965), Bakhtin describes "the grotesque body" as "a
body in the act of becoming."[32] That is to say, grotesquely exaggerated
body parts in Rabelais subvert the very principle of a holistic, integral
world with a pre-given cosmic order. The grotesque body challenges both
epistemological and social closure, the paradigm of an already established
harmonious totality, whether grounded in the divine destiny preached
in Rabelais' time or in the scientific rationalism of the Enlightenment.
Bakhtin suggests that if the world were already governed by a pre-given,
perfect order, such grotesque corporeal distortions would not exist.
Lichtenberg's hump not only shows he will remain childlike and thus
never a completely "mature" adult who accepts, and takes his place in,
the social, scientific, and academic order, but that his work and his very
being undermine — even if only at a tacit level — those very orders. Like

Bakhtin's Rabelais in connection with his age, Hofmann wants to show us an Enlightenment world that, contrary to its own self-perception, is continuously caught up in the process of becoming. Lichtenberg's hump also hints, much as Rabelais' grotesquely exaggerated noses, at the carnivalesque sexuality that will unfold when the scientist begins his relationship with his adolescent flower girl. Finally, it foregrounds his singularity, causing the "actions and events" that evolve in Hofmann's narrative "to be interpreted on the level of a single, individual life,"[33] a circumstance articulated by Bakhtin in the new corporeal canon of fifteenth-century literature exemplified by Rabelais.

Prior to Lichtenberg's transformative relationship with the young Stechard, Hofmann's novel portrays him as a highly neurotic, somewhat alienated hypochondriac, in keeping with the standard trope of the eccentric artist and scientist; *Die kleine Stechardin* illuminates both these facets in the dwarf's life and work. We see him in this early phase of the book as Blumenberg did, almost literally moving between the domains of experiment and diary, which is to say, between the scientific investigations he conducts through his huge array of instruments and his constant scribbling down of brilliantly witty remarks into notebooks that are not intended for public consumption (although they are the primary source of his posthumous fame). As Hofmann puts it in his characteristically pithy style, in a passage descriptive of Lichtenberg's bifurcated writing and belonging to the Stechard phase of the novel (for, rather than ending his dual career, his relationship with her simply added a third dimension to his life): "Es gab zwei verschiedene Arten, wissenschaftliche und andere. Für die wissenschaftlichen gab's ein Publikum, die anderen schrieb er für sich" (92; There were two different kinds, scientific and others. There was an audience for the scientific ones, he wrote the others for himself). As in *Die Vermessung der Welt* and *Das Ding an sich*, the scientific undertakings delineated in *Die kleine Stechardin* have a rather ridiculous quality, adding to the novel's subversion of the Enlightenment pursuit of quantitative, rational, and rationalizing knowledge. This tendency is enhanced by the "other" genre of Lichtenberg's writing, his diary entries, although, as Hofmann himself acknowledges (in a manner more blunt than Huizing's confession that his quotes are a mélange of genuine source material and invention), even some of the citations in *Die kleine Stechardin* are "erstunken und erlogen" (5; a pack of lies).

Be that as it may, Lichtenberg's utterances in the novel, whether stemming from the eighteenth-century aphorist or completely fabricated, sometimes provide a deconstructive counterpoint to his research endeavors, thereby undermining Enlightenment science, a purport consistent with the intent of the other two novels discussed here, but unique with respect to Hofmann's approach. This uniqueness is enabled by Lichtenberg's unusual eighteenth-century split identity as both a rationalist

pursuer of measurable scientific knowledge and an acerbic creator of aphorisms calling into question, among other things, the motives and validity
behind such pursuits. Thus, on the way to Hanover to survey territories
at the behest of the English monarch to whom they still belong, Lichtenberg takes along a telescope, precision watch, and quadrant. With the
telescope he constantly observes the heavenly firmament and counts the
stars, but only, as he puts it, "um sich seiner Nichtigkeit zu versichern"
(151; in order to assure himself of his nullity). In conversing with a Hungarian guest, Lichtenberg claims that thoughts, the background of the
world, must be prepared sensitively, like a good salad. This serves as his
metaphor for "die Redekunst," the art of speech. When the Hungarian
then asks what else he does (173), Lichtenberg says he "observed":

> Er observierte sowohl die tote wie auch die lebendige Welt. Von den
> Lebewesen observierte er sowohl die niederen als auch die hohen,
> und von den hohen, nun, . . . Er observierte Männer und Frauen,
> Pferde, junge Hunde, Katzen, da kannte er keinen Unterschied.

> [He observed the dead as well as the living world. From the living
> creatures he observed the lower as well as the higher, and from the
> higher, well. . . . He observed men and women, horses, young dogs,
> cats, here he did not know any difference.]

His heart then quickens when he reveals what really engages his observer's eye, namely, women in long skirts with narrow waists and in high
shoes (174). Lichtenberg thereby describes for the Hungarian his oscillation between aphoristic writing and detached, scientific observation,
except that the latter category is clearly ironized, for he reveals indifference to the Enlightenment project of distinguishing and categorizing
organic and inorganic natural phenomena, and shows himself interested
only in "observing" attractive women. If, as Blumenberg argued, the historical Lichtenberg constitutes a transitional figure into an age of scientific surveillance single-mindedly pursued, Hofmann imbues this aspect
of his personage with humor through Lichtenberg's droll metaphoric
description of the first sphere, writing, and the sexualization of his "theoretical curiosity" (Blumenberg) in connection with the second sphere,
"scientific" observation.

The relentless focus on Lichtenberg's diminutive stature, an effect of
the fairy-tale style in the novel that "undercuts" his stature as a serious
Enlightenment figure and makes his sexual relationship with a barely adolescent girl seem harmless, also lends a comical air to his unique scien-
tist/aphorist individuality and subversively contextualizes his theoretical
observations. At the outset, the narrator makes use of the childish rhetorical question device to describe Lichtenberg as follows: "Die Stirn, wenn
er drüberstrich, war hübsch gewölbt, doch was war dahinter? Jedenfalls

hatte er hübsche Händchen und Füßchen und blankgeputzte Augen, manchmal. Und eben einen großen Kopf mit Phantasie darin — 'wissenschaftlicher und anderer'" (9; the forehead, when he brushed over it, was attractively arched, but what was behind it? At any rate he had nice-looking little hands and feet and brightly shining eyes, sometimes. And likewise a large head with fantasy in it — "scientific and otherwise"). His elfin appearance, his little hands and feet, make his dual "stature" as scientist and man of letters, curtly alluded to at the conclusion to this passage, also seem simply one more droll, charming aspect of his character. When he later tells an Englishman who accompanies him on his survey expedition for the English king that humans are on earth to deal with its surface, that what involves depth and height is within the exclusive province of nature (161), he clearly subverts the Enlightenment view, held by Kehlmann's Humboldt, that the heavens and the bowels of the earth are also to be charted by the scientist, but this self-imposed limitation also seems linked through the novel's tone to Lichtenberg's diminutive physique and how this circumstance constricts his quotidian activities.

It is possible to regard the drolly simplistic remarks made by Lichtenberg to the Hungarian and the Englishman in a different light. Partly due to his deformity but also due to his eccentric brilliance, Lichtenberg is misunderstood and isolated in Göttingen and has only superficial social connections with his academic colleagues, who regard him as an odd specimen. He is a patient, loving teacher to Maria Stechard, and their mutual childlike qualities help cement their bond, but neither she nor the novel's other characters are his intellectual equals. Thus, his generally friendly but curt responses in conversation with most of them may reflect his sense that he would be otherwise misunderstood. As Carl Niekerk has noted, the historical Lichtenberg was deeply pessimistic that Enlightenment insights and discourse, particularly those of Kant, could ever be comprehended and practically applied by the masses. Lichtenberg found Kant too complex and thus without value for the common man. However, Lichtenberg also saw a general danger in Enlightenment education, comparing it in an aphorism to a fire that warms our winters and illuminates our nights, but that can also burn down our houses. He also asked what value the "light" of the Enlightenment had for people with no eyes to see it, or who deliberately closed their eyes. Niekerk sees Lichtenberg's views as symptomatic of a late Enlightenment pessimism signaling the end of the entire movement.[34] In the style of his verbal intercourse with others, Hofmann's Lichtenberg may reflect the historical figure's somewhat gloomy outlook regarding that age's dominant worldview.

Another aspect of Lichtenberg's thought that separated him from more mainstream Enlightenment philosophers like Kant was his defense of superstition. Niekerk argues that Lichtenberg believed superstitions were an "anthropological constant," unavoidable and indissoluble in humanity as a whole and a constituent element in his own nature, though he felt it had attained "monstrous" proportions in his personal case.[35] Hofmann's Lichtenberg reflects this counter-Enlightenment facet in the character of the scientist/aphorist. When an attractive young man who had performed personal services for the scholar seems to develop a romantic dalliance with his beloved Stechardin, Lichtenberg grills the girl on her relationship with the young man, Friedrich, and forces her to swear that she will eternally belong to him and him alone. She denies having had physical contact with him, and even pledges to die a miserable death if she is lying. Soon thereafter, she sickens and dies agonizingly of bilious fever. This causes Lichtenberg to ponder whether we are responsible for our own thoughts, and if they are stronger than we are (203–10). The association between her death and her oath is congruent with the fairy-tale economy of the novel, although, after a brief narration of Lichtenberg's subsequent illness and despair, it concludes with his marriage to another young woman he first employs as a servant, Margarethe Kellner, who bore him eight children (210–13). Despite this happy ending, the tacit nexus between an apparently violated oath, a painful demise suffered in consequence of this profanation, and Lichtenberg's subtly evoked suspicion — or superstition — of his complicity in this tragedy, resonates with the Romantic undertone of fated death and constitutes the final element subversive to Enlightenment rationalism in *Die kleine Stechardin*.

Lavater as Film Protagonist and as Key to Comprehensive Computer Surveillance

Jens Sparschuh's title character is the object of instrumentalization for three figures in *Lavaters Maske*. The narrator, a rather undisciplined author of middling fame, is attempting to write a movie script about him for a successful German film director. While doing research in Zurich's Central Library on his subject, he becomes acquainted with another researcher into Lavater, Magda Zabo, a somewhat ominous figure who believes she can decode one of the physiognomist's encrypted folios to discover a prototypically perfect face that would allow her company's computer program, Zorro, to determine how faces actually impact those who see them. Unlike Lavater, she is not interested in uncovering the putative harmony between outward facial appearance and inner spiritual essence, but rather in using the physiognomist's code to see what visages, for example, might strike the typical observer as reliable, even if the person behind the face does not actually possess this virtue (34). Finally, there is Lavater's servant Enslin, who, in the narrator's increasingly capricious reading of this figure, comes to manipulate his master for various nefarious purposes that might appeal to a movie audience, and

finally assumes Lavater's identity entirely. In the concluding chapter, the
now-apparently-insane narrator is depicted as believing that the historical Enslin did not actually commit suicide, but murdered his master and
appropriated his existence (253–61). In this instrumentalization of his
master, Enslin resembles the Eckermann figure in Sparschuh's novel *Der
große Coup*,[36] except that Sparschuh's earlier text is actually set during
Goethe's lifetime and this Eckermann is, during the narrative time frame,
only barely less marginalized, more proactive, and successful than the
amanuensis of Martin Walser's previously discussed radio play *In Goethes
Hand*. Through a conversation between the first-person author/narra-
tor and a pompous literary critic at one of the book readings that are
interspersed throughout *Lavaters Maske*, Sparschuh pokes ironic fun at
Jacques Derrida's idea that every text is only a pretext, an occasion for
interpretation (71) — an interpretation that might presumably address
the text's contemporary relevance and resonance, or lack thereof. Instead,
as Chloe Paver has argued, Sparschuh's two novels not only intend to
show Goethe and Lavater being "upstaged" by their presumed lackeys,
but also to demonstrate the foibles of the two great men and to "contest
the idea that their lives were necessarily richer and more worthy of attention than the lives lived around them."[37] Of course, there is also a distinction to be drawn *between* these two novels of Sparschuh. For while the
Eckermann figure of *Der große Coup* implicitly intervenes in Goethe's life
and works, the servant figure Enslin is himself revealed to be the product of ever-greater fabrication on the part of *Lavaters Maske*'s narrator/
author. For example, in one of the narrator's film scenarios, Enslin has a
secret plan to learn the mysterious nature of true beauty, having mistaken
Lavater's cabinet for a beauty institute. This plan, in turn, is based on
the narrator's decision to manipulate a reference to Enslin's "Hussar"-
like appearance (which occurs in Lavater's official report on his servant's
suicide) in order to justify disfiguring Enslin's visage in the movie (100).
In other words, Sparschuh's Enslin, unlike his Eckermann, is consciously
revealed to be a fictional construct.

In making use of Lavater's physiognomic studies, Zabo brings this
rather mystically oriented, anti-rationalist figure (who was portrayed as
such in Huizing's *Das Ding an sich*) into contiguity with eighteenth-
century Enlightenment rationalists such as Jeremy Bentham, who transformed the policing and disciplinary regulation of society from a reliance
on the spectacle of public torture to a methodology based on a network
of ceaselessly vigilant, omnipresent surveillance, a paradigm shift famously
delineated by Michel Foucault in his study *Surveiller et punir* (Disci-
pline and punish, 1975). Foucault's description of a power that utilizes
an instrument of surveillance that is exhaustive, permanent, omnipresent,
and capable of rendering everything visible while the power itself remains
invisible[38] allows us to read Zabo's Lavater-inspired decoding of faces as a

present-day extension of such literally cryptic all-encompassing, Enlightenment-born policing. In this sense, Sparschuh uses Lavater as a means to critique the Enlightenment along the lines of Theodor Adorno, who saw the Enlightenment as a permanent state of mind rooted in primal fear and the urge to control rather than as a discrete historical period.[39]

Lichtenberg as Enlightenment Hero

While the skewering of the Enlightenment through caricature, style, and ambience is a consistent thread in the novels of Kehlmann, Huizing, and Hofmann — providing evidence of an important tendency in contemporary German novels on figures associated with this movement — it is not the only approach to be found within this rather narrow genre, as has already been indicated through the discussion of Hein's short story on Humboldt. By way of further illustrating this, I will conclude this chapter by briefly examining another relatively recent Lichtenberg novel, Henning Boëtius's *Der Gnom*. This novel is more comprehensive in its engagement with Lichtenberg's life than is *Die kleine Stechardin*, as it spans almost the entirety of his existence, from early childhood to death. Though Boëtius captures the aphorist/scientist's eccentricities, he resorts neither to caricature nor parody, and Lichtenberg comes across as a brilliant defender of Enlightenment values without being cast as a one-dimensional rationalist like Kehlmann's Humboldt or Huizing's Kant. Indeed, Boëtius invents a speech Lichtenberg gives as a graduating high-school student in which he eloquently argues for the intimate, balanced relationship between poetry and science, claiming that poetry is as much cognition as science is imagination, and that both contribute to the exploration of life (26–27).[40] This imaginary speech sets the stage for a presentation of Lichtenberg as an intellectual who does not oscillate between science and imaginative writing, contrary to his presentation by Blumenberg and Hofmann, because they constitute for him two sides of one coin.[41] This metaphor is almost literally apt because Boëtius's Lichtenberg frequently draws upon it in articulating both the element of chance and the ideal holistic harmony he seeks in both his own life and that of humanity as a whole. Indeed, one chapter title, based on these ruminations, is entitled "Kopf oder Zahl 1774–1775" (227–74; Heads or tails 1774–1775).

As a man versed in letters as well as science, this Lichtenberg makes the acquaintance of Lessing and Friedrich Klopstock, though he is not terribly impressed by either writer. Most significant for our purposes are the intellectual relationships he develops with Goethe and Lavater. He rejects Goethe's theory of colors as unscientific dilettantism, even drivel. He feels it is laughable to write against Newton, the chief target of Goethe's wrath with respect to colors, and finds Goethe should stick to poetry and stay out of scientific research. He even writes Goethe an insultingly childish letter where his hostility is only thinly veiled (383–86). The defense of Newton against Goethe's aesthetically driven theory of colors is fully in line with Enlightenment values concerning scientific truth, as are Lichtenberg's scathing polemics against Lavater's popular notions concerning physiognomy. While Lichtenberg was a sensual man given to intensive reflection on the spiritual significance and character of the human face, he was incensed at the revival of physiognomy by Lavater, and sharply inveighed against him.[42]

In *Der Gnom*, the intense invective directed against Lichtenberg by Lavater's supporters — which draws on the Göttingen professor's physical deformities and his relationship with Stechard (who, in Boëtius's rendering, dies a virgin, having held out for a marriage that never takes place) — is underscored (306–9), although Lavater and Lichtenberg later have a somewhat reconciliatory meeting (369–71). In *Das Ding an sich*, Lavater is the author of three separate letters to Hamann entitled "Träume eines Geistersehers" (Dreams of a spirit-seer). These letters, while exhibiting Lavater's tendency toward eccentric rapture, also reveal the "truth" about the Adamic shard: Lavater recollects having read a text, apparently written by the Swedish mystic Emanuel Swedenborg, that seems to reveal the shard's Biblical origins (87–90, 124–26, and 160–64). While the second letter professes admiration for Kantian metaphysics (126), the collective title of the missives clearly pokes ironic fun at Kant's own treatise titled *Träume eines Geistersehers, erläutert durch Träume der Metaphysik* (Dreams of a spirit-seer, illustrated by dreams of metaphysics, 1766). This early essay was intended to debunk Swedenborgian occultism and speculative metaphysics. Kant attempts to show the supposed intersections and distinctions between these two, as well as their threat to his telos of a modern philosophy based on a stable, unselfish, empirically grounded intersubjectivity.[43]

While exploring Lichtenberg's own superstitions, foibles, and eccentricities, *Der Gnom* also presents him as the heroic explorer and defender of scientific truths, a debunker of the irrational in the mode of Kant in his 1766 essay, who exercises his satiric cudgel not only against celebrated writers like Lavater and Goethe when he finds they stray from such truths, but also against popular charlatans such as the contemporary magician Jacob Philadelphia (276–81). In general, Boëtius's novel, along with Hein's story about Humboldt, constitute a counterpoint to a more dominant trend in contemporary Germany — namely, an engagement in Enlightenment critique through caricature and parody, a trend evident in Heiner Müller's play *Leben Gundlings* and more recently manifested in the novels of Kehlmann, Huizing, Hofmann, and Sparschuh. Kehlmann and Huizing, in particular, cast the Enlightenment as the realization of a purely instrumentalized human reason that leads to the dominance over nature through overarching rational systems, perhaps unintentionally illustrating the arguments of Adorno and Max Horkheimer in this regard in their *Dialektik der Aufklärung* (Dialectic of enlightenment, 1947). Sparschuh utilizes Lavater's physiognomic principles to envision in the present day the realization of comprehensive human surveillance and social control, thus intensifying the panoptic trends Foucault traces, in *Surveiller et punir*, to the late eighteenth-century. Hein and Boëtius, on the other hand, portray their respective protagonists Humboldt and Lichtenberg as pursuers of cosmopolitan, humane, scientific inquiry, participants in the sort of *non*-instrumentalizing discourse that the philosopher Jürgen Habermas regards as a hallmark of the European Enlightenment, and that even Foucault saw as a positive, liberating aspect of Kant's definition of this movement.[44]

Conclusion

The predilections, scientific pursuits, and major figures associated with the Age of Enlightenment are targets of polemic narrative in a large number of fictional works situated in the Age of Goethe, perhaps second in number only to texts focused on Goethe himself. Technological advancement, objective standards for experimentation, the primacy of reason over belief and human emotions: These ideals, thoroughly articulated in the eighteenth century and pursued with fanatic zeal in the nineteenth, have been frequently associated in more contemporary decades with war, environmental degradation, the loss of natural habitat, and human exploitation. While these tendencies began well before the Age of Enlightenment, this period's ideology enabled their unchecked development and thus many of the enormous disasters that have befallen the twentieth and twenty-first centuries. For this reason, some narratives situated in the Age of Goethe are meant to be read proleptically. Seemingly benign and humorous discoveries, postulations, and inventions associated with the Enlightenment and propagated by fictional Humboldts and fictional Kants anticipate calamitous present-day trends. Sometimes these men are grotesquely caricatured, or at least shown to possess amusing eccentricities, as a means of subverting the scientific, philosophical, or political authority still associated with them today. Ambiguous fictionalized figures in this regard are the mathematician Gauß and the scientist/aphorist Lichtenberg — the former calls Humboldt's measuring mania into question through his postulates concerning curved space and his doubts about the benefits of his own surveying activities, while Lichtenberg's aphorisms and general diary jottings undermine the Enlightenment ideals of scientific progress and discovery he pursues in Hofmann's novel, ideals further subverted by the novel's fairy-tale ambience and tone.

To be sure, a counterdiscourse is also evident in Age-of-Goethe fiction from the 1970s to the present day. Hein's brief Humboldt narrative underscores the positive aspects of the Enlightenment, such as its tolerance and border-crossing cosmopolitanism. Boëtius portrays Lichtenberg almost unequivocally as an Enlightenment hero, as a debunker of the obscurantism purveyed not only by charlatans such as Jacob Philadelphia but also by Goethe in his color theory. Nevertheless, the more pronounced trend in fiction centered on the figures, discourse, and pursuits associated with the German Enlightenment is the portrayal of its foibles and weaknesses, presented with a prescient eye toward the contemporary age. In the case of Sparschuh's Lavater novel, this is done directly by situating the narrative's time frame *in* the present, as Lavater's ideas on physiognomy, articulated by flashbacks to his life and by a present-day researcher who wants to harness them to decode faces, illustrate Foucault's vision of all-encompassing, anonymous social surveillance. Thus, Age-of-Goethe fiction centered on the Enlightenment tends imaginatively to mirror contemporary critical discourse on this movement's dark side.

Notes

[1] Daniel Kehlmann, *Die Vermessung der Welt* (2005; Reinbek bei Hamburg: Rowohlt, 2007).

[2] Klaas Huizing, *Das Ding an sich: Eine unerhörte Begebenheit aus dem Leben Immanuel Kants* (Munich: Albrecht Knaus, 1998).

[3] Gert Hofmann, *Die kleine Stechardin* (1994; Munich: dtv, 1999).

[4] Heiner Müller, *Leben Gundlings Friedrich von Preußen Lessings Schlaf Traum Schrei: Ein Greuelmärchen*, in *Herzstück* (Berlin: Rotbuch, 1983), 9–40.

[5] Jens Sparschuh, *Lavaters Maske* (Cologne: Kiepenheuer & Witsch, 1999).

[6] Christoph Hein, "Die russischen Briefe des Jägers Johann Seifert," *Einladung zum Lever Bourgeois* (Berlin: Aufbau, 1980), 104–83.

[7] Henning Boëtius, *Der Gnom: Ein Lichtenberg Roman* (1989; Munich: btb, 1998).

[8] Christian Stahl, "Aus der Amazon.de-Redaktion," Amazon.de (15 December 2008) http://www.amazon.de/Die-Vermessung-Welt-Daniel-Kehlmann/dp/product-description/3499241005.

[9] See Heinz-Peter Preußer, "Zur Typologie der Zivilisationskritik: Was aus Daniel Kehlmanns Roman 'Die Vermessung der Welt' einen Bestseller werden ließ," *Text und Kritik* 177 (2008): 73.

[10] Arlene Akiko Teraoka, *The Silence of Entropy or Universal Discourse: The Postmodernist Poetics of Heiner Müller* (New York: Peter Lang, 1985), 73. Italics in the original.

[11] Hans Blumenberg, *Der Prozeß der theoretischen Neugierde* (Frankfurt am Main: Suhrkamp, 1973), 242–57.

[12] Hein, "Der neuere (glücklichere) Kohlhaas: Bericht über einen *Rechtshandel* aus den Jahren 1972/73," *Einladung zum Lever Bourgeois*, 82–103.

[13] See L. Kellner, *Alexander von Humboldt* (London: Oxford UP, 1963), 112, 225–27.

[14] Günther Drommer, "Typische Bemerkungen zu untypischen Texten," in Hein, *Einladung zum Lever Bourgeois*, 187.

[15] Marianne Krumrey, "Gegenwart im Spiegel der Geschichte: Christoph Hein, *Einladung zum Lever Bourgeois*," *Temperamente* 6.4 (1981): 144.

[16] Such allusions to Hein's contemporary GDR in the tale have been noted by Bernd Fischer, who accurately claims that Hein's Humboldt "is faced with problems which simultaneously concretize the historical situation and make allusion to the present," a GDR present marked by spying, all-encompassing state propaganda, and a repression of sexual behavior not in line with state mores. See Fischer, "*Einladung zum Lever Bourgeois*: Christoph Hein's First Prose Collection," in *Studies in GDR Culture and Society 4: Selected Papers from the Ninth New Hampshire Symposium on the German Democratic Republic*, ed. Margy Gerber et. al (Lanham, MD: UP of America, 1984), 130.

[17] Mark M. Anderson, "Der vermessende Erzähler: Mathematische Geheimnisse bei Daniel Kehlmann," *Text und Kritik* 177 (2008): 64.

[18] Preußer, "Zur Typologie der Zivilisationskritik," 76–77.

[19] Chenxi Tang, *The Geographic Imagination of Modernity: Geography, Literature, and Philosophy in German Romanticism* (Stanford, CA: Stanford UP, 2008), 83–84 and 197–98.

[20] Goethe's poem, titled "Ein Gleiches" (Sameness, 1780), a pendant to "Wanderers Nachtlied" (Wanderer's song at night, 1776) and sometimes referred to as "Wanderers Nachtlied II," is one of the most famous poems in the German language. It reads as follows: "Über allen Gipfeln / Ist Ruh, / In allen Wipfeln / Spürest du / Kaum einen Hauch; / Die Vögelein schweigen im Walde. / Warte nur, balde / Ruhest du auch" (In Goethe, *Gedenkausgabe* 2:69). A possible translation would be: Over all the hilltops / Is rest / In all the treetops / You feel / Hardly a breath / the little birds are silent in the forest / Only wait / Soon you too will rest. In *Die Vermessung der Welt*, Humboldt's literalizing Spanish version is "translated" by the narrator into an equivalent German, provoking astonishment among Humboldt's auditors: "Oberhalb aller Bergspitzen sei es still, in den Bäumen kein Wind zu fühlen, auch die Vögel seien ruhig, und bald werde man tot sein" (128; Above all the mountain peaks it is still, in the trees there is no wind to be felt, also the birds are quiet, and soon one will be dead).

[21] Kehlmann, "Wo ist Carlos Montúfar?," *Wo ist Carlos Montúfar?: Über Bücher* (Reinbek bei Hamburg: Rowohlt, 2005), 9–27.

[22] Ette, *Alexander von Humboldt*, 302–18.

[23] Nicolaas A. Rupke, *Alexander von Humboldt: A Metabiography* (Frankfurt am Main: Peter Lang, 2005), esp. 88–91, 116, 123, and 138.

[24] Michael Dettelbach. "Alexander von Humboldt between Enlightenment and Romanticism," *Northeastern Naturalist* 8. Special Issue 1 (2001), 9.

[25] James C. O'Flaherty, *Johann Georg Hamann* (Boston: Twayne, 1979), 21–25; John R. Betz, *After Enlightenment: The Post-Secular Vision of J. G. Hamann* (Oxford: Wiley-Blackwell, 2009), 29–32.

[26] The passage in Hamann's collected letters reads as follows: "Sie beten um Muth, nicht unter der Last der Geschäfte zu sinken — und mir vergeht aller Muth, unter der Last langer Weile" (You pray for courage not to sink under the burden of tasks and I am losing all courage under the burden of idleness). In Johann Georg Hamann, *Briefwechsel*, vol. 4, 1778–1782, ed. Arthur Henkel (Wiesbaden: Insel, 1959), 3. Huizing modifies this line only slightly in *Das Ding an sich*: "Sie beten in Ihrem letzten Brief um Mut, nicht unter der Last der Geschäfte zu versinken — und mir vergeht aller Mut unter der Last langer Weile" (119; You pray in your last letter for courage not to sink to the bottom under the burden of tasks and I am losing all courage under the burden of idleness).

[27] See O'Flaherty, *Johann Georg Hamann*, 82–86, and Erwin Metzke, "Kant und Hamann," in *Johann Georg Hamann*, ed. Reiner Wild (Darmstadt: Wissenschaftliche Buchgesellschaft, 1978), 233–63.

[28] Hamann, "Sokratische Denkwürdigkeiten: Für die lange Weile des Publikums zusammengetragen von einem Liebhaber der langen Weile. Mit einer doppelten Zuschrift an Niemand und an Zween," in *Sturm und Drang: Eine Auswahl theoretischer Texte*, ed. Erich Loewenthal, 3rd ed. (Heidelberg: Lambert Schneider, 1972), 61–84.

[29] Betz, *After Enlightenment*, 37.

[30] The complete line in *Das Ding an sich* reads as follows: "Es war einmal ein Handlungsreisender, ehemals Student der Theologie, Philosophie, Juristerei und Philologie in Königsberg, danach mäßig erfolgreicher Privatlehrer in Livland und Kurland, bis ein mitfühlender Freund aus Riga ihm unter die Arme griff, ihn in seiner Firma einstellte und genau zu dem Zeitpunkt, da Kant über die Frage brütete, 'Ob die Westwinde in unsern Gegenden darum feucht seien, weil sie über ein großes Meer streichen,' auf eine Reise über Berlin, Lübeck, Bremen und Amsterdam nach London schickte, um wichtige Geschäfte zu tätigen — und dieser Handlungsreisende hieß Johann Georg Hamann" (19; Once upon a time there was a business traveler, formerly a student of theology, philosophy, law, and philology in Königsberg, afterward a moderately successful private teacher in Livonia and Courland, until a sympathetic friend from Riga took him under his wing, placed him in his firm, and precisely at the moment of time that Kant was pondering the question "Whether the West Winds in our regions are humid because they blow over a large sea" sent him on a trip via Berlin, Lübeck, Bremen, and Amsterdam to London, in order to transact important business matters — and this business traveler was named Johann Georg Hamann).

[31] Klaus Harpprecht, "Der Krüppel und das Kind (*Die kleine Stechardin*)," in *Schauplatz Menschenkopf: Der Erzähler Gert Hofmann*, ed. Hans Christian Kosler (Munich: Carl Hanser, 1997), 193 and 196–97.

[32] Mikhail Bakhtin, *Rabelais and His World*, trans. Helene Iswolsky (Cambridge, MA: MIT Press, 1968), 317.

[33] Bakhtin, *Rabelais and His World*, 322.

[34] Carl Niekerk, *Zwischen Naturgeschichte und Anthropologie: Lichtenberg im Kontext der Spätaufklärung* (Tübingen: Max Niemeyer, 2005), 346–59.

[35] Niekerk, *Zwischen Naturgeschichte und Anthropologie*, 352.

[36] For a discussion of parallels between *Lavaters Maske* and *Der große Coup*, see Chloe E. M. Paver, "Lavater Fictionalized: Jens Sparschuh's *Lavaters Maske*," in *Physiognomy in Profile: Lavater's Impact on European Culture*, ed. Melissa Percival and Graeme Tytler (Newark: U of Delaware P, 2005), 217–29.

[37] Paver, "Lavater Fictionalized," 220.

[38] Michel Foucault, *Surveiller et punir: Naissance de la prison* (Paris: Gallimard, 1975), 215.

[39] See esp. Adorno's *Dialektik der Aufklärung* (Dialectic of enlightenment), co-authored with Max Horkheimer and first published in 1947.

[40] Boëtius acknowledges the fabricated character of this speech in a brief afterword, where all those writings ascribed in the novel to Lichtenberg that are pure inventions are listed (443).

[41] Nevertheless, on occasion, Lichtenberg finds himself uncomfortable at being half-scientist and half-writer (for example, 357).

[42] See Siegfried Frey, "Lavater, Lichtenberg, and the Suggestive Power of the Human Face," in *The Faces of Physiognomy: Interdisciplinary Approaches to Johann Caspar Lavater*, ed. Ellis Shookman (Columbia, SC: Camden House, 1993), 64–103.

[43] See Sarah Pourciau, "Disarming the Double: Kant in Defense of Philosophy (1766)," *Germanic Review* 81 (2006): 99–120.

[44] On this contrast in views on the Enlightenment between Habermas and Foucault on the one hand, and Adorno and Horkheimer on the other, see John A. McCarthy, "*Verständigung* and *Dialektik*: On Consensus Theory and the Dialectic of Enlightenment," in *Impure Reason: Dialectic of Enlightenment in Germany*," ed. W. Daniel Wilson and Robert C. Holub (Detroit, MI: Wayne State UP, 1993), 13–33. McCarthy draws on Lichtenberg in his own defense of the Enlightenment, citing the scientist's defense of reason, acknowledgement of its limits, and stress on the importance of skepticism, a balanced perspective McCarthy indicates is similar to that of Habermas (28–29).

Conclusion

WRITERS FREQUENTLY LOOK TO authors from the past for inspiration, guidance, and, conversely, as foils against whom they develop new styles, techniques, political perspectives, and themes. As demonstrated by the essays collected in the volume *The Author as Character*, discussed in the introduction, imaginative writers often make their literary precursors into fictional characters in pursuing their own diverse agendas. In the realm of cinema, the popular success of films such as *Shakespeare in Love* (1998) and the recent Jane Austen biopic *Becoming Jane* (2007) show author-as-character movies can generate mass cultural appeal. Not all such fiction stays within the national or even linguistic bounds of authors and their historical subjects. The English novelist Penelope Fitzgerald, for example, published a novel on the German Romantic poet Novalis (the pen name of Friedrich von Hardenberg), the *Blue Flower* (1995), the title of which is derived from Novalis's celebrated trope in his uncompleted novel *Heinrich von Ofterdingen* (1801).

While author-as-character fiction is clearly transnational in scope, German fiction on the leading literary and intellectual figures associated with the Age of Goethe has proven to be particularly rich, dynamic, prolific, and cogent. Although works belonging to this subgenre have been in evidence since the eighteenth century itself, when Lenz and Goethe portrayed their contemporaries by name in minor theatrical pieces, and prose of this sort by Büchner and Thomas Mann achieved canonic status, only since the 1970s has a wide-ranging and critically acclaimed body of such imaginative writing emerged. Eighteenth- and early nineteenth-century German authors were made fictional characters in these works to serve a variety of purposes, as was the case in such fiction prior to the 1970s, but one can nevertheless discern certain tendencies within the corpus examined in this book that allow it to emerge in its discrete and cohesive character.

Key to the development of fiction about Age-of-Goethe authors composed in the 1970s and the 1980s in both the Federal Republic of Germany and the German Democratic Republic was the hagiographic treatment of Goethe in the immediate aftermath of World War II. Both halves of the divided Germany competed with each other over whose political and ideological orientation most closely approximated that of the venerable statesman and poet. Both sides strove to be seen by the wider world as having erased the stain of National Socialism — so recently dominant in Germany at that time — through its replacement by the positive values attributed to

Goethe. The competition over Goethe was exemplified by the eager efforts of both the Eastern and Western zones of occupation to engage the services of the individual widely regarded as Goethe's contemporary ideological and artistic successor, Thomas Mann. This competition was especially evident in 1949, when the bicentennial of Goethe's birth occasioned prolific commemorations in both lands. At the dawn of the Nazi rise to power, Mann had composed an essay, "Goethe als Repräsentant des bürgerlichen Zeitalters" (Goethe as representative of the bourgeois age, 1932), in which, as the title indicates, he sought to establish Goethe as an exemplar of the middle class. However, where Mann saw Goethe's bourgeois values as being marked by humanism and cosmopolitanism, the National Socialists were able to emphasize a different aspect of Goethe's supposedly model citizenship by underscoring his selfless, devoted service to the state. In East Germany, Georg Lukács established what became the GDR artistic and intellectual orthodoxy by arguing, in part, that Goethean Classicism constituted a positive stage in the intellectual establishment of Marxism, while he accused Romantics such as Kleist of indulging in a decadent solipsism. Authors whose parents were mature adults during the Third Reich became suspicious of this too-facile instrumentalization of Goethe by the intellectuals temporally associated with National Socialist authoritarianism, even through some of these intellectuals had actively resisted the Nazis.

Negative views of Goethe and his influence were, of course, evident prior to the coming of age of the post-war generation of authors. In *Mimesis* (1946), composed during the war, Erich Auerbach vaguely linked Goethe's political quietism to the conditions allowing National Socialism to emerge. Thus, the stage was set for Goethe's transformation from a model citizen and literary exemplar in the Third Reich and then in East and West Germany into the bourgeois toady, sycophant, and even sexually perverse character evident in *Goethezeit* fiction by authors such as Peter Weiss and Martin Walser. More broadly speaking, the transvaluation of Goethean values enabled the two most dominant tendencies discussed in *Imagining the Age of Goethe*: the fictional savaging of the Sage of Weimar, and the concomitant valorization of eighteenth- and early nineteenth-century authors who had previously been either marginalized or treated with a degree of contempt by critical orthodoxy in both the FRG and the GDR, such as Kleist, Hölderlin, and Hamann, as well as largely neglected women writers such as Günderrode, Bettine Brentano, and Luise Gottsched. The pillorying of the privy counselor continued to be a major trend in post-unification German literature. This was also the case in the Goethe Year 1999, though this year also witnessed the publication of more nuanced, indeed affirmative, Goethe fiction. As the politically grounded rebellion against authoritarianism merged into the more amorphous suspicion of Enlightenment positivism in poststructuralist thought, a range of works skewering this movement's proclivities emerged, particularly in the domain of science, as we saw in chapter 5.

While the refutation of Goethe and the embrace of writers broadly (through perhaps not always accurately) associated with Romanticism took place in both halves of divided Germany in the 1970s, this trend was motivated by disparate circumstances in the two countries, as chapters 1 and 2 make evident. Scholars are in general agreement that what we might call the Romantic turn in the German Democratic Republic was precipitated by the so-called "Biermann affair," the decision of the nation's politburo to strip this singer/writer, committed to Communism but heterodox in his views, of his citizenship while he was engaged in a concert tour of West Germany in 1976. There had been a brief loosening of censorship in the GDR after Erich Honecker assumed power earlier in the decade, but a reimposition of tight oversight of the nation's intellectuals led dissidents to embrace, as comrades across the ages, another group of writers marginalized by the GDR intellectual establishment, the German Romantics. This turn led to an outpouring of fictional and nonfictional works by East German authors in which Romantics were sympathetically treated, and a perceived kinship between the GDR writers and their authorial subjects became manifest. The artistic high point of this trend was Christa Wolf's novel *Kein Ort. Nirgends*, the focus of chapter 1. Wolf's empathetic identification with the primary protagonists of her tale, Kleist and Günderrode, as well as with the seemingly secondary but subtextually central figure of Bettine Brentano, is established through both her unique intersubjective narrative approach and her deeply personal essays on these writers. The ideological underpinnings of Wolf's Romantic turn can be traced to her embrace of Anna Seghers, who defended the Romantics and other writers in her correspondence with Lukács. The latent martial violence of Romantic idealism, evident in the androgynous tendencies of Wolf's protagonists and inextricably linked to a holistic view of gender embraced by Wolf, is also a strong constitutive element in her novel. Romantic gender holism is also evident in an episode of Günter Grass's novel *Der Butt*.

The embrace of Kleist in the GDR in the 1970s is evident also in Günter Kunert's radio play *Ein anderer K.*, and Karin Reschke's novel on Kleist and the woman with whom he committed suicide, Henriette Vogel, shows he could be a figure of interest for West German feminists as well. Another writer who inspired authorial imagination on both sides of the internal German border was Hölderlin. Stephan Hermlin's radio play *Scardanelli* really inaugurated the Romantic turn in the GDR. Proleptically for subsequent GDR engagements with outcast authors from the Age of Goethe, Hermlin treated the poet as marginalized through political, social, and artistic circumstances. In Gerhard Wolf's *Der arme Hölderlin*, the political elements leading to the poet's insanity are emphasized, while a rather experimental style mixing third- and first-person narrative registers pushes this brief novel somewhat in the direction of his wife's intersubjective orientation in *Kein Ort. Nirgends*. In the FRG, the negative portrayal

of Goethe and the concomitant valorization of putatively rebellious figures such as Hölderlin made manifest the anti-establishment attitude of
the so-called 1968 generation of writers. Peter Weiss's drama on Hölderlin exhibits the deep disdain that certain individuals associated with the
West German Left came to feel toward Goethe: He is portrayed as an
opportunistic panderer to the nation's wealthy bourgeoisie and aristoc-
racy, and as the forerunner of establishment disdain toward long-haired
Western rebellious youth. Hölderlin, by contrast, is presented as a rabble-
rousing socialist ideologue. Weiss clearly bent established biographical
facts here to serve his political agenda. Peter Härtling's long novel on
the poet provides the most overt instance of personal identification with a
historical author among those examined in this book, as is evident in constant first-person narrative intrusions into *Hölderlin*. Härtling's novel also
exhibits the West German Left's ideological identification with Hölderlin,
albeit in a less polemical and more pessimistic fashion than is the case with
Weiss's play. While the GDR authors Wolf and Hermlin sympathize with
the poet as a fellow victim of censorship by a totalitarian regime, Weiss
and Härtling see him as a political visionary who anticipates the idealism
of the Western Left in the 1960s and 1970s.

With respect to author-as-character fiction situated in the Age of
Goethe, the novels of Renate Feyl bridge the gap between the late cold-
war era and the present age of globalization, for she published her novel
on Luise Gottsched when she was still a resident of the GDR, while her
subsequent historical fiction has appeared during the current era of the
Berlin Republic. Both *Idylle mit Professor* and her more recent novels have
a strong feminist dimension and demonstrate how determined women
such as Gottsched, Sophie La Roche, and Caroline von Wolzogen were
able to establish somewhat successful careers as writers despite the pressures of domestic life within the dictates of a paternalistic society. Nevertheless, there is some distance between the purport of Feyl's pre- and
post-GDR novels: While *Idylle mit Professor* continues in the tradition of
creating thinly veiled critiques of East German censorship (with Luise's
husband Johann Christoph serving as a metonym for the authoritarian
state), her subsequent work combines her feminist orientation with the
goal of enhancing German national identity in the current global age
by anchoring her novels in the discrete context of a core period in the
nation's intellectual and political history. In this blending of a national
(but not nationalistic) education with a feminist agenda, Feyl under-
takes a unique approach to the subgenre examined in this book. This is
also the case with respect to style: More than the other writers analyzed
in *Imagining the Age of Goethe*, she employs a realistic prose narrative and
pays close attention to period ambience and physical detail.

While I identify the anti-Goethe polemic as one of the two most
dominant tendencies in the subgenre under discussion — such that its

manifestations are treated in most of the book's chapters — it is the focus of most of chapter 4. The distinct lack of veneration, indeed antipathy, with which Goethe is treated as a historical figure in German literature from the 1970s to the present day is a consistent feature in GDR, FRG, and contemporary fiction. To be sure, the writers from these three German political entities had somewhat diverse priorities, shaped in part by the political conditions in which they were living. Although the primary focus of their Goethe fiction was his complex, somewhat duplicitous relationship with Charlotte von Stein, Peter Hacks (who evokes a comic element in this duplicity) and Johanna Hoffman (who concentrates her attention on its negative consequences) seem also at pains to counteract the early GDR's hagiographic treatment of Goethe by showing him to be neither a friend of the working class nor able to rise above his egotism in personal relationships, a circumstance also underscored by Sigrid Damm in her semi-fictional biography of his sister Cornelia. The FRG writer Martin Walser also draws attention to these perceived traits in Goethe's character, but ultimately seems more concerned with showing the negative personal and social consequences of treating Goethe as a cult figure in his drama *In Goethes Hand*. The destructively abject servitude displayed toward him by Eckermann in Walser's play evokes the negative side of the bourgeois Goethe cult Walser experienced in the FRG. Writing in the late postmodern age of the Berlin Republic, when veneration of elite literary culture and its practitioners has mostly disappeared, Walser changes his focus to the elderly Goethe's tragicomic love life in his recent novel *Ein liebender Mann*. Hanns-Josef Ortheil had already thrown the Goethe cult entirely into question by challenging the very notion that the poet possessed the discrete, coherent identity necessary for such veneration in his novel *Faustinas Küsse*. Nevertheless, even without a cult, Goethe's endless fascination for subsequent generations of writers shows no signs of abating, so that Goethe fiction will certainly continue to be published in future decades.

Rafik Schami's novel *Der geheime Bericht über den Dichter Goethe* provides a good example of a countertendency to negative treatments of the poet. This novel, as well as a few other contemporary works, tends to treat the poet with a certain veneration. While Otto Böhmer's novel *Der junge Herr Goethe*, also the product of the Goethe Year 1999, and Robert Löhr's two novels portraying Goethe as a flawed hero of the Napoleonic Wars, show other fiction continues to present this poet in a positive light, Schami's intent is unique. This Syrian-born German writer and his co-author Uwe-Michael Gutzschhahn wished to educate young Germans (and, presumably, their teachers) about both the genius and acculturative value of Goethe for contemporary pluralistic Germany by presenting a discussion of his works through an imaginative intercultural filter. Given this exceptional goal, Schami's novel may remain a unicum. Nevertheless, whether they turn out to be idiosyncratic or illustrative of broader trends, one can expect the continuation of German fictional literary engagements with Age-of-Goethe artists and intellectuals. For despite the ever-greater obsession with mass culture — usually American culture — in contemporary Germany, there is still no reason to assume the *Goethezeit* will lose its hold on the imagination of the nation's best writers.

Based on quantity of significant works, I identify (primarily antipathetic) Goethe fiction and, particularly in the pre-unification period, the valorization of alienated Romantic writers as the most dominant trends within the subgenre examined by this book. At least since the appearance of Theodor Adorno and Max Horkheimer's *Dialektik der Aufklärung* (Dialectic of enlightenment, 1947), a debunking of the Enlightenment's values of rationality and scientific progress has constituted a major thread in poststructuralist theoretical writing. With respect to contemporary German fiction situated in the Age of Goethe, the skewering of the Enlightenment is not as significant a tendency as the other two major trends, at least if quantity is the dominant consideration. Nevertheless, novels discussed in chapter 5 by Daniel Kehlmann, Gert Hofmann, and Klaas Huizing, all composed in the last two decades, show it may be in the process of developing into a popular approach to the subgenre. Consistent in their three novels is the subversion of Enlightenment science and philosophy through a humorous exaggeration of perceived eccentricities in historical paragons of the movement: Humboldt and Gauß (Kehlmann), Lichtenberg (Hofmann), and Kant (Huizing). Particularly in the case of Gauß and Lichtenberg, character dialectics (in Kehlmann's *Die Vermessung der Welt*) and a narrative voice imbued with a fairy-tale quality (Hofmann's *Der kleine Stechardin*) mitigate the protagonists' negative Enlightenment tendencies by portraying them in a sympathetic guise. As with the figure of Goethe drawn by Böhmer, Schami, and Löhr, works such as Hein's brief narrative concerning Humboldt's travels in Russia and Boëtius's portrayal of Lichtenberg as a scientific hero show an affirmative countertrend to negative representations of the Enlightenment. Nevertheless, Enlightenment scientific and/or geographic undertakings are seen in many works as futile, destructive, or both. In Sparschuh's *Lavaters Maske*, the title figure's physiognomic studies transform Enlightenment panopticism into a nightmare vision of all-encompassing social surveillance. Given particularly the success of Kehlmann's formula of imbuing Humboldt's adventures with the ambience of prophetic apocalypse, though presented in a humorous vein, one might expect a greater volume of works enacting this approach to imagining the age of Goethe in the future. Indeed, considering the fascination, marked by both antipathy and admiration, that the poets and intellectuals of this period continue to hold for Germany's contemporary authors, one can expect the future production of an enduring stream of author-as-character fiction devoted to what many still consider the "golden age" of German literature.

Bibliography

Primary Texts

Arnim, Bettine von. *Werke und Briefe*. Edited by Gustav Konrad and Joachim Müller. Frechen and Cologne: Bartmann, 1958–1963.

Bernhard, Thomas. "Goethe schtirbt." *Die Zeit*. 19 March 1982: 41–42.

———. "Immanuel Kant." In *Die Stücke 1969–1981*, 595–684. Frankfurt am Main: Suhrkamp, 1983.

Bernstein, F. W., Bernd Eilert, and Eckhard Henscheid. "Eckermann und sein Goethe: Ein Schau-/Hörspiel getreu nach der Quelle." In *Unser Goethe: Ein Lesebuch*, edited by Eckhard Henscheid and F. W. Bernstein, 975–1110. Zurich: Diogenes, 1982.

Boëtius, Henning. *Der Gnom: Ein Lichtenberg-Roman*. 1989: Munich: btb, 1998.

———. *Tod in Weimar*. 2nd ed. Gifkendorf: Merlin, 1999.

Böhmer, Otto A. *Der junge Herr Goethe*. Munich: Albrecht Knaus, 1999.

Bruyn, Günter de. *Das Leben des Jean Paul Friedrich Richter*. 5th ed. Halle-Leipzig: Mitteldeutscher Verlag, 1975.

Büchner, Georg. "Lenz." In *Werke und Briefe*, 69–89. Munich: dtv, 1980.

Damm, Sigrid. *Cornelia Goethe*. 3rd ed. Frankfurt am Main: Insel, 1989.

———. *Vögel, die verkünden Land: Das Leben des Jakob Michael Reinhold Lenz*. Berlin: Aufbau, 1985.

Feyl, Renate. *Aussicht auf bleibende Helle: Die Königin und der Philosoph*. Munich: Diana, 2008.

———. *Idylle mit Professor*. 6th ed. Munich: Diana, 2007.

———. *Die profanen Stunden des Glücks*. 7th ed. Munich: Diana, 2007.

———. *Das sanfte Joch der Vortrefflichkeit*. 9th ed. Munich: Diana, 2007.

Goethe, Johann Wolfgang von. *Gedenkausgabe der Werke, Briefe und Gespräche*. Edited by Ernst Beutler. 24 vols. Zurich: Artemis, 1948–54.

Grass, Günter. *Die Blechtrommel*. 6th ed. Frankfurt am Main: Fischer, 1962.

———. *Der Butt*. 6th ed. Darmstadt: Luchterhand, 1978.

Günderrode, Karoline von. *Gesammelte Werke*. Edited by Leopold Hirschberg. Vol. 1. Bern: Herbert Lang, 1970.

Hacks, Peter. *Ein Gespräch im Hause Stein über den abwesenden Herrn von Goethe*. In *Ausgewählte Dramen 2*, 389–454. Berlin: Aufbau, 1976.

———. *Musen: Vier Auftritte*. In *Ausgewählte Dramen 3*, 299–369. Berlin: Aufbau, 1981.

———. "Es ließe sich fragen . . . Zu *Ein Gespräch im Hause Stein über den abwesenden Herrn von Goethe*." In *Die Maßgaben der Kunst: Gesammelte Aufsätze*, 388–94. Dusseldorf: Claassen, 1977.

Hamann, Johann Georg. *Briefwechsel*. Edited by Arthur Henkel. Vol. 4, 1778–82. Wiesbaden: Insel, 1955–75.

———. "Sokratische Denkwürdigkeiten: Für die lange Weile des Publikums zusammengetragen von einem Liebhaber der langen Weile. Mit einer doppelten Zuschrift an Niemand und an Zween." In *Sturm und Drang: Eine Auswahl theoretischer Texte*, edited by Erich Loewenthal, 61–84. 3rd ed. Heidelberg: Lambert Schneider, 1974.

Härtling, Peter. *Die dreifache Maria: Eine Geschichte*. Darmstadt: Luchterhand, 1982.

———. "Das Ende der Geschichte: Über die Arbeit an einem 'historischen Roman.'" In *Meine Lektüre: Literatur als Widerstand*, edited by Klaus Siblewski, 112–23. Darmstadt: Luchterhand, 1981.

———. *Hoffmann oder Die vielfältige Liebe: Eine Romanze*. Cologne: Kiepenheuer & Witsch, 2001.

———. *Hölderlin: Ein Roman*. Darmstadt: Luchterhand, 1976.

———. "Mein Hölderlin." In *Zwischen Untergang und Aufbruch: Aufsätze, Reden, Gespräche*, 301–5. Berlin: Aufbau, 1990.

———. *Niembsch oder Der Stillstand: Eine Suite*. Stuttgart: Henry Goverts, 1964.

———. *Über Heimat*. Ludwigsburg: Verlag der Buchhandlung Aigner, 1982.

———. *Waiblingers Augen: Roman*. Darmstadt: Hermann Luchterhand, 1987.

Hein, Christoph. *Einladung zum Lever Bourgeois*. Berlin: Aufbau, 1980.

Hermlin, Stephan. "Gesang vom Künftigen: Zum hundertsten Todestag Friedrich Hölderlins." *Neue Schweizer Rundschau* 7 (1944): 390–401.

———. "Hölderlin 1944." In *Äußerungen 1944–1982*, edited by Ulrich Dietzel, 435–40. Berlin: Aufbau, 1983.

———. *In den Kämpfen dieser Zeit*. Berlin: Klaus Wagenbach, 1995.

———. *Scardanelli: Ein Hörspiel*. Berlin: Klaus Wagenbach, 1970.

Hesse, Hermann. *Der Steppenwolf*. 40th ed. Berlin: S. Fischer, 1931.

Hoffmann, Johanna. *Charlotte von Stein: Goethe und ich werden niemals Freunde*. 3rd ed. Berlin: Verlag der Nationen, 1991.

Hofmann, Gert. *Die kleine Stechardin*. 1994; Munich: dtv, 1999.

Hölderlin, Friedrich. *Sämtliche Werke*. Edited by Friedrich Beißner. Stuttgart: W. Kohlhammer, 1943–85.

Huizing, Klaas. *Das Ding an sich: Eine unerhörte Begebenheit aus dem Leben Immanuel Kants*. Munich: Albrecht Knaus, 1998.

Kant, Immanuel. "Der Streit der Fakultäten." In *Gesammelte Schriften*, edited by Königlich Preußischen Akademie der Wissenschaften, 1–116. Vol. 7. Berlin: Georg Reimer, 1907.

Kehlmann, Daniel. *Die Vermessung der Welt*. 2005; Reinbek bei Hamburg: Rowohlt, 2007.

———. "Wo ist Carlos Montúfar?" *Wo ist Carlos Montúfar?: Über Bücher*, 9–27. Reinbek bei Hamburg: Rowohlt, 2005.

Kleist, Heinrich von. "Penthesilea." In *Werke und Briefe in vier Bänden*, edited by Siegfried Streller, 5–120. Vol. 2. Berlin: Aufbau, 1978.

Kunert, Günter. *Ein anderer K*. Stuttgart: Philipp Reclam, 1977.

————. "Heinrich von Kleist — Ein Modell." In *Diesseits des Erinnerns*, 36–62. Munich: Carl Hanser, 1982.

————. "Pamphlet für K." In *Die Schreie der Fledermäuse*, edited by Dieter E. Zimmer, 333–42. Munich: Hanser, 1979.

Löhr, Robert. *Das Erlkönig-Manöver*. 4th ed. Munich: Piper, 2010.

————. *Das Hamlet-Komplott*. Munich: Piper, 2010.

Mann, Thomas. *Gesammelte Werke in zwölf Bänden*. Oldenbourg: S. Fischer, 1960.

Müller, Heiner. *Leben Gundlings Friedrich von Preußen Lessings Schlaf Traum Schrei: Ein Greuelmärchen*. In *Herzstück*, 9–40. Berlin: Rotbuch, 1983.

Ortheil, Hanns-Josef. *Faustinas Küsse*. Munich: Luchterhand, 1998.

Reschke, Karin. *Verfolgte des Glücks: Findebuch der Henriette Vogel*. 1982; Hamburg: Rotbuch, 1996.

Schami, Rafik, and Uwe-Michael Gutzschhahn. *Der geheime Bericht über den Dichter Goethe, der eine Prüfung auf einer arabischen Insel bestand*. Munich: Hanser, 1999.

Schelling, Friedrich. "Philosophische Briefe über Dogmatismus und Kritizismus (1795)." In *Werke*, edited by Manfried Schröter, 205–65. Vol. 1. Munich: C. H. Beck and R. Oldenbourg, 1927.

Schiller, Friedrich. *Werke*. *Nationalausgabe*. Edited by Eberhard Haufe. Vol. 25. Weimar: Hermann Böhlaus Nachfolger, 1979.

Schmidt, Arno. "Goethe und Einer seiner Bewunderer." In *Das erzählerische Werk in 8 Bänden*, 31–62. Vol. 6. Bargfeld: Arno Schmidt Stiftung, 1985.

Sparschuh, Jens. *Der große Coup: Aus den geheimen Tage- und Nachtbüchern des Johann Peter Eckermann*. 2nd ed. Cologne: Kiepenheuer & Witsch, 1996.

————. *Lavaters Maske*. Cologne: Kiepenheuer & Witsch, 1999.

Struzyk, Brigitte. *Caroline unterm Freiheitsbaum: Ansichtssachen*. Darmstadt: Luchterhand, 1988.

Walser, Martin. *Brandung*. Frankfurt am Main: Suhrkamp, 1985.

————. *Ein liebender Mann*. Reinbek bei Hamburg: Rowohlt, 2008.

————. *In Goethes Hand: Szenen aus dem 19. Jahrhundert*. Frankfurt am Main: Suhrkamp, 1982.

Walser, Robert. "Kleist in Thun." In *Das Gesamtwerk*, edited by Jochen Greven, 174–85. Vol. 1. Geneva: Helmut Kossodo, 1972.

Weiss, Peter. "Hölderlin." In *Stücke vol. 2/2*, 265–416. Frankfurt am Main: Suhrkamp, 1977.

Wieland, C. M. "Der Herausgeber an die Leser." In Sophie von La Roche, *Melusinens Sommerabende*. 1806; Reprint, Eschborn: Dietmar Klotz, 1992.

Wolf, Christa. *Die Dimension des Autors: Essays und Aufsätze, Reden und Gespräche 1959–1985*. Darmstadt: Luchterhand, 1987.

————. *Kein Ort. Nirgends*. 2nd ed. Darmstadt: Luchterhand, 1979.

————. *Kein Ort. Nirgends: Mit einem Kommentar von Sonja Hilzinger*. Frankfurt am Main: Suhrkamp, 2006.

Wolf, Christa, and Gerhard Wolf. *Ins Ungebundene gehet eine Sehnsucht: Gesprächsraum Romantik*. Berlin: Aufbau, 1985.

————. "Nicht beendetes Gespräch: Zum 60. Geburtstag Stephan Hermlins 1975." In Hermlin, *In den Kämpfen dieser Zeit*, 105–8.

Wolf, Gerhard. *Der arme Hölderlin*. Darmstadt: Luchterhand, 1982.

Secondary Sources

Adelson, Leslie A. *Making Bodies, Making History: Feminism and German Identity*. Lincoln: U of Nebraska P, 1993.

Allan, Seán. "'Mein ist die Rache spricht der Herr': Violence and Revenge in the Works of Heinrich von Kleist." In *A Companion to the Works of Heinrich von Kleist*, edited by Bernd Fischer, 227–48. Rochester, NY: Camden House, 2003.

Anderson, Mark M. "Der vermessende Erzähler: Mathematische Geheimnisse bei Daniel Kehlmann." *Text und Kritik* 177 (2008): 58–67.

Arnds, Peter O. "Orientalizing Germany in Rafik Schami's *Die Sehnsucht der Schwalbe* and *Sieben Doppelgänger*." *Seminar* 41 (2005): 275–88.

————. *Representation, Subversion, and Eugenics in Günter Grass's* The Tin Drum. Rochester, NY: Camden House, 2004.

Aust, Hugo. *Der historische Roman*. Stuttgart: J. B. Metzler, 1994.

Bakhtin, Mikhail. *Rabelais and His World*. Translated by Helene Iswolsky. Cambridge, MA: MIT Press, 1968.

Baldwin, Claire. *The Emergence of the Modern German Novel: Christoph Martin Wieland, Sophie von La Roche, and Maria Anna Sagar*. Rochester, NY: Camden House, 2002.

Bartle, Gamin. "Displacing Goethe: Tribute and Exorcism in Thomas Mann's the *Beloved Returns*." In Franssen and Hoenselaars, *The Author as Character*, 195–212.

Bauer Pickar, Gertrud, and Sabine Cramer, eds. *The Age of Goethe Today: Critical Reexamination and Literary Reflection*. Munich: Wilhelm Fink, 1990.

Beckermann, Thomas, and Volker Canaris, eds. *Der andere Hölderlin: Materialien zum "Hölderlin" Stück von Peter Weiss*. 2nd ed. Frankfurt am Main: Suhrkamp, 1979.

Benn, Maurice B. *The Drama of Revolt: A Critical Study of Georg Büchner*. Cambridge: Cambridge UP, 1976.

Berghahn, Daniela. *Hollywood behind the Wall: The Cinema of East Germany*. Manchester: Manchester UP, 2005.

Bertaux, Pierre. "Hölderlin und die Französische Revolution." In Beckermann and Canaris, *Der andere Hölderlin*, 65–100.

Berwald, Olaf. *An Introduction to the Works of Peter Weiss*. Rochester, NY: Camden House, 2003.

Betz, John R. *After Enlightenment: The Post-Secular Vision of J. G. Hamann*. Oxford: Wiley-Blackwell, 2009.

Bird, Stephanie. *Recasting Historical Women: Female Identity in German Biographical Fiction*. Oxford, UK: Berg, 1998.

Block, Richard. *The Spell of Italy: Vacation, Magic, and the Attraction of Goethe*. Detroit, MI: Wayne State UP, 2006.

Blumenberg, Hans. *Der Prozeß der theoretischen Neugierde.* Frankfurt am Main: Suhrkamp, 1973.

Boa, Elizabeth, and Rachel Palfreyman. *Heimat — A German Dream: Regional Loyalties and National Identity in German Culture 1890–1900.* Oxford: Oxford UP, 2000.

Bohm, Arnd. "Authority and Authorship in Luise Adelgunde Gottsched's *Das Testament.*" *Lessing Yearbook* 18 (1986): 129–40.

Borchardt, Edith, and Jennifer Wright. "Androgyny: The Search for Wholeness in Karoline von Günderrode and Heinrich von Kleist. Christa Wolf's Novel *Kein Ort. Nirgends.*" *Journal of the Fantastic in the Arts* 11 (2001): 245–56.

Bovenschen, Silvia. *Die imaginierte Weiblichkeit: Exemplarische Untersuchungen zu kulturgeschichtlichen und literarischen Präsentationsformen des Weiblichen.* Frankfurt am Main: Suhrkamp, 1980.

Brady, Philip. "On Not Being Intimidated: Socialist Overhauling of a Classic." In *Goethe Revisited: A Collection of Essays,* edited by Elizabeth M. Wilkinson, 31–52. London: John Calder, 1984.

Braunbeck, Helga G. *Autorschaft und Subjektgenese: Christa Wolfs Kein Ort, Nirgends.* Vienna: Passagen, 1992.

Bridge, Helen. "Biographical Fiction by GDR Women Writers: Reassessing the Cultural Heritage." In Durrani and Preece, *Travellers in Time and Space,* 155–65.

———. *Women's Writing and Historiography in the GDR.* Oxford: Clarendon, 2002.

Brockmann, Stephen. *German Literary Culture at the Zero Hour.* Rochester, NY: Camden House, 2004.

Butler, Judith. "Performative Acts and Gender Constitution: An Essay in Phenomenology and Feminist Theory." In *Performing Feminisms: Feminist Critical Theory and Theater,* edited by Sue-Ellen Case, 270–82. Baltimore, MD: Johns Hopkins UP, 1990.

Cohen, Robert. *Peter Weiss in seiner Zeit: Leben und Werk.* Stuttgart: J. B. Metzler, 1992.

Cohn, Dorrit. *The Distinction of Fiction.* Baltimore, MD: Johns Hopkins UP, 1999.

Dettelbach, Michael. "Alexander von Humboldt between Enlightenment and Romanticism." *Northeastern Naturalist* 8. Special Issue 1 (2001): 9–20.

Dick, Elizabeth Margaret. "Rewriting the Past: Goethe and Contemporary Literature." PhD diss., Washington University, 2004.

Dierks, Manfred. "Thomas Mann's Late Politics." In *A Companion to the Works of Thomas Mann,* edited by Herbert Lehnert and Eva Wessell, 203–19. Rochester, NY: Camden House, 2004.

Dietrick, Linda. "Appropriating Romantic Consciousness: Narrative Mode in Christa Wolf's *Kein Ort. Nirgends.*" In *Echoes and Influences of German Romanticism: Essays in Honor of Hans Eichner,* edited by Michael S. Batts, Anthony W. Riley, and Heinz Wessel, 211–23. New York: Peter Lang, 1987.

Doane, Heike A. "Love. vs. Life: Martin Walser describes Johann Peter Eckermann's Development." In Bauer Pickar and Cramer, *The Age of Goethe
Today,* 154–70.

Drommer, Günther. "Typische Bemerkungen zu untypischen Texten." In
Hein, *Einladung zum Lever Bourgeois,* 185–90.

Durrani, Osman. "Introduction." In Durrani and Preece, *Travellers in Time
and Space,* i–ix.

Durrani, Osman, and Julian Preece, eds. *Travellers in Time and Space:
The German Historical Novel/Reisende durch Zeit und Raum: Der
deutschsprachige historische Roman.* Amsterdam: Rodopi, 2001.

Durzak, Manfred. "Ein Gespräch im Hause Hacks über den anwesenden
Herrn von Goethe: Goethe-Einflüsse und Goethe-Adaptionen in Stük-
ken von Peter Hacks." In Bauer Pickar and Cramer, *The Age of Goethe
Today,* 130–53.

Dwars, Jens-Fietje. *Und dennoch Hoffnung. Peter Weiss: Eine Biographie.* Berlin: Aufbau, 2007.

Eggert, Hartmut. *Studien zur Wirkungsgeschichte des deutschen historischen
Romans 1850–1875.* Frankfurt am Main: Vittorio Klostermann, 1971.

Ellis, Roger. *Peter Weiss in Exile: A Critical Study of his Works.* Ann Arbor: U
Michigan Research P, 1987.

Ester, Hans, and Guillaume van Gemert, eds. *Künstler-Bilder: Zur Produktiven Auseinandersetzung mit der schöpferischen Persönlichkeit.* Amsterdam: Rodopi, 2003.

———. "Zum Geleit." In Ester and van Gemert, *Künstler-Bilder,* 7–9.

Ette, Ottmar. *Alexander von Humboldt und die Globalisierung: Das Mobile des
Wissens.* Frankfurt am Main: Insel, 2009.

Fehervary, Helen. *Hölderlin and the Left: The Search for a Dialectic of Art and
Life.* Heidelberg: Carl Winter, 1977.

Fenves, Peter. "The Scale of Enthusiasm." In Klein and La Vopa, *Enthusiasm
and Enlightenment in Europe,* 117–52.

Fetz, Gerald A. "Cultural History on Stage: *In Goethes Hand.*" In *Martin Walser: International Perspectives,* edited by Jürgen E. Schlunk and
Armand E. Singer, 145–55. New York: Peter Lang, 1987.

Fischer, Bernd. "*Einladung zum Lever Bourgeois:* Christoph Hein's First
Prose Collection." In *Studies in GDR Culture and Society 4: Selected
Papers from the Ninth New Hampshire Symposium on the German Demo-
cratic Republic,* edited by Margy Gerber et al., 125–36. Lanham, MD:
UP of America, 1984.

Foucault, Michel. *Surveiller et punir: Naissance de la prison.* Paris: Gallimard,
1975.

Franssen, Paul, and Ton Hoenselaars, eds. *The Author as Character: Representing Historical Writers in Western Literature.* Cranbury, NJ: Associated University Presses, 1999.

———. "The Author as Character: Defining a Genre." In Franssen and
Hoenselaars, *The Author as Character,* 11–35.

Frey, Siegfried. "Lavater, Lichtenberg, and the Suggestive Power of the Human Face." In *The Faces of Physiognomy: Interdisciplinary Approaches to Johann Caspar Lavater*, edited by Ellis Shookman, 64–103. Columbia, SC: Camden House, 1993.

Gailus, Andreas. *Passions of the Sign: Revolution and Language in Kant, Goethe, and Kleist.* Baltimore, MD: Johns Hopkins UP, 2006.

Geppert, Hans Vilmar. *Der 'andere' historische Roman: Theorie und Strukturen einer diskontinuierlichen Gattung.* Tübingen: Max Niemeyer, 1976.

Gerlach, Rainer, and Matthias Richter, eds. *Peter Weiss im Gespräch.* Frankfurt am Main: Suhrkamp, 1986.

Gerhard, Melitta. "Ursache und Bedeutung von Goethes 'Entsagung.'" *Jahrbuch des freien deutschen Hochstifts* (1981): 110–15.

Gersdorff, Dagmar von. *"Die Erde ist mir Heimat nicht geworden": Das Leben der Karoline von Günderrode.* Frankfurt am Main: Insel, 2006.

Gerstenberger, Katharina. *Writing the New Berlin: The German Capital in Post-Wall Literature.* Rochester, NY: Camden House, 2008.

Hahn, Hans-Joachim. "Hermann Hesse's Goethe." In *A Companion to the Works of Hermann Hesse*, edited by Ingo Cornils, 395–420. Rochester, NY: Camden House, 2009.

Hanenberg, Peter. *Peter Weiss: Vom Nutzen und Nachteil der Historie für das Schreiben.* Berlin: Erich Schmidt, 1993.

Harpprecht, Klaus. "Der Krüppel und das Kind (*Die kleine Stechardin*)." In *Schauplatz Menschenkopf: Der Erzähler Gert Hofmann*, edited by Hans Christian Kosler, 192–97. Munich: Hanser, 1997.

Håstad, Disa. "*Hölderlin* beginnt mit Marats Tod: Gespräch mit Peter Weiss. Ende 1972." Translated by Michael Kanning. In Gerlach and Richter, *Peter Weiss im Gespräch*, 192–201.

Hatfield, Henry. *Crisis and Continuity in Modern German Fiction: Ten Essays.* Ithaca, NY: Cornell UP, 1969.

Hell, Julia. *Post-Fascist Fantasies: Psychoanalysis, History, and the Literature of East Germany.* Durham, NC: Duke UP, 1997.

Henkel, Arthur. *Entsagung: Eine Studie zu Goethes Altersroman.* Tübingen: Max Niemeyer, 1954.

Herminghouse, Patricia. "Die Wiederentdeckung der Romantik: Zur Funktion der Dichterfiguren in der neueren DDR-Literatur." Translated by Reinhart Jost. In Hoogeveen and Labroisse, *DDR-Roman und Literaturgesellschaft*, 217–48.

Hilzinger, Sonja. "'Avantgarde ohne Hinterland': Zur Wiederentdeckung des Romantischen in Prosa und Essayistik der DDR." *Text + Kritik, Sonderband: Literatur in der DDR: Rückblicke.* Edited by Heinz Ludwig Arnold (1991): 93–100.

Hock, Lisabeth M. *Replicas of a Female Prometheus: The Textual Personae of Bettina von Arnim.* New York: Peter Lang, 2001.

Hoesterey, Ingeborg. *Pastiche: Cultural Memory in Art, Film, Literature.* Bloomington: Indiana UP, 2001.

Hoffmeister, Donna L. "Rewriting Literary History Through Fiction: Karin Reschke and Christa Wolf." *South Atlantic Review* 49 (1984): 3–17.

Hoffmeister, Gerhart. "Rhetorics of Revolution in West European Romanticism." In *The French Revolution and the Age of Goethe*, edited by Gerhart Hoffmeister, 91–106. Hildesheim: Georg Olms, 1989.

Holquist, Michael. Introduction to *The Dialogic Imagination: Four Essays*, by M. M. Bakhtin, xv–xxxiii. Edited by Michael Holquist. Translated by Caryl Emerson and Michael Holquist. Austin: U of Texas P, 1981.

Hoogeveen, Jos, and Gerd Labroisse, eds. *DDR-Roman und Literaturgesellschaft*. Amsterdam: Rodopi, 1981.

Jehlen, Myra. "Archimedes and the Paradox of Feminist Criticism." In *The "Signs" Reader: Women, Gender & Scholarship*, edited by Elizabeth Abel and Emily K. Abel, 69–95. Chicago: U of Chicago P, 1983.

Johnstone, Richard. "The Rise of Faction." *Quadrant* (April 1985): 76–78.

Kellner, L. *Alexander von Humboldt*. London: Oxford UP, 1963.

Kittler, Friedrich. "Writing into the Wind, Bettina." Translated by Marilyn Wyatt. *Glyph 7* (1980): 32–69.

Klein, Lawrence E., and Anthony J. La Vopa. *Enthusiasm and Enlightenment in Europe 1650–1850*. San Marino, CA: Huntington Library, 1998.

Komar, Kathleen L. "Klytemnestra in Germany: Re-visions of a Female Archetype by Christa Reinig and Christine Brückner." *Germanic Review* 69 (1994): 20–27.

Kontje, Todd. *German Orientalisms*. Ann Arbor: U of Michigan P, 2004.

———. *Women, the Novel, and the German Nation 1771–1871: Domestic Fiction in the Fatherland*. Cambridge: Cambridge UP, 1998.

Koopmann, Helmut. *Goethe und Frau von Stein: Geschichte einer Liebe*. Munich: C. H. Beck, 2002.

Kord, Susanne. *Little Detours: The Letters and Plays of Luise Gottsched (1713–1762)*. Rochester, NY: Camden House, 2000.

Krauss, Hannes. "Die Kunst zu erben — zur romantischen Rezeption (nicht nur) romantischer Literatur: Über Sigrid Damm, Christa Moog und Brigitta Struzyk." In *Neue Ansichten: The Reception of Romanticism in the Literature of the GDR*, edited by Howard Gaskill, Karin McPherson, and Andrew Barker, 41–52. Amsterdam: Rodopi, 1990.

Krimmer, Elisabeth. "The Gender of Terror: War as (Im)Moral Institution in Kleist's *Hermannschlacht* and *Penthesilea*." *German Quarterly* 81 (2008): 66–85.

———. *In the Company of Men: Cross-Dressed Women around 1800*. Detroit, MI: Wayne State UP, 2004.

Krumrey, Marianne. "Gegenwart im Spiegel der Geschichte: Christoph Hein, *Einladung zum Lever Bourgeois*." *Temperamente* 6.4 (1981): 143–47.

Kruse, Jens. "'Goethe' und Adenauer als Dioskuren: die Goethe-Fiktionen der fünfziger Jahre." *Germanic Review* 63 (1988): 189–96.

———. "The Political Uses of 'Goethe' during the Nazi Period: Goethe Fictions between 1933 and 1945." *New German Review* 19 (2003–4): 12–29.

———. "Walsers Eckermann-Stück: Goethe-Schelte oder Liebeserklärung?" *Monatshefte* 79 (1987): 439–48.

Kuhn, Anna K. "Peter Hacks' *Ein Gespräch im Hause Stein über den abwesenden Herrn von Goethe*: A Feminist Reinterpretation of the *Geniebegriff*." *Germanic Review* 60 (1985): 91–97.

Kurpanik-Malinowska, Gizela. "Stil und Traditionsbezüge gehören zusammen: Zu Christa Wolfs Aufarbeitung der deutschen Romantik." In Tunner, *Romantik — Eine lebenskräftige Krankheit*, 135–44.

La Vopa, Anthony. "The Philosopher and the *Schwärmer*: On the Career of a German Epithet From Luther to Kant." In Klein and La Vopa, *Enthusiasm and Enlightenment in Europe*, 85–115.

LaCapra, Dominick. *History and Criticism*. Ithaca, NY: Cornell UP, 1985.

Lajarrige, Jacques. "Wahnsinn mit Gänsefüßchen: Zur Rehabilitierung Heinrich von Kleists in Günter Kunerts *Ein anderer K.*" In Tunner, *Romantik — Eine lebenskräftige Krankheit*, 145–58.

Lohan, Robert, ed. *The Golden Age of German Literature*. New York: Frederick Ungar, 1945.

Lukács, Georg. "Hölderlins *Hyperion*." In Beckermann and Canaris, *Der andere Hölderlin*, 19–47.

———. *Probleme des Realismus*. Berlin: Aufbau, 1955.

———. *Werke*. Vol. 6, *Probleme des Realismus 3: Der historische Roman*. Neuwied: Luchterhand, 1965.

Mandelkow, Karl Robert. *Goethe in Deutschland: Rezeptionsgeschichte eines Klassikers. Band 2: 1919–1982*. Munich: C. H. Beck, 1989.

Martens, Lorna. *The Promised Land? Feminist Writing in the German Democratic Republic*. Albany: SUNY P, 2001.

McCarthy, John A. "*Verständigung* and *Dialektik*: On Consensus Theory and the Dialectic of Enlightenment." In *Impure Reason: Dialectic of Enlightenment in Germany*, edited by W. Daniel Wilson and Robert C. Holub, 13–33. Detroit, MI: Wayne State UP, 1993.

McCormick, Richard W. *Politics of the Self: Feminism and the Postmodern in West German Literature and Film*. Princeton, NJ: Princeton UP, 1991.

Meinecke, Friedrich. *Weltbürgertum und Nationalstaat*. 6th ed. Munich: R. Oldenbourg, 1922.

Menke, Timm Reiner. *Lenz-Erzählungen in der deutschen Literatur*. Hildesheim: Georg Olms, 1984.

Metzge, Erwin. "Kant und Hamann." In *Johann Georg Hamann*, edited by Reiner Wild, 233–63. Darmstadt: Wissenschaftliche Buchgesellschaft, 1978.

Meyer, Franziska. *Avantgarde im Hinterland: Caroline Schlegel-Schelling in der DDR-Literatur*. New York: Peter Lang, 1999.

Mix, York-Gothart. "Mit Goethe und Diderot gegen die Pächter des klassischen Erbes: U. Plenzdorfs *Die neuen Leiden des jungen W.*, V. Brauns Texte zu *Hinze und Kunze* und die Kontrolle der literarischen Kommunikation in der DDR." *Jahrbuch der deutschen Schillergesellschaft* 42 (1998): 401–20.

Molinelli-Stein, Barbara. *Thomas Mann: Das Werk als Selbstinszenierung eines problematischen Ichs. Versuch einer psycho-existenziellen Strukturanalyse zu den Romanen* Lotte in Weimar *und* Doktor Faustus. Tübingen: Stauffenburg, 1999.

Nethersole, Reingard. "Models of Globalization." *PMLA* 116 (2001): 638–49.

Niekerk, Carl. *Zwischen Naturgeschichte und Anthropologie: Lichtenberg im Kontext der Spätaufklärung.* Tübingen: Max Niemeyer, 2005.

Niggl, Günter. *Zeitbilder: Studien und Vorträge zur deutschen Literatur des 19. und 20. Jahrhunderts.* Wurzburg: Königshausen & Neumann, 2005.

O'Flaherty, James C. *Johann Georg Hamann.* Boston: Twayne, 1979.

Øhrgaard, Per. "He, Butt! Das ist deine andere Wahrheit: Die Romantik als Bezugspunkt in der deutschen Gegenwartsliteratur." *Text & Kontext* 18 (Supp.: 1983): 128–45.

Onderdelinden, Sjaak. "'So kann es gewesen sein': Peter Härtlings Künstlerromane." In Ester and van Gemert, *Künstler-Bilder*, 129–48.

Oppen, Karoline von. "'Man muß jetzt laut schreien, um gehört zu werden': Stefan Heym, Walter Jens, Helga Königsdorf: An Intellectual Opposition?" In *Textual Responses to German Unification: Processing Historical and Social Change in Literature and Film*, edited by Carol Anne Costabile-Heming, Rachel J. Halverson, and Kristie A. Foell, 109–29. Berlin: Walter de Gruyter, 2001.

Osterkamp, Ernst. "Karin Reschke *Verfolgte des Glücks: Findebuch der Henriette Vogel*." *Kleist-Jahrbuch* (1984): 163–75.

Paulson, William. *Literary Culture in a World Transformed: A Future for the Humanities.* Ithaca, NY: Cornell UP, 2001.

Paver, Chloe E. M. "Lavater Fictionalized: Jens Sparschuh's *Lavaters Maske.*" In *Physiognomy in Profile: Lavater's Impact on European Culture*, edited by Melissa Percival and Graeme Tytler, 217–29. Newark: U of Delaware P, 2005.

Peterson, Brent O. "Mühlbach, Ranke, and the Truth of Historical Fiction." In *A Companion to German Realism 1848–1900*, edited by Todd Kontje, 53–84. Rochester, NY: Camden House, 2002.

Pizer, John. "'Man schaffe ihn auf eine sanfte Manier fort': Robert Walser's *Lenz* as a Cipher for the Dark Side of Modernity." In *Space to Act: The Theater of J. M. R. Lenz*, edited by Alan C. Leidner and Helga S. Madland, 141–49. Columbia, SC: Camden House, 1993.

Ponzi, Mauro. "Zur Entstehung des Goetheschen Motivs der 'Entsagung.'" *Zeitschrift für Germanistik* 7 (1986): 150–59.

Pourciau, Sarah. "Disarming the Double: Kant in Defense of Philosophy (1766)." *Germanic Review* 81 (2006): 99–120.

Presner, Todd Samuel. *Mobile Modernity: Germans, Jews, Trains.* New York: Columbia UP, 2007.

Preußer, Heinz-Peter. "Zur Typologie der Zivilisationskritik: Was aus Daniel Kehlmanns Roman 'Die Vermessung der Welt' einen Bestseller werden ließ." *Text und Kritik* 177 (2008): 73–85.

Razbojnikova-Frateva, Maja. *Fiktionale Frauenbiographien in der Gegenwartsliteratur: Das Reden vom Geschlecht im Text hinter dem Text.* Berlin: trafo, 2003.

Reid, J. H. *Writing without Taboos: The New East German Literature.* New York: Berg, 1990.

Richel, Veronica C. *Luise Gottsched: A Reconsideration.* Bern: Peter Lang, 1973.

Richter, Simon. *Missing the Breast: Gender, Fantasy, and the Body in the German Enlightenment.* Seattle: U of Washington P, 2006.

Richter-Schröder, Karin. *Frauenliteratur und weibliche Identität: Theoretische Ansätze zu einer weiblichen Ästhetik und zur Entwicklung der neuen deutschen Frauenliteratur.* Frankfurt am Main: Hain, 1986.

Roberts, David. "The Modern German Historical Novel: An Introduction." In *The Modern German Historical Novel: Paradigms, Problems, Perspectives,* edited by David Roberts and Philip Thomson, 1–17. Oxford, UK: Berg, 1991.

Roos, Peter. "[Gespräch mit] Peter Weiss. [1978]." In Gerlach and Richter, *Peter Weiss im Gespräch,* 227–30.

Rosellini, Jay. "Zur Funktionsbestimmung des historischen Romans in der DDR-Literatur." In Hoogeveen and Labroisse, *DDR-Roman und Literaturgesellschaft,* 61–101.

Rupke, Nicolaas A. *Alexander von Humboldt: A Metabiography.* Frankfurt am Main: Peter Lang, 2005.

Sabin, Stefana. "Im Schatten des Objekts: Über Peter Härtlings literatur-historische Figuren in den Romanen *Niembsch oder Der Stillstand, Hölderlin* und *Die dreifache Maria.*" In *Peter Härtling: Auskunft für Leser,* edited by Martin Lüdke, 53–68. Darmstadt: Luchterhand, 1988.

Said, Edward W. *Orientalism.* New York: Vintage Books, 1979.

——. "2003 Preface to the Twenty-Fifth Anniversary Edition." 5 Nov. 2002. http://www.princeton.edu/~paw/web_exclusives/plus/plus_110503orient. html.

Savage, Robert. *Hölderlin after the Catastrophe: Heidegger — Adorno — Brecht.* Rochester, NY: Camden House, 2008.

Schlenstedt, Silvia. *Stephan Hermlin: Leben und Werk.* West Berlin: deb, 1985.

Schulz-Jander, Eva-Maria. "'Das Gegenteil von Gebrechlichkeit ist Übereinkunft': Christa Wolf's *Kein Ort. Nirgends.*" In Bauer Pickar and Cramer, *The Age of Goethe Today,* 232–44.

Şenocak, Zafer. "Das Buch mit den sieben Siegeln. Über die vergessene Sprache der osmanischen Dichtung." *War Hitler Araber? IrreFührungen an den Rand Europas. Essays.* Berlin: Babel, 1994, 34–47.

——. "Wann ist der Fremde zu Hause? Betrachtungen zur Kunst und Kultur von Minderheiten in Deutschland." *Atlas des tropischen Deutschland. Essays.* 2nd ed. Berlin: Babel, 1993, 64–75.

Seret, Roberta. *Voyage into Creativity: The Modern Künstlerroman.* New York: Peter Lang, 1992.

Sharman, Gundula. *Twentieth-Century Reworkings of German Literature: An Analysis of Six Fictional Reinterpretations from Goethe to Thomas Mann.* Rochester, NY: Camden House, 2002.

Simpson, Patricia Anne. *The Erotics of War in German Romanticism.* Lewisburg, PA: Bucknell UP, 2006.

Skow, Katya. "Goethe Lite: The Fictionalization of German Literati." *Popular Culture Review* 17 (2006): 21–30.

Stahl, Christian. "Amazon.de — Rezension." 15 December 2008. http:/lesetipps. com/LesetippsG-L/Werke/Daniel_Kehlmann/Daniel_Kehlmann.

Strich, Fritz. *Goethe und die Weltliteratur*. Bern: Francke, 1946.

Sudau, Ralf. *Werkbearbeitung, Dichterfiguren: Traditionsaneignung am Beispiel der deutschen Gegenwartsliteratur*. Tübingen: Max Niemeyer, 1985.

Tang, Chenxi. *The Geographic Imagination of Modernity: Geography, Literature, and Philosophy in German Romanticism*. Stanford, CA: Stanford UP, 2008.

Tautz, Birgit. "Paths of Orientation: Gisela Kraft's turn to Romanticism circa 1990." *Colloquia Germanica* 38 (2005): 175–94.

Teraoka, Arlene Akiko. *The Silence of Entropy or Universal Discourse: The Postmodern Poetics of Heiner Müller*. New York: Peter Lang, 1985.

Thornham, Sue. "Introduction: Telling Stories; Feminism and Cultural Studies." In *Feminist Theory and Cultural Studies: Stories of Unsettled Relations*, edited by Sue Thornham, 1–15. London: Arnold, 2000.

Tunner, Erika, ed. *Romantik — Eine lebenskräftige Krankheit: Ihre literarischen Nachwirkungen in der Moderne*. Amsterdam: Rodopi, 1991.

Vaget, Hans Rudolf. "Thomas Mann, Schiller, and the Politics of Literary Self-Fashioning." *Monatshefte* 97 (2005): 494–510.

Varsamopoulou, Evy. *The Poetics of the* Künstlerinroman *and the Aesthetics of the Sublime*. Burlington, VT: Ashgate, 2002.

Visser, Anthonya. "Hanns-Josef Ortheils *Faustinas Küsse* — ein postmoderner Künstlerroman?" In Ester and van Gemert, *Künstler-Bilder*, 187–205.

Waldstein, Edith. "Christa Wolf's *Kein Ort. Nirgends*: A Dialogic Re-Vision." In *The Enlightenment and Its Legacy: Studies in German Literature in Honor of Helga Slessarev*, edited by Sara Friedrichsmeyer and Barbara Becker-Cantarino, 181–93. Bonn: Bouvier, 1990.

Wallenborn, Markus. *Frauen. Dichten. Goethe.: Die produktive Goethe-Rezeption bei Charlotte von Stein, Marianne von Willemer und Bettina von Arnim*. Tübingen: Max Niemeyer, 2006.

Wilson, W. Daniel. *Das Goethe-Tabu: Protest und Menschenrechte im klassischen Weimar*. Munich: dtv, 1999.

———. "'Humanitätssalbader': Goethe's Distaste for Jewish Emancipation, and Jewish Responses." In *Goethe in German-Jewish Culture*, edited by Klaus L. Berghahn and Jost Hermand, 146–64. Rochester, NY: Camden House, 2001.

Woodmansee, Martha. *The Author, Art, and the Market: Rereading the History of Aesthetics*. New York: Columbia UP, 1994.

Zima, Peter V. *Der europäische Künstlerroman: Von der romantischen Utopie zur postmodernen Parodie*. Tübingen: A. Francke, 2008.

Ziolkowski, Theodore. "Das Treffen in Buchenwald oder Der vergegenwärtigte Goethe." *Modern Language Studies* 31 (2001): 131–50.

Index

Abusch, Alexander, 114, 117
Adam, 168
Adelson, Leslie A., 27n40
Adorno, Theodor, 113, 180, 186n44
Adorno, Theodor, works by: *Dialektik der Aufklärung* (co-author), 182, 192
Agamemnon, 94
Alcoforcado, Marie, 83–84n19
Anderson, Edith, 42
Anderson, Mark, 165
Anna Amalia, Duchess of Weimar, 12, 122
Arnds, Peter O, 151n18, 154n69
Arnim, Achim von, 49, 134, 144
Arnim, Bettine von. *See* Brentano, Bettine
Arnim, Siegmund von, 112, 134
artist novel. *See Künstlerrroman*
Auerbach, Erich, works by: *Mimesis*, 188
Aust, Hugo, 5–6
Austen, Jane, 187
Authenrieth, Eugen, 72–73, 76
author-as-character fiction, 10, 187, 190, 192

Bakhtin, Mikhail, works by: *The Dialogic Imagination*, 90; *Rabelais and his World*, 174–75
Baldwin, Claire, 109–110n23
Balzac, Honoré de, 4
Bartle, Gamin, 14
Bayle, Pierre, works by: *Dictionnaire*, 93, 94
Becher, Johannes R., 114, 117
Becher, Johannes R., works by: *Schlacht um Moskau*, 60–61
Becoming Jane (movie), 187
Beethoven, Ludwig von, 17, 59
Beißner, Friedrich, 58

Benn, Maurice, 13
Bentham, Jeremy, 179
Berens, Christoph, 170, 172
Berghahn, Daniela, 67
"Berlin Republic," 22–24, 87, 97, 98, 107, 111, 115, 150, 191
Bernhard, Thomas, 9
Bernhard, Thomas, works by: "Goethe schtirbt," 25n25, 155n77; *Immanuel Kant*, 25–26n25
Bernstein, F. W., Bernd Eilert, and Eckhard Henscheid, works by: "Eckermann und sein Goethe: Ein Schau-/Hörspiel getreu nach der Quelle," 153–54n55
Berteaux, Pierre, 58, 59, 61, 66, 68, 70, 71, 78
Berwald, Olaf, 72
Betz, John, 171, 172
Beulwitz, Friedrich Wilhelm Ludwig, 101, 110n28
Biermann, Wolf, 23, 38, 45, 51, 56, 57, 61, 64, 189
Bird, Stephanie, 105, 123, 125
Bloch, Ernst, works by: *Das Prinzip Hoffnung*, 63–64
Block, Richard, 136
Bloom, Harold, 38
Blumenberg, Hans, 22, 162–63, 170, 175, 176, 180
Blumenberg, Hans, works by: *Prozeß der theoretischen Neugierde*, 156, 159–60, 165
Bobrowski, Johannes, works by: "Boehlendorff," 64
Bodmer, Johann Jakob, 92, 95
Boëtius, Henning, works by: *Der Gnom*, 22, 157, 180–82, 183, 186n40, 192; *Tod in Weimar*, 21, 112, 134, 137, 154n56, 154n57

Böhlendorff, Casimir, 64
Bohm, Arnd, 97
Böhmer, Otto, works by: *Der junge Herr Goethe*, 21, 112, 137, 191, 192
Böhmer-Schlegel-Schelling, Caroline, 20, 23, 89, 105–7, 108, 123
Bonpland, Aimé, 165, 168, 169, 170
Börne, Ludwig, 2, 128
Bovenschen, Silvia, 99
Brady, Philip, 115–16
Braun, Volker, works by: *Hinze und Kunze* texts, 114–15
Braunbeck, Helga G., 38, 41
Brentano, Bettine, 18, 19, 28–31, 48–51, 55n58, 99–100, 101, 112, 134, 144, 146, 188, 189
Brentano, Bettine, works by: *Clemens Brentanos Frühlingskranz*, 37, 50; *Goethes Briefwechsel mit einem Kind*, 31, 37, 48, 50, 134; *Die Günderrode*, 31, 35, 36–37, 42, 50
Brentano, Clemens, 29, 37, 49, 99–100, 101
Bridge, Helen, 91, 109n16, 119, 120, 121, 122, 123, 125
Brockmann, Stephen, 151n14
Brothers Grimm, 49, 173. *See also* Grimm, Jacob
Brückner, Christine, 94
Bruyn, Günter de, 38, 56
Bruyn, Günter de, works by: *Das Leben des Jean Paul Friedrich Richter*, 123
Büchner, Georg, 39, 187
Büchner, Georg, works by: *Lenz*, 12–14, 17, 26n28; *Woyzeck*, 72
Bürger, Gottfried August, 39
Butler, Judith, 28, 30, 49–50

Carl August, Duke of Weimar, 135, 145
Cixous, Hélène, 38
Clytemnestra, 94
Cohen, Robert, 68
Cohn, Dorrit, 123, 152n35

Congress of Vienna, 1
Corday, Charlotte, 85n37
Creuzer, Friedrich, 35, 42

Damm, Sigrid, 13, 56
Damm, Sigrid, works by: *Christiane und Goethe: Eine Recherche*, 122, 123; *Cornelia Goethe*, 20, 56, 91, 106, 112, 117, 122–25, 126–27, 152n36, 191; *Goethes letzte Reise*, 122–23; *Das Leben des Friedrich Schiller: Eine Wanderung*, 122; *Vögel, die verkünden Land: Das Leben des Jakob Michael Reinhold Lenz*, 122
Dedenroth, Eugen Hermann von, works by: "Ein Sohn Alexander's von Humboldt oder der Indianer von Maypures," 18
Deicke, Günther, 59
Derrida, Jacques, 179
Dettelbach, Michael, 167–68
Dick, Elizabeth Margaret, 153n54, 154n57
Doane, Heike, 127
Drommer, Günther, 161
Durrani, Osman, 6
Durzak, Manfred, 118, 119

Ebers, Georg, 6
Ebersbach, Volker, works by: *Caroline*, 105, 106
Eckermann, Hännchen, 126, 132, 133
Eckermann, Johann Peter, 20–21, 112, 126–29, 130, 131, 132–33, 134, 150, 153n43, 153n54, 153n55, 179, 191
Eckermann, Johann Peter, works by: *Gespräche mit Goethe*, 112, 128, 133, 139, 153n55
Eckermann, Karl, 126
Eco, Umberto, 6
Eggert, Hartmut, 25n21
Ehrenberg, Christian, 163
Eilert, Bernd. *See* Bernstein, F. W.
Ellis, Roger, 70

Enlightenment, 1, 21–22, 50, 58, 92, 156–83, 186n44, 188, 192
Enslin, Gottward Siegfried, 178–79
Ester, Hans, 8
Ette, Ottmar, 18, 162, 166–67
Euripides, works by: *Alcestis*, 11

Federal Republic of Germany (FRG), 5, 6, 19, 22–24, 47, 57, 61, 68, 80, 103, 107, 111, 113–15, 125–26, 150, 187–88, 189–90, 191
Fehervary, Helen, 60, 63–64, 80, 81, 84n24, 85n36
Fenves, Peter, 35–36, 52n13
Fetz, Gerald, 126
Feuchtwanger, Lion, 102
Feuerbach, Ludwig, 89
Feyl, Renate, 6, 19, 23, 82, 87–108, 108n1, 125, 144, 190
Feyl, Renate, works by: *Ausharren im Paradies*, 96; *Aussicht auf bleibende Helle: Die Königin und der Philosoph*, 20, 88, 89–90, 104–5; *Idylle mit Professor*, 20, 87, 90, 91–96, 98, 102, 106, 190; *Der lautlose Aufbruch: Frauen in der Wissenschaft*, 89; *Die profanen Stunden des Glücks*, 20, 88, 96–100, 101, 102, 110n25, 111; *Das sanfte Joch der Vortrefflichkeit*, 20, 88, 90, 91, 100–105, 110n28, 111, 145; *Sein ist das Weib, Denken der Mann: Ansichten für und wider die gelehrten Frauen* (editor), 89
Fichte, Johann Gottlieb, 66, 68
Fischer, Bernd, 184n16
Fitzgerald, Penelope, works by: *The Blue Flower*, 187
Fix, Peter, 116–17
Fleming, Paul, 95
Forster, Georg, 107, 110n37
Foucault, Michel, 22, 38, 186n44
Foucault, Michel, works by: *Surveiller et punir*, 179–80, 182, 183
Fouché, Joseph, 149
Fouqué, Friedrich de la Motte, 46
Franssen, Paul, 10
Freiligrath, Ferdinand, 128–29

French Neoclassicism, 90
French Revolution, 32, 33, 40, 58, 59, 60, 62, 64, 66–67, 68, 70, 71, 80, 114, 167
Freud, Sigmund, 41
Friedrich I, Elector of Brandenburg, King of Prussia, 105
Friedrich II, King of Prussia (Friedrich the Great), 11, 95, 158
Friedrich Wilhelm I, King of Prussia, 158
Fühmann, Franz, 38

Gailus, Andreas, 32–33
Gauss, Carl Friedrich, 7, 21, 23, 157, 163–66, 168, 169–70, 182, 192
Gauss, Carl Friedrich, works by: *Disquisitiones Arithemeticae*, 168
Gauss, Eugene, 163
Geertz, Clifford, 90
Gemert, Guillame van, 8
George, Stefan, 47
Geppert, Hans Vilmar, 4–5
German Democratic Republic (GDR), 5, 6, 12, 19, 22–24, 38–40, 44, 45, 56, 58, 61, 68, 72, 81, 87–96, 97, 102, 103, 106, 107, 111–12, 113–15, 116–23, 125, 150, 160, 161, 163, 167, 184n16, 187–88, 189, 190, 191; Romantic turn in, 23, 38, 51, 56–57, 59, 61, 64, 67, 82, 111, 123, 189
Gerstenberger, Katharina, 2–3
Goethe, August, 15, 39, 127, 129
Goethe, Cornelia, 13, 20, 99, 112, 122–25, 127
Goethe, Frau Rat (Catharine Elizabeth), 37, 99, 124
Goethe, Johann Caspar, 124, 125
Goethe, Johann Wolfgang von, 1, 2, 5, 8, 9, 11, 12, 14–17, 18, 19, 20–21, 23, 24n1, 25n25, 37, 39, 40, 44, 58, 59, 60, 67–72, 78–80, 81, 82, 84–85n35, 85n36, 90, 99, 100, 101, 102, 104, 111–50, 151n14, 152n31, 153n50, 153n55, 157, 158, 163, 179, 180–81, 182, 187, 188, 189, 190, 191, 192

Goethe, Johann Wolfgang von, works by: "Auf Miedings Tod," 148; "Der Erlkönig," 146; *Die Farbenlehre*, 139, 180–81, 183; *Faust*, 115, 118, 139, 146, 148; "Ein Gleiches/Wandrers Nachtlied," 184n20; *Götter, Helden und Wieland*, 10–11, 187; "Das Göttliche," 146, 155n78; *Iphigenie*, 122; *Italienische Reise*, 136–37; *Die Leiden des jungen Werthers*, 16, 84n29, 110n25, 115, 135, 139, 149; *Das Märchen*, 146; *Marienbader Elegie*, 129, 131; *Reineke Fuchs*, 139; *West-östlicher Divan*, 138–43; *Wilhelm Meisters Lehrjahre*, 68, 139, 149; *Wilhelm Meisters Wanderjahre oder die Entsagenden*, 131, 148

Goethe, Ottilie, 127, 130
Goldammer, Peter, 45–46
Gontard, Suzette, 63, 83–84n19
Gottsched, Johann Christoph, 20, 88, 89, 92–96, 97, 107, 109n16, 190
Gottsched, Luise, 19–20, 88, 91–96, 97, 99, 101, 105, 188, 190
Gottsched, Luise, works by: *Geschichte der lyrischen Dichtkunst der Deutschen*, 97; *Das Testament*, 94
Grass, Günter, works by: *Die Blechtrommel*, 115; *Der Butt*, 19, 29, 48–51, 189
Grimm, Jakob, 49. *See also* Brothers Grimm
Gruner, Justus, 46
Grützke, Johannes, 134
Günderrode, Karoline von, 18, 24, 28–33, 35–39, 41–45, 48–49, 50, 51, 61, 66, 108, 188, 189
Günderrode, Karoline von, works by: *Darthula nach Ossian*, 36; "Timur," 43–44
Gundling, Johann Paul Freiherr von, 158
Gutzschhahn, Uwe-Michael, 21, 112, 142, 191

Habermas, Jürgen, 182, 186n44
Hacks, Peter, 137

Hacks, Peter, works by: *Ein Gespräch im Hause Stein über den abwesenden Herrn von Goethe*, 20, 84n29, 111, 116–18, 119, 120, 121, 127, 128, 134, 152n30, 158, 191; *Das Jahrmarksfest zu Plundersweilen*, 115; *Musen: Vier Auftritte*, 118, 119; *Pandora, Drama nach J. W. von Goethe*, 115; "Saure Feste," 118
Hafiz, 138, 140
Haller, Albrecht, 92
Hamann, Johann Georg, 7, 21–22, 157, 159, 160, 168–72, 173, 181, 185n26, 188
Hamann, Johann Georg, works by: *Sokratische Denkwürdigkeiten*, 172
Hanenberg, Peter, 72
Hardenberg, Karl August von, 46
Hardenberg, Friedrich von. *See* Novalis
Harnack, Otto, 153n53
Harpprecht, Klaus, 174
Härtling, Peter, 5, 6, 7, 64, 87, 88
Härtling, Peter, works by: *Die dreifache Maria*, 74, 81; "Das Ende der Geschichte," 75, 76, 77; *Das Familienfest*, 75; *Hoffmann oder Die vielfältige Liebe*, 74, 77, 81, 86n62; *Hölderlin*, 9–10, 19, 57, 60, 67, 73–82, 87, 174, 190; "Mein Hölderlin," 78, 80; *Niembsch oder der Stillstand*, 73, 75, 81, 85n48; *Schubert: Zwölf Moments musicaux und ein Roman*, 74; *Schumanns Schatten: Variationen über mehrere Personen*, 74; *Über Heimat*, 85–86n50, 86n60; *Waiblingers Augen*, 73–74, 81
Hatfield, Henry, 17
Haza, Sophie, 47
Hegel, Georg Wilhelm Friedrich, 4, 19, 41, 58, 59, 60, 66, 68–69
Heidegger, Martin, 73
Hein, Christoph, 56, 144
Hein, Christoph, works by: "Einladung zum Lever Bourgeois," 161; *Einladung zum Lever Bourgeois*, 22, 157, 160; "Der neuere (glücklichere) Kohlhaas: Bericht

über einen Rechtshandel aus den Jahren 1972/73," 160–61; "Die russischen Briefe des Jägers Johann Seifert," 22, 157, 161–63, 164, 165, 167, 168, 180, 181, 182–83, 184n16, 192
Heine, Heinrich, 1, 141
Hell, Julia, 38, 39
Henkel, Arthur, 131, 153n53
Henscheid, Eckhard. *See* Bernstein, F. W.
Herder, Johann Gottfried, 100, 102
Herminghouse, Patricia, 43
Hermlin, Stephan, 58, 63, 70, 78, 82, 190
Hermlin, Stephan, works by: "Gesang vom Künftigen: Zum hundertsten Todestag Friedrich Hölderlins," 61–63; "Hölderlin 1944," 61–63; *Scardanelli*, 19, 57, 59–63, 64, 65, 66, 67, 69, 76, 80, 81, 85n36, 189
Hesse, Hermann, works by: *Der Steppenwolf*, 16–17
Hilzinger, Sonja, 56, 57, 61
historical novel, 3–7, 9–10, 19, 20, 73–77, 87–91, 95, 96, 97, 101–4, 108n2, 125, 157, 159
Hitler, Adolph, 12
Hoenselaars, Ton, 10
Hoffmann, E. T. A., 12, 74, 77, 81, 82, 86n62
Hoffmann, Johanna, works by: *Goethe und ich werden niemals Freunde*, 20, 106, 112, 119–22, 123–24, 127, 134, 191
Hoffmeister, Donna, 48
Hoffmeister, Gerhart, 66–67
Hofmann, Gert, works by: *Die kleine Stechardin*, 22, 156, 157, 158, 159, 160, 173–78, 180, 181, 182, 192
Hoesterey, Ingeborg, 144, 155n77
Hölderlin, Friedrich, 9, 13, 19, 23, 29, 33, 36, 38, 39, 56–82, 111, 126, 150, 188, 189, 190
Hölderlin, Friedrich, works by: *Empedokles*, 80; *Hyperion*, 58–59, 68, 69, 70, 72, 80, 83–84n19; "Das Schicksal," 84n28

Hölderlin, Karl, 66
Hölderlin Society, 58, 61, 62, 68, 81
Holocaust, 114
Holquist, Michael, 90
Honecker, Erich, 51, 56, 189
Horkheimer, Max, works by: *Dialektik der Aufklärung* (co-author), 182, 192
Hoyer, Charlotte, 118, 119
Huizing, Klaas, 7, 175
Huizing, Klaas, works by: *Das Ding an sich*, 7, 21, 156, 157, 158, 159, 160, 168–72, 173, 180, 181–82, 185n26, 185n30, 192
Humboldt, Alexander von, 7, 18, 21, 22, 23, 144, 156, 157, 159, 160, 161–68, 177, 180, 181, 182, 184n16, 184n20, 192
Humboldt, Wilhelm von, 103, 164

Ivan the Terrible, 145

Jahn, Friedrich Ludwig (Turnvater), 163
Jean Paul, 66, 123
Jefferson, Thomas, 165
Jehlen, Myra, 94
Joyce, James, 6
Joyce, James, works by: *Portrait of the Artist as a Young Man*, 3, 6, 9

Kalb, Charlotte von, 70
Kalb, Fritz von, 70
Kant, Immanuel, 5, 7, 21–22, 25–26n25, 31–35, 40, 52n16, 98, 99, 102, 156, 157, 159–60, 165, 168–72, 173, 177, 180, 181, 182, 192
Kant, Immanuel, works by: *Kritik der reinen Vernunft*, 171, 172; *Der Streit der Fakultäten*, 32–33, 34; *Träume eines Geistersehers, erläutert durch Träume der Metaphysik*, 181; "Was ist Aufklärung?," 160
Katte, Hans Hermann von, 158
Kaufmann, Hans, 42
Kehlmann, Daniel, 4

Kehlmann, Daniel, works by: *Die Vermessung der Welt*, 7, 18, 21, 23, 90, 156, 157, 158, 159, 160, 162, 163–68, 169–70, 177, 180, 181–82, 192; "Wo ist Carlos Montúfar?," 166

Kellner, Margarethe, 178

Kestner, Charlotte Buff, 15

Kleist, Heinrich von, 5, 17, 18, 19, 23, 28–48, 49, 51, 56, 61, 82, 144, 145–46, 147, 148, 149, 158, 159, 188, 189

Kleist, Heinrich von, works by: *Die Familie Schroffenstein*, 30; *Michael Kohlhaas*, 32–33, 53n22, 158, 160–61; *Penthesilea*, 30, 33–34, 36, 41, 42, 43, 47, 53n20; *Phoebus* (co-editor), 47; *Prinz Friedrich von Homburg*, 34; *Der zerbrochene Krug*, 145–46

Klopstock, Friedrich, 92, 99, 180

Komar, Kathleen L., 94, 109n14

Konstantin (Weimar Prince), 121

Kontje, Todd, 96, 100, 139

Kord, Susanne, 97, 109n15

Körner, Christian Gottfried, 167

Kraft, Gisela, 83n2

Kraft, Gisela, works by: *Prolog zu Novalis*, 83n2

Krauss, Hannes, 123

Krimmer, Elizabeth, 29–31, 48

Krumrey, Marianne, 163

Kruse, Jens, 11–12

Kühn, Sophie von, 83n2

Kulmus, Luise Adelgunde Victoria. *See* Gottsched, Luise

Kunert, Günter, 56

Kunert, Günter, works by: *Ein anderer K.*, 29, 45–47, 51, 189; "Heinrich von Kleist — Ein Modell," 46

Künstlerroman, 3, 7–10, 74, 85n49

La Roche, Georg Michael Frank von, 96–98, 101

La Roche, Maximiliane, 100

La Roche, Sophie, 20, 88, 93, 96–100, 101, 102, 105, 111, 190

La Roche, Sophie, works by: *Geschichte des Fräuleins von Sternheim*, 96, 98, 99, 100, 101, 110n25; *Melusinens Sommerabende*, 98, 99; *Pomona* (editor), 97, 98, 100

Labbé, Louise, 83–84n19

Lacan, Jacques, 38

LaCapra, Dominick, 74

Lampe, Martin, 160, 168, 169, 170, 172

Lavater, Johann Kaspar, 22, 157, 169–70, 171, 178–80, 181, 182, 183, 192

Leibnitz, Gottfried Wilhelm, 20, 25n25, 88, 104–5, 158

Lenau, Nikolaus, 73, 74, 81

Lenin, Vladimir, 59

Lenz, Jakob Michael Reinhold, 11, 12–14, 39, 99, 122

Lenz, Jakob Michael Reinhold, works by: *Pandämoneum Germanicum*, 11, 187

Lessing, Gotthold Ephraim, 95, 97, 100, 103, 158, 159, 180

Lessing, Gotthold Ephraim, works by: *Emilia Galotti*, 158; *Nathan der Weise*, 158

Levetzow, Amalie von, 130, 131

Levetzow, Ulrike von, 112, 129–32, 153n50

Lévi-Strauss, Claude, 172

Lichtenberg, Georg Christoph, 22, 156, 157, 159, 173–78, 180–82, 183, 186n40, 186n41, 186n44

Lohan, Robert, 1

Löhr, Robert, works by: *Das Erlkönig-Manöver*, 21, 112, 137, 143–47, 148–49, 191, 192; *Das Hamlet-Komplott*, 21, 112, 137, 143–44, 147–49, 191, 192

Louis XVI, 32

Louise, Queen of Prussia, 48

Lukács, Georg, 18, 23, 29, 37–40, 44, 56, 57, 59, 68, 70, 81, 82, 103, 111, 188, 189

Lukács, Georg, works by: *Der historische Roman*, 3–5, 102; "Hölderlins Hyperion," 57–59, 60, 62, 63, 67, 68

Luther, Martin, 32

Madison, James, 165, 167
Mandelkow, Karl Robert, 114, 118, 125–26, 151n14
Mann, Thomas, 6, 8, 24n1, 113, 114, 188
Mann, Thomas, works by: *Dr. Faustus*, 7; "Goethe als Repräsentant des bürgerlichen Zeitalters," 188; *Lotte in Weimar*, 13, 14–16, 20, 54n35, 116, 134, 187; "Schwere Stunde," 13, 14, 15, 17; *Der Tod in Venedig*, 134, 154n57; *Tonio Kröger*, 3
Marat, Jean-Paul, 72
Maria Theresa, 96
Mark, Julia, 86n62
Martens, Lorna, 23–24, 94
Marx, Karl, 58, 70, 72, 128, 140–41
McCarthy, John A., 186n44
McCormick, Richard W., 27n40
Meinecke, Friedrich, works by: *Die deutsche Katastrophe*, 2, 113; *Weltbürgertum und Nationalstaat*, 1–2, 113
Mendelssohn, Moses, 167
Menke, Timm Reiner, 26n28
Mesmer, Franz, 169
Meyer, Franziska, 110n37
Meyer, Maria, 74
Michaelis, Johann David, 106
Mirabeau, Honoré de, 32, 33
Mix, York-Gothart, 114–15, 119
Mohnelli-Stein, Barbara, 15
Montúfar, Carlos, 166
Morgner, Irmtraud, 92
Mörike, Edward, 74, 81, 82
Moritz, Karl Philip Emanuel, 135, 136
Mozart, Wolfgang Amadeus, 17
Mozart, Wolfgang Amadeus, works by: *Don Giovanni*, 82; *Die Zauberflöte*, 17
Mühlbach, Luise, 25n21
Mühlbach, Luise, works by: *Deutschland in Sturm und Drang*, 11, 25n21; *Fürsten und Dichter*, 11, 18
Muhrbeck, Friedrich, 80
Müller, Adam, 47, 48

Müller, Adam, works by: *Phoebus* (co-editor), 47
Müller, Heiner, works by: *Leben Gundlings Friedrich von Preußen Lessings Schlaf Traum Schrei: Ein Greuelmärchen*, 22, 156, 158–59, 181
Muncker, Franz, 106

Napoleon, 1, 2, 4, 12, 15–16, 21, 36, 39, 40, 50, 58, 65, 90, 102–3, 113, 137, 143, 145, 147, 149, 150. *See also* Napoleonic Wars
Napoleonic Wars, 49, 150, 191
National Socialism, 1, 2, 11–12, 15–16, 39, 57, 61–62, 81, 113–14, 115, 124, 167, 187, 188
Nethersole, Reingard, 104
Neuffer, Christian, 60, 71, 78–79, 81
Newton, Sir Isaac, 180–81
Niekerk, Carl, 177–78
Nietzsche, Friedrich, 157, 158
Niggl, Günter, 128
Novalis, 66, 83n2, 187
Novalis, works by: *Heinrich von Ofterdingen*, 187

Oberlin, Johann Friedrich, 13
O'Flaherty, James, 171
Øhrgaard, Per, 49
Onderdelinden, Sjaak, 85n49
Opitz, Martin, 95
Ortheil, Hans Josef, works by: *Faustinas Küsse*, 21, 23, 112, 134–37, 158, 191
"Ossian," works by: "Darthula," 42

Paulson, William, 143
Paver, Chloe, 179, 186n36
Peterson, Brent O., 11, 18
Philadelphia, Jacob, 181, 183
Pietism, 171
Pizer, John, 26n28
Plenzdorf, Ulrich, works by: *Die neuen Leiden des jungen W.*, 84n29, 114–15, 116, 149
Plievier, Theodor, 113
Preußer, Heinz-Peter, 166
Proust, Marcel, 8

Rabelais, François, 174–75
Racine, Jean, 161
Ransmayr, Christoph, 9
Rasputin, 115
Razbojnikova-Frateva, Maja, 110n35
Reid, J. H., 92, 93, 95
Reinig, Christa, 94
Renaissance, 58
Renfranz, Hans Peter, works by: *Eckermann feiert Goethes 100. Geburtstag*, 132
Reschke, Karin, works by: *Verfolgte des Glücks: Findebuch der Henriette Vogel*, 18–19, 23, 29, 47–48, 51, 108, 189
Revolution of 1848, 1, 128
Richel, Veronica, 97
Richter, Jean Paul Friedrich. *See* Jean Paul
Richter, Simon. 34, 41, 53n20
Richter-Schroeder, Karin, 23
Riemer, Friedrich Wilhelm, 118
Roberts, David, 6
Robespierre, 59
Romantics, Romanticism, 23, 28–29, 31, 32, 37, 38, 39, 44, 48–51, 55n60, 58, 63, 64, 66–67, 69, 76, 80, 81, 82, 105–7, 118, 134, 140, 147–48, 156, 166, 167, 168, 173–74, 178, 188, 189, 192. *See also* German Democratic Republic, Romantic turn in
Rose, Gustav, 163
Rosellini, Jay, 102
Rousseau, Jean-Baptiste, 95
Rousseau, Jean-Jacques, 167
Runge, Phillip Otto, 49, 50
Rupke, Nicolaas, 167
Russian Revolution, 114

Sabin, Stefana, 74
Said, Edward, works by: *Orientalism*, 138, 140–41
Sartre, Jean-Paul, 8
Savage, Robert, 59, 68, 73
Savigny, Friedrich Carl von, 42–43, 48
Schabert, Ina, 123
Schami, Rafik, 133, 154n69

Schami, Rafik, works by: *Der geheime Bericht über den Dichter Goethe, der eine Prüfung auf einer arabischen Insel bestand*, 21, 100, 112, 137, 138–43, 191, 192
Schelling, Friedrich, 33, 35, 36, 66, 68, 75, 105, 107, 163
Schelling, Friedrich, works by: *Philosophische Briefe über Dogmatismus und Kritizismus*, 35
Schiller, Charlotte, 101–4, 110n28
Schiller, Friedrich, 2, 11, 14, 15, 18, 58, 67–71, 79–80, 84–85n35, 85n36, 88, 90, 98, 99, 100–105, 110n28, 122, 123, 132, 144, 145–46, 147, 158, 159, 167
Schiller, Friedrich, works by: *Demetrius*, 145; *Don Carlos*, 14; *Die Räuber*, 101; "Der Spaziergang," 158; *Thalia* (editor), 70
Schlegel, August Wilhelm, 105, 107, 144, 147–48, 149
Schlegel, Friedrich, 76
Schlegel, Friedrich, works by: *Über die Sprache und Weisheit der Inder*, 138
Schlenstedt, Silvia, 61, 63
Schlosser, Johann Georg, 124, 125
Schlosser, Lulu, 124
Schmid, Siegfried, 69
Schmidt, Arno, works by: *Goethe und Einer seiner Bewunderer*, 12, 115
Schubert, Franz, 17, 74
Schumann, Robert, 74
Scott, Walter, 3, 5
Scott, Walter, works by: *Waverly*, 4
Seghers, Anna, 18, 23, 29, 37–39, 40, 44, 56, 57, 58, 59, 61, 63, 189
Seifert, Johann, 157, 161–63, 164, 167
Senoçak, Zafer, 138–39, 142
Senoçak, Zafer, works by: "Das Buch mit den sieben Siegeln. Über die vergessene Sprache der osmanischen Dichtung," 142; "Wann ist der Fremde zu Hause? Betrachtungen zur Kunst und Kultur von Minderheiten in Deutschland,"142–43
Seret, Roberta, 7

Setzwein, Bernhard, works by: *Nicht kalt genug*, 157, 158
Seven Years' War, 93, 94–95, 97
Shakespeare, William, works by: *Hamlet*, 148, 149
Shakespeare in Love (movie), 187
Sharman, Gundela, 9, 114
Simplicissimus (journal), 14
Simpson, Patricia, 29–31, 48
Sinclair, Isaak, 80
Skow, Katya, 137
Sophie Charlotte (Queen of Prussia), 20, 88, 104–5
Sparschuh, Jens, works by: *Der große Coup*, 21, 112, 132–33, 153n54, 179, 186n36; *Lavaters Maske*, 22, 156–57, 178–80, 181, 183, 186n36, 192
Staël, Germaine de, 1, 144, 148, 149
Staël, Germaine de, works by: *De l'Allemagne*, 1, 144, 148
Stahl, Christian, 157
Stein, Charlotte von, 20, 112, 116–18, 119–22, 123, 124, 125, 127, 128, 134, 152n31, 191
Stein, Charlotte von, works by: *Dido*, 117
Stein, Fritz, 122
Stein, Josias, 116, 119, 121
Stechard, Maria Dorothea, 22, 174–78, 181
Stefan George Circle, 57
Storm and Stress, 11, 39, 116, 122, 156
Strich, Fritz, works by: *Goethe und die Weltliteratur*, 1, 113
Struzyk, Brigitte, works by: *Caroline unterm Freiheitsbaum*, 20, 23, 89, 105–7, 108, 110n37, 123
Sudau, Ralf, 9–10
Swedenborg, Emanuel, 181

Tang, Chenxi, 166
Teraoka, Arlene, 158
Third Reich. *See* National Socialism
Thornham, Sue, 87
Tieck, Ludwig, 76, 144, 147, 148, 149

Tieck, Ludwig, works by: *Der blonde Eckbert*, 148; *Der gestiefelte Kater*, 148
Timur, 141
Tischbein, Johann Heinrich Wilhelm, 135, 136
Trotsky, Leon, 72

Vaget, Hans, 14
Varsamopoulou, Evy, 7–8
Visser, Anthonya, 135–36
Vogel, Henriette, 19, 23, 46, 47–48, 51, 108, 189
Voltaire, 95, 147
Von den Fischer un siene Fru (fairy tale), 49, 50
Vulpius, Christiane, 102, 111, 118, 122, 127

Waiblinger, Wilhelm, 60, 65, 67, 73–74, 81, 82
Walser, Martin, 58, 114, 125, 137, 158, 188
Walser, Martin, works by: *Brandung*, 129–30, 131; *Ein fliehendes Pferd*, 129; "Goethes Anziehungskraft," 127; "Imitation oder Realismus," 126; *In Goethes Hand: Szenen aus dem 19. Jahrhundert*, 20–21, 112, 126–29, 130, 131, 132, 153n54, 179, 191; *Ein liebender Mann*, 21, 112, 129–32, 153n50, 191
Walser, Robert, works by: "Kleist in Thun," 26n28, 29, 45; *Lenz*, 14, 26n28
Weigel, Sigrid, 94, 109n14
Weimar Classicism, 67, 68, 101–2, 103–4, 111, 113, 115, 118, 133, 147, 188
Weiss, Peter, 4, 6, 9, 64, 78, 82, 107, 117
Weiss, Peter, works by: *Hölderlin*, 10, 19, 23, 57, 58, 59, 67–73, 76, 79, 80, 81, 84–85n35, 85n36, 111, 128, 188, 190; *Marat/Sade*, 69, 72; *Trotzki im Exil*, 72
Wieland, Christoph Martin, 10–11, 12, 97–99, 100, 101

Wieland, Christoph Martin, works by: *Alceste*, 11; "Briefe an einen Freund über das Singspiel," 11; preface to *Geschichte des Fräuleins von Sternheim*, 99, 109–110n23; preface to *Melusinens Sommerabende*, 99; *Teutschen Merkur* (editor), 98

Wilson, W. Daniel, 128, 153n47

Wittgenstein, Ludwig, 25n25

Wolf, Christa, 55n60, 61, 63, 82, 87, 92

Wolf, Christa, works by: *Die Dimension des Autors*, 34, 41–42, 44–45, 48, 50, 53n22, 54n37, 55n60; *Ins Ungebundene gehet eine Sehnsucht: Gesprächsraum Romantik* (co-editor), 64; *Kassandra*, 28; *Kein Ort. Nirgends*, 18, 19, 23, 24, 28–45, 46, 48–51, 56, 57, 64, 65, 67, 87, 89, 108, 111, 123, 144, 189; *Nachdenken über Christa T.*, 63; "Selbstversuch," 42; *Störfall*, 28

Wolf, Friedrich, 113

Wolf, Gerhard, 38, 58, 70, 78, 82

Wolf, Gerhard, works by: *Der arme Hölderlin*, 19, 23, 38, 57, 63–68, 70, 76, 79, 80, 81, 187, 189, 190; *Ins Ungebundene gehet eine Sehnsucht: Gesprächsraum Romantik* (co-editor), 64

Wollstonecraft, Mary, 87

Wolzogen, Caroline von, 20, 88, 93, 100–104, 105, 111, 190

Wolzogen, Caroline von, *Agnes von Lilien*, 88

Wolzogen, Wilhelm von, 101

Woodmansee, Martha, 97–99, 100n25

World War II, 1, 16, 19, 61, 113, 133, 150, 187

Young Germany, 2, 128, 167

Zenge, Wilhelmine von, 41

Zima, Peter, 8–9

Zimmer, Ernst, 64, 76

Ziolkowski, Theodore, 132, 150n1, 153n43, 153–54n55

Zola, Emile, 4